FOR THE ENRICHMENT OF COMMUNITY LIFE

FOR THE ENRICHMENT OF COMMUNITY LIFE

GEORGE EASTMAN AND THE FOUNDING OF THE EASTMAN SCHOOL OF MUSIC

Vincent A. Lenti

MELIORA PRESS

An Imprint of the University of Rochester Press

First published 2004

Meliora Press is an imprint of the
University of Rochester Press
668 Mt. Hope Avenue, Rochester, NY 14620, USA
www.urpress.com

and Boydell & Brewer, Ltd.
P.O. Box 9, Woodbridge, Suffolk IP12 3DF, UK
www.boydellandbrewer.com

ISBN 1–58046–169–7 (Hard cover)
ISBN 1–58046–199–9 (Soft cover)

Library of Congress Cataloging-in-Publication Data
Lenti, Vincent.
    For the enrichment of community life : George Eastman and the founding of the Eastman School of Music / Vincent A. Lenti.
        p. cm.
    Includes bibliographical references and index.
    ISBN 1–58046–169–7 (hardcover : alk. paper)
    1. Eastman School of Music.   I. Title.
MT4.R6E245 2004
780′.71′174789–dc22   2004014975

British Library Cataloguing-in-Publication Data
A catalogue record for this item is available from the British Library

Printed in the United States of America
This publication is printed on acid-free paper

To Victor and Anna, my parents

Contents

Part Two: The Beginning of the Hanson Years

A Parallel Development

Figures

Preface

This book represents the first part of the history of the Eastman School of Music, beginning with the events that led to the establishment of the school in 1921 and ending in 1932 with the death of the school's benefactor, George Eastman. It was the fulfillment of a long-held dream when James Undercofler, the dean of the Eastman School of Music, asked me to serve as historian for the purpose of producing a history of the school. Whatever other qualifications I may have in undertaking this responsibility, I can at least claim to have known intimately the Eastman School for almost a half century. I now enter my forty-eighth year at this marvelous institution, having experienced the school as an undergraduate student, graduate student, member of the faculty, and member of the administration. Because of my long tenure at Eastman, I have had the good fortune to know personally many of the legendary faculty members who contributed so much toward making Eastman one of the world's most prestigious centers for musical training. And I have also had the distinction of working under all but one of the school's five directors.

My initial interest in the school's origins came during the mid-1970s, about a half-dozen years after I had been appointed director of the Preparatory Department (predecessor of the Community Education Division). That initial interest took the form of a paper that traced the origins of the Eastman School and the subsequent history of the Preparatory Department through the year 1953, a paper I read for the members of the Rochester Historical Society in 1978. The project proved to be so interesting and fascinating that it stimulated my desire to learn more about the history of music in Rochester. This, in turn, led to the publication of several articles in *Rochester History*, a quarterly edited by the city historian and published by the Rochester Public Library. The research involved in the preparation of those articles has provided me with important background information for the writing of this book.

I have been able to make considerable use of my earlier notes and sources, especially a series of recorded interviews from 1977 and 1978. The people whom I interviewed were all associated with the Eastman School of Music in its earliest days, including several

who were either students or members of the faculty when the
school first opened. Although it is sad to note that every one of
them is now gone, listening once again to these recordings that
I made a quarter century ago has been not only informative but also
quite inspiring. The enthusiasm with which they all spoke about
their experiences at Eastman has helped me to understand and
appreciate more fully the excitement that surrounded the opening
of the school and theater in the early 1920s.

The decision to relate the Eastman history in several volumes
was taken almost immediately after I had been asked to undertake
this project. Part of the reason for this was the practical considera-
tion that I am researching and writing this history while still maintaining a full-time teaching schedule at the school. Confining
myself to a reasonable period of time in the school's history would
certainly lead to an earlier publication than any attempt to relate the
entire story in a single volume. Readers of this book, therefore, will
need to be patient in awaiting the next installment, which I anticipate will deal with the years from the death of George Eastman in
1932 to the retirement of Howard Hanson in 1964 after his long
tenure of forty years as the school's second director.

A few specific comments are perhaps needed concerning the
chapters that follow. Readers will note that I have included the
dates for the famous musical figures who are mentioned in the text
as teachers of people associated with the Eastman School of Music
and/or its predecessor institutions, as well as for the famous musicians who appeared in Rochester concerts and recitals. Such information is included only when such an individual is first mentioned
in the text, and it is my hope that these dates will be helpful in plac-
ing such musicians in proper historical context. Titles of musical
works are customarily noted as they appeared in contemporary
programs or publicity. For example, the titles of Italian or German
operas may given in English, especially when reference is specifically being made to an opera performance presented in English
translation. Thus, I have used *The Marriage of Figaro* instead of *Le
Nozze di Figaro* and *The Abduction from the Seraglio* instead of *Die
Entführung aus dem Serail*, to cite two examples.

Readers will note a number of quotations from newspapers and
other periodicals. One of the great resources available to me at the
Sibley Music Library has been a very large collection of scrapbooks
with many newspaper clippings concerning the early years of the
Eastman School and Eastman Theatre. Without exception my
quotations are taken from items contained in those scrapbooks. As
a result, citations in the notes may not include all of the customary

information. In almost all cases, however, the name and date of the newspaper or journal is provided, although occasionally such information was impossible to discern from the content of the scrapbook.

I have had access to three major sources of archival material in the writing of the present volume: the George Eastman Archive and Study Center at the George Eastman House in Rochester; the Department of Rare Books, Special Collections, and Preservation, Rush Rhees Library at the University of Rochester; and the Ruth T. Watanabe Special Collections and Eastman School of Music Archives, Sibley Music Library at the Eastman School of Music. When mentioned in the notes, these collections are abbreviated simply as GEH (George Eastman House), RRL (Rush Rhees Library), and SML (Sibley Music Library).

My chief obligation in writing this book is to James Undercofler, dean and fifth director of the Eastman School of Music, for his interest and encouragement, and for the confidence he expressed in appointing me historian and asking me to undertake this project. I would be remiss if I fail to note also the encouragement I received from his predecessor, Robert Freeman, who always demonstrated a great personal interest in the research that I pursued during his tenure as director of the Eastman School of Music. My obligations to local archivists are considerable: to Kathleen Connor, curator at the George Eastman Archive and Study Center at the George Eastman House in Rochester; to Nancy Martin, manuscript librarian and archivist at the University of Rochester's Rush Rhees Library, and to her predecessor Karl S. Kabelac; and to David Peter Coppen, Special Collections Librarian at the Sibley Music Library and Eastman School archivist. This book could not have been written without the generous assistance and professional courtesy they consistently extended to me. Since the majority of my research has been in the Sibley Music Library, I am especially indebted to David, not only for his help and advice in guiding me through the resources at the Sibley Music Library, but also for his friendship, which I deeply appreciate. I am also much obliged to Louise Goldberg for the important contributions that she made to the chapter on the Sibley Music Library.

I would like to thank Ruth Rosenberg-Naparsteck, city historian and editor of *Rochester History*, for allowing me to borrow rather freely from my previously published articles. The quarterly publication that she now edits has been in print since 1939 and has a long and distinguished history of documenting the history of Rochester and its surrounding area. It has been a valuable experience to contribute to several issues, and I thank Ruth for her encouragement and support over a period of a number of years. Sincere thanks are also due to Timothy Madigan for being such a supportive editor and for being such a good friend during the many months leading up to the publication of this book.

Finally, I should express my heartfelt thanks to my wife and daughter, who have shown exemplary patience and understanding as I have become more and more immersed in this project. I am sure that I have spent far too much time away from family responsibilities, especially during the countless number of hours I sat in front of the computer at home, and I am grateful to them for their forbearance and for their support of this book.

All photographs unless otherwise indicated are from the Eastman School of Music Archives, Eastman School of Music, University of Rochester, and are used by permission. The photographs taken by Alexander Leventon are in the Alexander Leventon Collection, Ruth T. Watanabe Department of Special Collections, Sibley Music Library, Eastman School of Music. They are used by permission of the Leventon family.

Vincent A. Lenti
January 2004

Introduction

The Eastman School of Music has long enjoyed a well-deserved reputation as one of the world's most prestigious centers for musical training and musical scholarship. Founded in 1921, it built upon an existing music school that had been opened eight years earlier by two enterprising musicians who aspired to provide the citizens of their adopted city with an opportunity for serious and productive music study. Although they were able to employ a number of excellent teachers and attract an adequate number of students, their school struggled financially from year to year. It is unlikely that it could have survived, much less thrived, except for the almost providential intervention of two very remarkable, yet very different men. Each may have had a completely different motivation, but their involvement in the affairs of this struggling little music school would have far-reaching consequences in the history of musical training in America. While others may have had important roles in the creation of the Eastman School of Music, it was a millionaire industrialist by the name of George Eastman and a remarkable university president by the name of Rush Rhees who really made it all possible. Without Eastman and Rhees, the project would never have succeeded.

By the early years of the twentieth century, George Eastman had established himself as the wealthiest and most influential person in Rochester, New York. Born in 1854, he was only five years old when he arrived in town with his family. Eastman's earliest years in his adopted city were difficult ones, especially after the premature death of his father, but in 1880 he leased the third floor of a building to begin manufacturing his recently patented dry plates for photographers. In a short while he perfected a system of roll film for cameras, and, in doing so, forever transformed photography by making it an affordable and accessible pastime for practically everyone. When Eastman introduced the Kodak camera in 1889, he coined the very appropriate slogan, "You press the button, we do the rest." The resulting explosion of interest in photography soon made the Eastman Kodak Company the world's leading manufacturer of photographic film, while also making George Eastman a multimillionaire.

Rush Rhees could not have been a more different person. An ordained Baptist minister, he arrived in town to become president of the University of Rochester in 1900. Rhees had had no experience as a university administrator, and his collegiate background consisted solely of an eight-year term as chair of New Testament studies at Newton Theological Institution. The university that selected Rhees as its president had first opened its doors to students on November 5, 1850, and during its first fifty years it had developed very slowly, being limited to what its founders had called "The Collegiate Department." When Rush Rhees retired thirty-five years after his inauguration as the University of Rochester's third president, he had guided the institution through a remarkable three and a half decades of unprecedented expansion.

The astonishing growth of the university was achieved not only because of the vision of its gifted president, but also through that president's cultivation of support from Rochester's wealthiest citizen, George Eastman. Gaining Eastman's confidence and support was crucial to realizing any ambitions that Rhees might have entertained for his university. He worked patiently toward that goal over a period of many years, fully understanding the significance of the fact that George Eastman was a bachelor and had no children to whom he could leave his fortune. Rhees succeeded probably beyond his wildest expectations, since George Eastman's generosity to the University of Rochester eventually exceeded $35,000,000 in gifts and bequests, an amount equivalent today to about $300,000,000. Those millions made possible not only the Eastman School of Music in 1921 but also the university's School of Medicine and Dentistry in 1926. At the time of Rhees's retirement in 1935, the University of Rochester had become the fifth most heavily endowed university in the United States.

George Eastman has sometimes been described as being musically tone-deaf, and he himself often commented on his lack of musical ability. Why should such a man decide to establish and endow a music school? Part of the answer to this question can be found in the simple observation that Eastman was not the musical "ignoramus" that people have often assumed him to be. Although he was certainly uneducated in musical matters, he had defined musical tastes and appreciated the importance of music and its value to society. Faced with the necessity of disposing of his fortune, he chose to invest in something for the betterment of the community in which he lived. As Rochester's most distinguished citizen, he undoubtedly wished to leave behind some kind of permanent monument by which people might remember him for his generosity and kindness, something more than the company that he had founded. That monument was to be the Eastman School of Music and its adjoining Eastman Theatre.

The Eastman School of Music is not the oldest music school in the United States, nor is it the largest. Nonetheless, it has had an enormous influence on music education in the United States. Creating a professional music school within the context of a university was a bold experiment at the time. American music education had traditionally followed the European model of training performers in conservatories and creating musical scholars in universities. The Eastman School would be a home to both performer and scholar, as well as being a home to both composer and educator. It would offer instruction to students whose interests were purely avocational, while also offering training to those preparing for a professional career in music. It would be a professional music school, but one committed to a broadly based education leading not to a professional diploma but to a baccalaureate degree. The Eastman School would be in the forefront of national efforts to establish and regulate the curriculum for the bachelor of music degree. It would be a leader in the training of musicians at the graduate level through the awarding of the master of music degree and through the creation of a new professional doctorate in music, which would be known as the doctor of musical arts degree.

Even more important, however, was the effort to establish the Eastman School as a truly American institution, dedicated to American ideals and to the encouragement and support of American music. When it first opened its doors in 1921, the school was rather typical of musical institutions of its time in having a faculty that was somewhat dominated by European and European-trained musicians. Some came to the United States during the great years of immigration at the end of the nineteenth century, seeking a better life in the New World. Others came following the devastation of the First World War. Some were exiles from their native country, especially Russians who fled in the aftermath of the Bolshevik Revolution. The European influence at the Eastman School lessened, however, especially after Rush Rhees deliberately sought to appoint an American as the school's second director in 1924. The man he chose was Howard Hanson, who led the school for the next forty years. Under his leadership the Eastman School of Music became a truly American institution, one known throughout the world for its advocacy and support of American music.

It is the story of the earliest years in the history of the Eastman School of music that forms the subject of this book. The story to be related, however, is not simply that of a music school. It also involves a symphony orchestra, an American opera company, a ballet company, a school of dance and drama, a music library, and a commercial radio station dedicated to broadcasting live classical music. The story includes efforts to support the musical education of Rochester's elementary and secondary school children and the involvement of the symphony orchestra in their musical education. It is the story of a magnificent new theater that became the location of concerts and recitals by the world's greatest musicians, a theater that featured annual series of performances presented by the Metropolitan Opera Company of New York.

Upon the facade Eastman Theatre are inscribed the words, "For the Enrichment of Community Life." The inscription was selected by Rush Rhees with the intent of dedicating the theater to that purpose. In a broader sense, however, these words embody the mission of a great music school. The founders of the Eastman School of Music were convinced that the life of the community could be enriched through the art of music. All of the endeavors associated with the founding of the school—opera, dance, drama, concerts, radio broadcasts—were part of the great idea that was unfolding in Rochester during the 1920s. That great idea led to the development of a great music school, the history of which we now begin to relate.

Part One

The Origins of the
Eastman School of Music

Chapter 1

1913–1918
Alf Klingenberg Opens
a Music School

The Eastman School of Music opened in 1921, a little more than one hundred years after the first permanent settlers arrived in Rochester. Founded in 1817 and incorporated as a city in 1834, Rochester has had a long and distinguished musical history. Situated along the Erie Canal—"The Gateway to the West"—the city quickly grew in population, reputation, and affluence. There is much evidence to suggest that, from Rochester's very beginnings, music always formed an important part of its social life. The city's first instrumental band was formed the same year that the city was founded. The first church organ was installed only eight years later. The first public concerts took place during the 1820s in Eagle Tavern, located in the center of town at the corner of State Street and Buffalo Road (now Main Street). Subsequent years witnessed the construction of several theaters for popular and serious entertainment. Quite a few of these were situated along South Avenue and Exchange Street. The city's first music store opened for business in 1836, only two years after Rochester was incorporated. During the same year, the first local choral society came into existence with the organization of the Rochester Academy of Sacred Music. The original Rochester Philharmonic had origins in 1865,[1] less than half a century after the appearance of the first permanent settlers. Throughout the nineteenth century, the presence of ever-increasing numbers of musical organizations and musical activities gave

---

[1]   The early Rochester Philharmonic was incorporated seven years after it was founded and presented many concerts in Rochester until it was disbanded in the early 1880s. The present Rochester Philharmonic Orchestra has no historic connection with this earlier group.

evidence of a population that greatly appreciated the value and importance of music in the cultural and social life of their city.

Not all of the music in early Rochester was "homegrown," however. The cultural life of the city was greatly enhanced by an influx of famous European artists who were willing to risk the hazards of an ocean voyage and the rather unpredictable behavior of American audiences for the financial rewards that American tours offered to them. One of the first to tour the New World was Ole Bull (1810–80), the famous Norwegian violinist. He appeared in Rochester for a concert in June of 1844, soon to be followed by the German pianist Leopold de Meyer (1816–83), who was considered to be one of Europe's greatest virtuosi. De Meyer was initially engaged to play only six concerts in New York City, his debut taking place on October 20, 1845. These recitals led to an extensive two-year tour of the United States. De Meyer was quickly followed by Henri Herz (1803–88), who enjoyed a wide reputation in Europe as a pianist, composer, teacher, and manufacturer of pianos. He arrived in America a year and a day after De Meyer and made his American debut in New York on October 29, 1846. Herz concertized in America from the fall of 1846 until January 1848, and he then returned for additional concerts during the 1848–49 season and once more in 1850. His only Rochester appearance was on August 18, 1847.

Perhaps the most memorable event in the musical history of nineteenth-century Rochester was the concert offered by Jenny Lind (1820–87), the "Swedish Nightingale," in July 1851. She appeared under the sponsorship of the famous P. T. [Phineas Taylor] Barnum (1810–91), later associated with Barnum and Bailey, the most famous circus in American history. With Barnum's sense of showmanship, tickets for Lind's Rochester concert were sold at the unheard of prices of two, three, and five dollars. Other visiting performers during the 1850s included pianists Louis Moreau Gottschalk (1829–69) and Sigismond Thalberg (1812–71), and the nine-year-old Italian soprano, Adelina Patti (1843–1919), who was to become one of the greatest coloratura singers of the nineteenth century, with a career that spanned more than a half-century. Thalberg's tour of America, if nothing else, was a remarkable testimony to his physical endurance, since he appeared in more than three hundred concerts, beginning in New York on November 10, 1856, and concluding in Peoria, Illinois, on June 12, 1858. His American concerts included three in Rochester: April 21, 1857, June 12 of the same year, and May 7, 1858.

Visiting artists continued to appear in Rochester following the Civil War, including Anton Rubinstein (1829–94), widely considered to be the greatest pianist in the world, and Henryk Wieniawski (1835–80), the famous Polish violinist and composer. They toured America together and presented a recital in Rochester on November 23, 1872, a little more than two months after their sensational New York debut. Other visiting artists included Hans von Bülow (1830–94), Teresa Carreño (1853–1917), and Moritz Rosenthal (1852–1946). Bülow arrived in Boston on October 18, 1875, after Anton Rubinstein had encouraged him to concertize in America. By this time he had recovered from the humiliation he had suffered when his wife Cosima left him to marry Richard Wagner (1813–83). His motivation for an American tour was reportedly to earn enough money to avoid poverty in his final years. This goal was surely fulfilled, since he performed 139 concerts in seven months, including a Rochester recital on April 21, 1876.

The rich musical life of the city made it perhaps inevitable that there should be a music school established in Rochester. The earliest schools were, in fact, only private studios offering specialized instruction. But in 1906, John D. Beall, a well-known voice teacher from the Ithaca Conservatory, started commuting to Rochester to give lessons. The following year, he opened the Rochester School of Music, occupying rooms in a building on the corner of South Clinton Avenue and Court Street. From Ithaca Beall also brought W. Grant Egbert to teach violin and Sophie Fernau to teach piano. He soon moved his school to new facilities in the Cornwall Building on Main Street, where it had a faculty of over one dozen teachers. Beall was able to offer instruction in piano, voice, violin, organ, elocution, Italian, German, and physical culture, as well as courses in solfege, harmony, and theory.

In December 1907, however, competition for Beall's school arose with the incorporation of the Rochester Conservatory of Music. The charter members of this new endeavor were Floyd Spencer, H. C. Saehlenlow, and Edith Compton, who soon married Floyd Spencer. The following March, Beall's school became what was then politely described as "financial embarrassed," and its assets were purchased by the Rochester Conservatory, which also paid off Beall's debts. The conservatory then increased its capital stock from $10,000 to $75,000 and engaged Beall as musical director. It also hired W. Grant Egbert as president and head of the violin department, with Floyd Spencer serving as treasurer and manager. John Beall retired from his position as musical director on July 1, 1909, citing ill health, and moved to a large private house at 86 Clinton Avenue South.

The following year, the Rochester Conservatory of Music secured necessary capital to purchase new facilities in the center of the city, at 81 South Fitzhugh Street. Its faculty was sufficient for the conservatory to be able to offer instruction in piano, organ, voice, violin, cello, harp, clarinet, and cornet, as well as in mandolin, banjo, and guitar. Courses were also offered in harmony, composition, history of fine arts, ensemble, elocution, English, German, French, and Italian. The conservatory curricula included a four-year collegiate course, a two-year collegiate course specifically designed for the training of teachers, and a children's department for students of precollegiate age.

Among the faculty members were Floyd Spencer and his wife, Edith Compton Spencer. Spencer taught voice, while his wife was one of three piano teachers on the faculty. Her credentials were certainly not without merit, since she had studied piano in Europe with Liszt's famous student Rafael Joseffy (1852–1915), as well as with the noted English pianist Harold Bauer (1873–1951). The violin teachers included W. Grant Egbert and Ludwig Schenck. Schenck was a native Rochesterian, whose training had been in Dresden, Germany. Before returning to his native city, he had a successful and varied career, including playing in the Symphony Orchestra of New York and in the Theodore Thomas Orchestra,[2] as well as serving as a member of the Dannreuther Quartet.[3] In Rochester he settled into a prominent position through his work on the conservatory faculty, as conductor of the Rochester Symphony Orchestra,[4] and as director of orchestral studies for the city high schools.

Of all the members of the faculty, however, perhaps the most significant for the future of music education in Rochester may have been George Barlow Penny, who served as musical director (John Beall's former position) as well as being a teacher of piano, organ, voice, harmony, composition, and the history of fine arts. Unlike his European, conservatory-trained faculty colleagues, Penny was a musician with solid academic credentials, being a graduate of Cornell University. He had also completed music study at Syracuse University, studying there with Percy Goetschius (1853–1943). Penny had built a fine reputation for himself by organizing and

---

[2] Theodore Thomas (1835–1905) began conducting in 1859 and was largely responsible for introducing and popularizing European orchestral music in the United States.
[3] The Dannreuther Quartet, an important early string quartet in America, was founded in 1884 by Gustav Dannreuther (1853–1923). The ensemble was originally known as the Beethoven String Quartet, its name being changed in 1894.
[4] The Rochester Symphony Orchestra, founded in 1901, comprised amateurs and students. It performed free concerts in Rochester until disbanded in the 1920s.

developing the School of Fine Arts at the University of Kansas, where he served as Dean from 1890 to 1903. He subsequently organized the School of Fine Arts at Washburn College before coming to Rochester in 1907.

Penny was an accomplished organist and choral conductor, having held a number of positions including at Grace Cathedral in Kansas City and with the Topeka Oratorio Society. After coming to Rochester he became conductor of the Rochester Oratorio Society and a lecturer in music at the University of Rochester, all of this in addition to his many teaching and administrative responsibilities at the Rochester Conservatory. A widely traveled man, Penny had made two trips to the Far East and five trips to Europe. It is unclear exactly what brought him to Rochester, but his interest in music training within the context of a university education proved to be of considerable influence during the next few years. Sometime during the summer months of 1912, George Barlow Penny and his wife were dinner guests at the home of Rush Rhees, the president of the University of Rochester. The specific occasion of the dinner party was to entertain Alf and Alexandra Klingenberg, who were visiting the Pennys at the time. This dinner party brought together for the first time three men—Rhees, Penny, and Klingenberg—who soon would have a major role in the events leading to the establishment of the Eastman School of Music.

Alf Klingenberg was a Norwegian pianist who had personally known the composer Edvard Grieg (1843–1907), and who had been a student at the Hochschule für Musik in Berlin. His teachers in Germany had included Bernard Stavenhagen (1862–1914) and Karl Barth (1847–1922).[5] Klingenberg came to the United States at the turn of the century and accepted a position at Hardin College in Mexico, Missouri. Some of his students at Hardin were from Topeka, Kansas, and he soon relocated there, where he maintained a private piano teaching studio. After a few years, however, he gave up his private studio to become head of the piano department at the School of Fine Arts at Washburn College in Topeka, where George Barlow Penny was Dean. It was at Washburn, therefore, that Klingenberg and Penny first became acquainted. After several years

---

[5] Barth had a very prominent career as a teacher in Germany. His most notable students included Artur Rubinstein (1887–1982) and Wilhelm Kempff (1895–1991), as well as the famous Soviet pianist and teacher Heinrich Neuhaus (1884–1964), whose own students included Emil Gilels (1916–85) and Sviatoslav Richter (1915–97).

Figure 1. Alf Klingenberg, first director of the Eastman School, in his office at the D.K.G. Institute of Musical Art.

Klingenberg left Washburn, but he was recruited back to the college to become the new dean of the School of Fine Arts following Penny's departure. In addition to these positions in Missouri and Kansas, he taught for a while in Portland, Oregon.

Frequent changes in his career suggested a man in search of a mission in life. Alf Klingenberg has been described by many as a quiet and reserved man, but an exceptionally fine musician, pianist, and teacher. Alexandra Klingenberg was, by all reports, neither quiet nor reserved. In some ways an ideal partner for her more passive husband, she had the more dominating and assertive personality. The circumstances behind their visit with George Barlow Penny and his wife are unknown, although it may have been in connection with a Rochester concert engagement for Klingenberg. Whatever the reasons for the visit, it resulted in a decision for Klingenberg to relocate in Rochester and accept a position in September 1912 as head of the piano faculty at the Rochester Conservatory of Music.

The following year Alf Klingenberg left the Rochester Conservatory to open his own music school, a move that he and his wife had probably contemplated since first coming to Rochester. The new school was opened in partnership with violinist/conductor Hermann Dossenbach. The choice of Dossenbach as a partner in the new venture was particularly astute since he was perhaps Rochester's most prominently known musician at the time. He was the son of Mathias Dossenbach, who had come from Germany in the mid-1800s and originally settled in Niagara Falls before relocating in Rochester. Mathais had four sons who were all musically gifted, although the career of the eldest was prematurely ended due to illness. But the other three sons, especially Hermann, all contributed a great deal to the musical of life of Rochester. Hermann Dossenbach's most important accomplishment had been to give the city its first professional orchestra, which, after somewhat humble beginnings, had achieved impressive financial and civic backing and was in the forefront of local musical activity.[6]

As a location for their school, Klingenberg and Dossenbach chose a building at 47 Prince Street, which they purchased from William Gleason of Gleason Works, an important local manufacturing concern. Klingenberg's choice of location was as astute as his choice of partner, since the new school was situated adjacent to the campus of

---

[6]   Originally known as the Dossenbach Orchestra, the group gave its first concert on February 5, 1900, and soon established itself as a professional symphony orchestra in Rochester. Renamed as the Rochester Orchestra in 1912, it disbanded after giving its final concert on March 17, 1919.

THE

ROCHESTER
ORCHESTRA

HERMANN DOSSENBACH, *Conductor*

Dr. Rush Rhees   -   -   .   -   -   -   *President*
Mrs. E. R. Willard   -   -   -   -   - *Vice-President*
Mrs. E. W. Mulligan   -   -   -   -   -   *Treasurer*
Hon. W. S. Hubbell -   -   -   -   -   *Secretary*

Announcement
Season of 1917-18
Convention Hall

Dates and Soloists

Monday, October 22d   -   -   Mabel Garrison, *Soprano*

Monday, November 19th   - Schumann-Heink, *Contralto*

Monday, December 17th   - David Hochstein, *Violinist*

Monday, January 21st   -   Clarence Whitehill, *Baritone*

Monday, February 18th   -   -   - Anna Case, *Soprano*

Monday, March 18th   -   -   - Josef Hofmann, *Pianist*

Figure 2. Season announcement for Hermann Dossenbach's Rochester Orchestra, 1917–18. (Collection of the author.)

the University of Rochester and diagonally across the street from Sibley Hall, which housed the Sibley Musical Library.[7] This collection, given to the university in 1904 by Hiram W. Sibley, was an invaluable resource, and its nearby location was of obvious advantage to the new school. The school building provided rather modest teaching facilities. The main entrance of the institute led directly into a long corridor, with Klingenberg's office to the left in the front of the building and his teaching studio to the right. Another teaching studio was located to the rear of the building, along with a couple of small practice rooms equipped with upright pianos. Additional studios were located on the second floor. To provide much-needed additional space, a large rectangular building was constructed at the rear of the property. It contained an auditorium and stage for recitals; the auditorium was equipped with a pipe organ and two grand pianos. George Barlow Penny also held his classes in this building.

The Dossenbach-Klingenberg School of Music opened in the fall of 1913 and was provisionally chartered by the Regents of the University of the State of New York. In their application for the provisional charter, dated September 18, 1913, the owners stated that the new corporation was being established for the following purpose:

> To establish an educational institution in which persons of both sexes may be taught the art, science, and the practice of music in all its branches, to impart instruction and conduct examinations in all branches of music and of history, the languages and elocution, in so far as it may be necessary or proper to impart instruction and conduct examinations therein in connection with instruction in any branch of vocal or instrumental music.
>
> To grant and issue diplomas in any and all of the branches or subjects theretofore enumerated or referred to under and in accordance with the laws of the State of New York, and the rules and regulations of the Regents of the University of the State of New York.[8]

The music school was authorized to issue capital stock in the amount of $10,000, consisting of one hundred shares each with a par value of $100, but the corporation was to begin business with capital of only $1,000, represented by ten shares. Alf Klingenberg held five of these shares, while Hermann Dossenbach held four, the

[7] See "Hiram W. Sibley and His Music Library," p. 231.
[8] [Application for Provisional Charter] 18 September 1913, The University of the State of New York, The State Education Department, Albany, N.Y.

remaining single share being held by Dossenbach's wife, Daisy. The three shareholders, along with Alexandra Klingenberg, formed the directors of the corporation.

The Dossenbach-Klingenberg School of Music had a history that was quite as turbulent and unsettled as that of the Rochester Conservatory of Music. Had it not been for the fact that it was the immediate predecessor of the Eastman School of Music, its existence undoubtedly would be only an interesting footnote in Rochester history. After only one year of operation, the corporation was reorganized by bringing in a new partner, a voice teacher whose name was Oscar Gareissen. Gareissen was a prominent voice teacher who had previously taught for six years at Michigan State Normal College, and who had enjoyed considerable success as a recital soloist. In bringing in a new partner for the music school, Dossenbach and Klingenberg still retained equal ownership of the property rights, but the three men held equal shares in the corporation. Apparently, new capital stock was issued in the amount of twenty-four shares, each partner holding eight. To reflect the new partnership, the name of the school was changed to the D.K.G. Institute of Musical Art, the initials reflecting the surnames of the three directors. This change of name was requested on September 16, 1914, in a formal petition to the Regents of the University of the State of New York, which approved the request at its meeting of September 24.

There was a further change two years later when, in the fall of 1916, the Rochester Conservatory of Music was consolidated with the institute, the annual catalogue-title reading "D.K.G. Institute of Music Art and Rochester Conservatory of Music." John C. Bostlemann, Jr., who had succeeded Floyd Spencer as musical director of the conservatory, became a "director" along with Dossenbach, Klingenberg, and Gareissen, but the terms of agreement stipulated that Bostlemann's tenure would last only until July 1, 1917. In fact, he severed his connections with the institute before the end of the 1916–17 academic year. The consolidation was apparently only a means of absorbing the older school into the institute, and future catalogues dropped all mention of the conservatory. Shortly afterwards, Bostlemann unsuccessfully attempted to sue the institute and its three directors for reasons that are now unclear.

In the summer of 1917, a further change took place. Klingenberg became the sole owner of both the property and corporate rights. First of all, he purchased the capital stock held by both Dossenbach and Gareissen for a sum of $100 per share, each man thereby receiving $800. Second, he purchased Dossenbach's share of the property rights by agreeing to pay $6,200 and to assume two existing mortgages,

Figure 3. The D.K.G. Institute of Musical Art, predecessor of the Eastman School.

one for $5,000 and the other for $3,000. The agreement also verified that Alf Klingenberg would hereafter be considered the sole owner of the D.K.G. Institute of Musical Art.

All of the foregoing suggests that the institute was a rather shaky business venture. However, the school was not lacking in proper friends who must have brought a high level of advice and expertise to its operation. Klingenberg's Board of Advisors was headed by University of Rochester President Rush Rhees, a man of vision and genuine administrative accomplishment. Other advisors included the Honorable James C. Cutler, former mayor of Rochester; Harper Sibley, grandson of the founder of Western Union; the Honorable Walter S. Hubbell, a former state assemblyman; and William Bausch of Bausch and Lomb, the optical company.

Klingenberg was also supported by a surprisingly fine faculty. When he and Dossenbach opened the school in 1913, there were twenty-one faculty members. A prominent member of the faculty was the well-known tenor, Tom Karl, who had sung at La Scala in Milan. Born in Dublin on January 19, 1846, he had received his training in England and Italy, and then enjoyed considerable success in Italian opera. He later turned his talents towards light opera, and was one of the founders of the "Bostonians," the most famous and successful light-opera company of its time. Karl retired in 1896 and finally settled in Rochester, where he accepted Klingenberg's invitation to join the faculty of the new Dossenbach-Klingenberg School of Music. He died on March 19, 1916.

For a short while, Klingenberg was able to secure Eduardo Barbieri as a teacher of violin. A graduate of the Conservatorio di Musica in Milan, Barbieri had been a member of the orchestra at La Scala and had taught at the Royal College of Music in London. In Rochester he soon came to the conclusion that he could make more money teaching privately and opened a studio on East Avenue. In addition to his Rochester students, Barbieri taught many others in places as far east as Albany, spending three days on the road each week to give lessons to these aspiring young violinists. Among his Rochester students in the 1920s was a teenager named John Celentano, who would later enjoy a long and fruitful career as a member of the faculty at the Eastman School of Music. Other important faculty members at the institute included pianist Edith McMath (a graduate of the Stern Conservatory in Berlin) and cellist Emil Knoepke (a former member of both the Pittsburgh and Cincinnati Symphonies). Klingenberg also secured the services of Ludwig Schenck and of his friend George Barlow Penny, both of whom were faculty members at the rival Rochester Conservatory of Music.

A significant local talent among the original faculty members was John Adams Warner. He was the son of J. Foster Warner and the grandson of Andrew J. Warner, who were both among Rochester's most successful architects. His brother, also named Andrew J. Warner (but known as "Jack" or "A.J."), became a newspaper writer and a highly influential music critic in Rochester. The Warner family was well established and had all of the proper social connections. Their home was on Prince Street just off East Avenue, and it was known simply as "The Mansion." It had a lovely music room, which was the setting for many private concerts and impromptu gatherings of local musicians.

Young John Warner had been sent off to Harvard for his education. After graduating in 1909, he spent considerable time studying with several of the leading piano teachers in Europe, including Giuseppe Buonamici (1846–1914) in Italy, Harold Bauer in Paris, and Leopold Godowsky (1870–1938) in Innsbruck. He also studied organ with Charles-Marie Widor (1844–1937) and, accordingly, taught both piano and organ for Klingenberg. Warner was by all accounts a very gifted musician, but in 1917 he suddenly abandoned what might have been a promising musical career to become the fourth man to join the newly formed New York State Police. Six years later he was appointed superintendent (a post he held for about twenty years), and in 1927 he married Governor Al [Alfred Emanuel] Smith's daughter, Emily. He never totally left music, however, and continued to perform, including a 1940 appearance in New York's Carnegie Hall as a concerto soloist.

Another significantly talented local musician who joined the faculty was David Hochstein, who taught at the institute during the 1915–16 school year. Born in Rochester in 1892, he showed an unusual talent for the violin at an early age and was sent to Ludwig Schenck for lessons. He also worked for a time with Aloys Trnka, a highly gifted violinist who had recently studied with Otakar Ševčik (1852–1934) in Vienna. It is unclear exactly why Trnka came to Rochester, but it was to David Hochstein's great advantage to have such a highly talented musician as his teacher during his high school years. While in high school Hochstein formed a very close friendship with John Adams Warner, and through the Warner family he was introduced to Emily Sibley Watson. She was the daughter of Hiram Sibley, one of the founders of Western Union.[9] She became

---

[9]   Emily Sibley Watson, therefore, was the sister of Hiram W. Sibley, the founder of the Sibley Music Library.

Hochstein's patroness and secured the funding that would permit Hochstein to continue his studies in Europe.

In 1909 Hochstein was sent to study in the *Meisterschule* taught by Ševčik in Vienna. When he graduated from the Akademie für Musik und darstellende Kunst in 1911, he was the first student ever to win both the "One Thousand Crown Award" and the "First State Prize." In addition to his studies with Ševčik, Hochstein also worked with Leopold Auer (1845–1930), first in Loschwitz during the summer months of 1911, and then in St. Petersburg in the fall of 1913. Thus, Hochstein received his training from the two most prominent and important violin teachers in Europe. The critical acclaim he gained for concerts given in Berlin, London, Boston, New York, and elsewhere is clear evidence that his was an extraordinary talent, and he was befriended by such distinguished musicians as Myra Hess (1880–1965) and Harold Bauer. A brilliant career was not to be, however, as his life was tragically cut short by an artillery shell during the First World War. Among Hochstein's many admirers was the American author, Willa Cather (1876–1947). After his tragic death in 1918, Cather used Hochstein as inspiration for the character, David Gebhardt, in her 1922 Pulitzer Prize–winning novel, *One Of Ours*.

The strangest faculty appointment at the institute may have been Rosita Renard, who came in the fall of 1916. This tremendously gifted woman was born in Santiago, Chile, on February 8, 1894, and she had studied with Martin Krause (1853–1918) in Berlin, where she was a classmate of the famous pianist, Edwin Fischer (1886–1960). Two years after completing her diploma (when she was only twenty-two years old) she was invited to become a member of the faculty at the "D.K.G." Arriving from Chile with her mother and sister, she was informed that she would receive compensation only by means of a commission on all the pupils she taught. Renard soon learned, however, that she had only one assigned student. Facing an impossible financial situation, she left Rochester and attempted to establish a performing career, first in America where she enjoyed considerable success and a short while later in Europe. The postwar years in Europe, however, were not kind to musical careers, and she was soon forced to return to the United States.

During the mid-1920s Renard came back to Rochester to perform George Gershwin's *Rhapsody in Blue* with the Eastman Theatre Orchestra. (She may have been one of the earliest pianists to include the piece in her concert repertoire.) Her appearance in Rochester involved six consecutive days of performances during the afternoon and evening Eastman Theatre shows. In other words, she was the entertainment that preceded the showing of the feature film. This kind of professional engagement clearly demonstrates that Renard's career had seriously faltered since the initial success she had enjoyed in America just a few years earlier.

It is not surprising, therefore, that Renard soon decided to return to Santiago to teach. Then in 1945, she was suddenly rediscovered by the noted conductor Erich Kleiber (1890–1956), and her career began to blossom. Her concert engagements included a Carnegie Hall recital on January 19, 1949, which was a huge sensation.[10] Finally on the threshold of the success that always seemed to elude her, she was suddenly taken ill and diagnosed with sleeping sickness (encephalitis). She did not respond to treatment and died on May 24, 1949, only four months after her triumph in Carnegie Hall. Her brief Rochester tenure was only one chapter in an unfulfilled career and tragic life. The circumstances behind Renard's appointment to the faculty of the "D.K.G." are unclear, although she may have become acquainted with Edith McMath during the latter's student days in Berlin. It is possible, therefore, that McMath recommended Renard to Alf Klingenberg.

The Klingenberg school essentially offered three programs, somewhat similar to those of the older Rochester Conservatory: a preparatory course for younger students, a four-year course leading to a diploma, and a public school course, graduates of which were qualified to teach music in New York State schools. Students in the four-year course received two private lessons each week. Required courses included solfeggio, dictation, theory, harmony, analysis, counterpoint, composition, and orchestration in addition to ancient, medieval, and modern music history. The first graduates of the four-year course were Jean Ingelow and Ernestine Klinzing in 1915. Both had done the first two years of their diploma program elsewhere, presumably at the Rochester Conservatory. The following year diplomas were awarded to five pianists, as well as to two additional students who were graduated from the "Department of Public School Music." By the time of its eighth and final commencement in 1921, the institute had graduated twenty-six students from the four-year course and twenty-one from the public school course. The two original graduates from 1915 remained in the Rochester area for the remainder of their careers. Ingelow was active as a church organist in the upstate New York area for many

---

[10] A recording of Renard's Carnegie Hall has been available, first on long-playing record and more recently on compact disc (VAI Audio 1028-2, 1993).

years, while Klinzing joined the institute faculty and later became a valued teacher at the Eastman School of Music.

The D.K.G. Institute of Musical Art, despite its noble purposes and an excellent faculty in many regards, was a rather modest and provincial undertaking as a music school. Rapidly occurring changes in corporate structure and changes in faculty indicate that it was a troubled school, too. When Klingenberg became the sole director in 1917, he faced long-term debts of over $12,000, not an inconsiderable sum for the times; he also had to deal with the regular operational expenses of the school. As an institution it was certainly trying to fulfill the purpose for which it claimed to have been founded: "to meet the demands of the musical public of Rochester for a school of music of the highest standard." Yet, for all its good intentions and good results, question must have existed as to whether or not the school could survive. Help, however, was forthcoming in a manner that would dramatically change the nature of music education in Rochester and have a very broad impact on music education in general.

Chapter 2

1918–1919
George Eastman Becomes Involved

Early in 1918 George Eastman is said to have posed the following question to Rush Rhees: "Why don't you have a music school?" His proposal was to buy the D.K.G. Institute of Musical Art for the University of Rochester. Eastman's question, perhaps first quoted in John Rothwell Slater's biography of Rush Rhees,[1] does not appear in earlier commentaries, such as Stewart Sabin's essays for the Rochester Historical Society[2] or Carl Ackerman's 1930 biography of George Eastman.[3] Slater and others who have written since his time have used the question to suggest that the Eastman proposal was quite unanticipated by Rhees. Eastman faculty member Ernestine Klinzing, in a 1967 essay, even added that she had recalled "hearing Mrs. Klingenberg say that President Rhees was not very receptive to the idea, feeling that a professional school had no place in a university atmosphere."[4]

The context in which Rhees may have made such a comment to Alexandra Klingenberg is difficult to understand, since the idea of a university music school apparently had been around for a long time. According to Slater, the idea dated back to 1904, when Rush Rhees had written his consulting architects that they might begin

---

[1]   John Rothwell Slater, *Rhees of Rochester* (New York and London: Harper and Brothers, 1946), 169.
[2]   Stewart B. Sabin, "Music in Rochester from 1909 to 1924," in *Rochester Historical Society Publication Fund Series*, vol. 3, ed. Edward R. Foreman (Rochester, 1924); Stewart B. Sabin, "A Retrospect of Music in Rochester," in *Centennial History of Rochester, New York*, vol. 2, ed. Edward R. Foreman (Rochester, 1932).
[3]   Carl W. Ackerman, *George Eastman* (Boston and New York: Houghton Mifflin Co., 1930).
[4]   Ernestine N. Klinzing. "Music in Rochester: A Century of Musical Progress: 1825–1925," *Rochester History* 29, no. 1 (January 1967): 24.

Figure 4. George Eastman, benefactor and founder of the Eastman School. (Photograph by Alexander Leventon. Used by permission.)

Figure 5. Rush Rhees, president of the University of Rochester. (Photograph by Alexander Leventon. Used by permission.)

thinking about a possible building for a music school, adding, however, that the realization of such a building would probably be sometime in the "distant future."[5] The date 1904 is significant in that it coincides with Eastman's donation of $77,000 to the

---

[5] Slater, *Rhees*, 57. Slater does not give a specific date for this correspondence. The letter to G. L. Heins of Heins & LaFarge suggested plans for a new science building,

University for the construction of a new biology/physics building, his first contribution to the university and the beginning of his long association with Rhees. This was the only occasion when Rush Rhees directly asked George Eastman for money, a remarkable observation considering the extraordinary amount that Eastman eventually gave to the university.

The University of Rochester was extremely fortunate to have a great educator and a man of vision and leadership as its president at this critical time in its history. An ordained Baptist minister, he had received his general education at Amherst College and his theological training at Hartford Theological Seminary. His selection by the trustees of the University of Rochester was partly a reflection of an unwritten rule at the time which required the appointment of a Baptist minister as the University's president.[6] However, the selection of Rhees proved to be a particularly wise choice. Rhees's accomplishments as president were made possible only through his cultivation of George Eastman's generosity, but he had to exercise great patience in dealing with the Rochester millionaire, who initially showed little interest in committing himself to any large-scale support of the university. In the years following his 1904 gift to the university, Eastman demonstrated a growing interest and deepening commitment toward music. In the fall of 1905 he engaged Hermann Dossenbach to provide a chamber music ensemble for a series of Thursday evening and Sunday afternoon musicales in his home.[7] These musicales became an extraordinarily important part of Rochester social life, and Rush Rhees and his wife were among the regularly invited guests. In addition to employing Dossenbach at his home, Eastman also provided important support for his orchestral aspirations. Eastman's mother had been one of the original patronesses of the Dossenbach Orchestra when it was founded in 1900. When the Musical Council, of which Rhees was President, sent Dossenbach to Europe for study during the 1911–12 season,

---

an engineering building, a chapel and auditorium, an art museum, a geological museum, a group of dormitories, and a Rochester Academy of Medicine, in addition to the possibility of a music school.

[6]   Although the University of Rochester was not officially affiliated with any particular church denomination, it had been founded by the American Baptist Church and its previous presidents had all been Baptist ministers.

[7]   The Dossenbach ensemble was initially paid $5,600 a year for playing at Eastman's home during a forty-week "season." Part of their contract required them to be available to play at the homes of Eastman's friends, such as the Mulligans, when he was out of town.

Eastman was the principal contributor to a fund established in support of the sabbatical. He also made annual contributions to Ludwig Schenck's Rochester Symphony and assisted David Hochstein by purchasing for him two violins, including a priceless Stradivarius. In many of these activities, Eastman worked closely with Rush Rhees. As the years passed, a genuine friendship developed between the two men, a friendship supported by mutual admiration and many common interests.

As the D.K.G. Institute of Musical Art continued to struggle financially, it was perhaps only natural that Eastman would become involved. Three institute graduates, who later became associated with the Eastman School of Music, all credited the Klingenbergs with eliciting Eastman's interest in the music school project. Ernestine Klinzing, in her 1967 essay, stated, "The credit for interesting George Eastman in the establishment of a music school endowed and connected with the University belongs in part to Mrs. Alf Klingenberg and to Mr. Hermann Dossenbach, who both worked toward that end."[8] Arthur See, interviewed by Roger Butterfield in 1950, commented:

> It was the Klingenbergs who gave him the motivation he was seeking—a project providing the long-range benefits that were a pre-requisite to any gift of GE's. It was only natural that they should suggest a school of music, a suggestion that reveals their perception of GE's philanthropic propensities.
>
> Once the idea of a music school took root, GE's energy and imagination brought it to full bloom in no time. The genius that had built a world-wide industry out of a revolutionary plan played with full force over the new field. Almost at once GE saw the project in its entirety.[9]

But it was Mildred Brownell Mehlenbacher who provided the most interesting and revealing information when, in a 1977 interview, she stated that George Eastman had been financially helping the Klingenbergs prior to his eventual decision to purchase the

[8] Klinzing, *Music in Rochester*, 23.
[9] Eastman-Butterfield Collection RRL. The collection consists of extensive notes assembled in the early 1950s by Roger Butterfield as a resource for a proposed biography of George Eastman (which was never published). Arthur See, a graduate of the D.K.G. Institute of Musical Art, where he studied with Alf Klingenberg, became secretary of the institute in 1918.

school for the university.[10] According to Mehlenbacher, Alexandra Klingenberg seized the initiative and went directly to Eastman's office to seek his support. After visiting the Prince Street school, he apparently agreed to offer some kind of financial assistance. There is good reason to accept Mehlenbacher's recollection of these events. She was a 1916 graduate of the D.K.G. Institute and the daughter of Frank Brownell, the man on whom Eastman relied for camera design. At an earlier date Eastman had bought out Brownell's own business for $150,000 and hired him at an impressive salary of $12,000 a year to head the experimental department at Kodak. Therefore, the Brownells were frequent guests in George Eastman's home, and their daughter's understanding of Eastman's earliest involvement with the Klingenbergs may have arisen as much from the family's social connections as from her own status as a student at the D.K.G. Institute of Musical Art.

Although any early Eastman involvement with the institute is not well documented, Mehlenbacher's testimony was corroborated by Harriet Seelye Rhees in her 1942 essay for the Rochester Historical Society. In it she referred to the institute when stating, "This struggling school was helped a little by Mr. Eastman."[11] Since her husband was the head of the institute's board of advisors, it is logical to assume that both Rush Rhees and his wife would have been aware of any financial assistance that Eastman was giving to the Klingenbergs. That assistance may have taken the form of providing scholarships for deserving students, and there is some suggestion that Eastman might have contributed to the costs of constructing the auditorium located to the rear of the Prince Street music school.

No direct evidence exists, of course, that would present an accurate account of the time frame and events that finally led Eastman to purchase the Institute for the University. It is highly probable, however, that conversations occurred between Eastman and Rhees on an ongoing basis concerning the future of music in Rochester, conversations motivated by their mutual interest in music. Then, following Eastman's tentative involvement in the affairs of the Prince Street school, a decision was finally reached that the most expedient manner of fulfilling hopes for music education in Rochester would be

---

[10] Mildred Brownell Mehlenbacher, interviewed by the author. Tape recording, Rochester, 16 November 1977.

[11] Mrs. Rush (Harriet Seelye) Rhees, "Rochester at the Turn of the Century" in *The Rochester Historical Society Publications*, vol. 20, compiled by Dexter Perkins (Rochester, 1942), 84.

to build upon what Klingenberg had already achieved by allowing the institute to pass under university ownership.

One possible scenario emerges from a rather fascinating story told by Jean Ingelow,[12] who related that George Barlow Penny took his orchestration class on a picnic in the spring of 1915, her senior year at the institute. According to Ingelow, Professor Penny spoke at length with his students at this picnic, telling them about a new school of music which Mr. Eastman was going to build. This conversation, if it took place, happened three years prior to the supposed question of "Why don't you have a music school?" Oral history is always somewhat suspect in the absence of any supporting evidence, and Ingelow's recollections came more than six decades after the alleged conversation by Professor Penny. Nonetheless, it is interesting to speculate whether, even as early as the spring of 1915, Eastman had already committed himself to building a new school for the Klingenbergs, although perhaps not with any intention at that date of affiliating the school with the University of Rochester. The full story has never been told, nor will it ever be related, since the only people who really knew are long since gone. All that remains are fascinating bits of information that can lead to endless speculation.

In any event, the decision to act in 1918 was most expeditious. The institute's provisional charter was about to expire, to be replaced by an absolute charter only if the school could give evidence of acquiring resources and equipment deemed suitable and sufficient by the Regents for its chartered purpose. The charter difficulties must have been at the forefront of concerns confronting the institute's advisors, including Rush Rhees. Acquisition by the University of Rochester would be a major step toward putting music education on a firmer basis in the City of Rochester. On March 27, 1918, Rush Rhees addressed the following letter to Augustus Downing, Assistant Commissioner of the State Department of Education in Albany:

> You are doubtless acquainted with the D.K.G. Institute of Musical Art in the City of Rochester, in which case you know that at present it is a proprietary institution operated for the profit of the proprietors.
>
> Some friends of musical education in Rochester are considering the wisdom of putting the institution on a different

---

[12] Jean Ingelow, interviewed by the author. Tape recording, Lakeville, N.Y., 7 May 1977.

basis as a distinctly educational institution owned by a
Board of Trustees and operated in the interests of the institution and of musical education exclusively. If this reorganization is realized it is probable that the University of
Rochester will affiliate with the institution so far as the
work conducted by it is of collegiate grade, by which I
mean that on completion of work suitable for the degree
Bachelor of Music by students who have pursued these
studies for four years after completing the necessary college preparation in a high school, the University will
stand ready to confer the music degree, as is done now by
Yale and I believe also by Syracuse.

You will do me a kindness if you will put me in pos-
session of all the information that I may need in order to
explain to the friends who are interested in the matter
what steps should be taken to effect this reorganization so
far as your department is concerned. Please tell me also
whether your Department has in its practice established
a minimum number of trustees for such an educational
institution.

Those who are interested in this project believe that the
de-personalizing of the school will make it possible for it
to render a larger service to the community. They are
interested in the matter because of their appreciation of
the service which has already been rendered by the
Institute under its present organization.[13]

Downing replied on April 1, 1918, in a detailed three-page letter which included the following note of caution:

I ought to say, however, that in studying your charter in
order to write you as intelligently as might be possible,
grave question arises as to whether the University of
Rochester has any right to enter into affiliated relations
with this or any other institution to confer degrees.[14]

Further correspondence ensued, but matters of real importance did
not develop until April 27, the date upon which the executive
committee of the university's Board of Trustees had its eighth
meeting of the year. At this meeting, Rhees referred to the possibility of establishing a music degree program by affiliating with the
D.K.G. Institute of Musical Art. Curiously, Rhees made no mention
of the fact that George Eastman was prepared to purchase the

---

[13]   Rush Rhees, Letter to Augustus Downing, 27 March 1918, RRL.
[14]   Augustus Downing, Letter to Rush Rhees, 1 April 1918. RRL

Institute for the university, even though that decision had been confirmed earlier in the month. The executive committee responded to
Rhees's report by passing a resolution favoring affiliation and
authorizing a committee to study possible charter revision.

Charter revision, however, was not the road upon which Rhees
opted to travel. On the same day on which he met with the trustees,
he addressed yet another letter to Augustus Downing, setting forth
an argument that the University of Rochester was already empow-
ered by its charter to confer music degrees. He argued that the university's provisional charter of 1850 granted "all the powers of
conferring degrees possessed by the trustees of similar collegiate
institutions in this State,"[15] a provision subsequently confirmed in
the later permanent charter. Among the other collegiate institutions
of the time was Columbia College which, by an Act of 1787, had
seen the privileges of its original 1754 Royal Charter confirmed.
This original charter, by which King George II had founded
Columbia as Kings College, authorized that institution to confer
those degrees "granted by any or either of our universities or colleges in that part of our kingdom called England."[16] Rhees had been
able to confirm that Oxford had conferred bachelor of music
degrees in the mid-eighteenth century. He reasoned that Kings
College had similar authority under Royal Charter, that Columbia
College inherited this authority by the Act of 1787, and that the
University of Rochester, therefore, possessed this same authority by
virtue of its own charter.

Augustus Downing was undoubtedly bedazzled by this line of
reasoning and could only reply on April 29 that he was very much
interested in this matter and would make a complete study of it. As
a preliminary step, Downing sent Rhees another letter on April 30,
enclosing a six-page brief which started by posing the question,
"Has the University of Rochester charter rights that warrant it in
organizing and affiliating with other schools; or of conferring other
degrees, undergraduate and graduate, than those in arts and science?" This question was followed by a one-word reply, "No." The
brief ended with five conclusions:

> 1. Rochester University [*sic*] has corporate power to
>   organize college instruction in courses leading to
>   degrees in arts and science only.

---

[15] Rush Rhees, Letter to Augustus Downing, 27 April 1918. RRL.
[16] Ibid.

2. Has no charter authority to organize other schools or colleges.
3. Has no authority to enter into affiliation with other corporations.
4. That the trustees of corporations created by the Regents (sec. 68 E.L.) may "grant such degrees and honors as are specifically authorized by their charter."
5. That colleges of liberal arts and science chartered by the Regents have power to confer undergraduate and graduate degrees in arts and science only.[17]

On May 21 Downing made his final reply to Rush Rhees in a two-page letter in which he simply reiterated his previous conclusions concerning the university's charter rights:

> I am quite firm in the opinion that Rochester University [*sic*] does not possess the power to confer a degree in music, and until its charter rights are extended the institution is not warranted in announcing courses leading to the proposed degree.[18]

Rhees acknowledged Downing's letter on May 22, confessing that he still did not understand Downing's interpretation of the facts, but he added that his inability to understand Downing's reasoning was probably due to his "torpidity of mind."[19] He next acted to gain Regent's authority to affiliate with the Institute as well as authority to conduct instruction leading to a bachelor of music degree. Two resolutions were duly submitted to Downing following the June meeting of the university's Board of Trustees.

The great haste with which Rush Rhees had proceeded during the spring months of 1918 suggests that he was anxious to acquire the institute and begin operating it in time for the opening of the 1918–19 school year. His dealings with Augustus Downing necessitated a delay in that affiliation, but apparently Klingenberg's desire to sell the school could not wait. Accordingly, on July 19, 1918, George Eastman purchased the school for $28,000. For this sum he acquired both the property and corporate rights of the institute, and for the next 315 days Eastman was the sole owner of the music

---

[17]   Augustus Downing, Letter to Rush Rhees, 30 April 1918. RRL.
[18]   Augustus Downing, Letter to Rush Rhees, 21 May 1918. RRL.
[19]   Rush Rhees, Letter to Augustus Downing, 22 May 1918. RRL.

school. Eleven days after the purchase, he wrote a curious letter to his niece, Ellen Dryden:

> Since having the codicil to my will drawn relating to the music school, I have come to the conclusion that the proper disposition of the 900 East Av [*sic*] property—That is the house and lot with fixtures and such furnishings as you do not want—would be to give it to the University of Rochester for a music school. As I have not time to have another codicil drawn, I shall rely on you to carry out this planning.[20]

The suggestion that the university should use his home for a music school, made after he had purchased the institute for the university, would seem to give indication that, as of the summer months of 1918, Eastman may have made no commitment to provide a new building for the institute. It would also seem to contradict Jean Ingelow's recollections of 1915. The thought that no construction plans were in the offering is supported by the fact that Rhees had not referred either to Eastman or to any pending construction when reporting to the executive committee of the Board of Trustees on April 29.

Further support of this contention may be found in the catalogues of the institute itself. The 1918–19 catalogue, issued for the fall following Eastman's purchase, made the following announcement:

> It is with great satisfaction that the Director upon completion of the School's fifth year of existence can announce that the interest in the school has grown to such an extent that a number of public spirited citizens of Rochester have offered a generous support to insure its continued progress.
>
> This is in the first place made possible through the generosity of Mr. Eastman who bought the Institute and its buildings for the University of Rochester.
>
> While the exact nature of the Institute's affiliation with the University is still to be determined, announcement can be made that arrangements are in progress, whereby students who have met the college entrance requirements will be enabled to work for a bachelor's degree from the

---

[20] George Eastman, Letter to Ellen Dryden, 30 July 1918. GEH.

> University by adding to the regular Four Year's course of
> the Institute the necessary academic studies.[21]

What is contained in the foregoing paragraphs is simply a reitera-
tion of Rush Rhees's statements that an affiliation between the institute and university was pending. The consistent reference to
affiliation for the purpose of offering a music degree and the
absence of any comment concerning future plans for a new music
school building does not give any indication that long-range plans
for the music school project had been discussed or formulated in
conjunction with Eastman's purchase of the institute. Furthermore,
during the entire period of 1918, no correspondence apparently
exists that refers to either land acquisition or new construction.
Such matters were to develop only later and would unfold quite
dramatically in 1919.

For Alf Klingenberg, however, it was business as usual when
the institute reopened in September 1918. He remained director of
the school, and no noticeable change in faculty or curricula could be
observed under the new ownership. Rush Rhees, however, was
anxiously awaiting Regents approval of the amendment to the university charter. This was finally accomplished on December 12,
1918, and the new provisions sanctioned

> the establishment and maintaining of undergraduate and
> graduate college departments, professional, technical,
> vocational, and other departments; the designation of
> any department of the University as schools and with
> appropriate distinguishing names; the placing of any
> such departments under specific management, auxiliary
> and subordinate to that of the University trustees. . . .[22]

Although Rush Rhees received written confirmation from
Downing of the amendment's approval in a letter dated December
24, 1918, he was anxious to have a certified copy and sent a
telegram to Albany requesting this. In response to this telegram, he
was mistakenly sent two copies of the bill pending in the State
Assembly which would amend the charter of the city of Rochester.
He rather impatiently requested correction of the matter in a letter

---

[21] *The Institute of Musical Art* [Catalogue] (Rochester [1918]), unpaginated. SML.
[22] University of the State of New York, Amendment to Charter of University of
Rochester. Dated December 12, 1918, by the Regents of the State of New York,
executed under their seal and recorded in their office. SML.

dated January 16, 1919, received an immediate apology, and finally obtained the desired document on January 21. In the history of the University of Rochester, the date of January 21, 1919, is of genuine importance. Albany had claimed, with some justification, that the University of Rochester was a university in name only. The amendment to its charter, as finally received by President Rhees on that cold and wintery January day, made the institution a university in fact as well as in name.

Chapter 3

1919–1921
Planning the New School
and Theater

In February 1919—eleven months after Rush Rhees's initial inquiry to Augustus Downing concerning the feasibility of the university affiliating with the Institute of Musical Art, and six months after Eastman's purchase of the Prince Street music school—Rochester's newspapers announced that Eastman was committing himself to providing the university with a new concert hall and school of music "surpassed by no other in the world." Plans had unfolded rapidly, and land for new buildings had been selected on the city's east side in an area bordered by Main Street on the north, Barrett Alley on the south, Gibbs Street on the west, and Swan Street on the east.

The executive committee of the university's Board of Trustees passed a resolution at its meeting of February 28, 1919, which approved options for the sale and transfer to the university of several parcels of land, the purchase price of which George Eastman had generously offered to pay. The committee further passed a resolution of thanks to Eastman:

> Resolved, That the Executive Committee of the Trustees of the University of Rochester express to Mr. George Eastman their high appreciation of his magnificent provision for a new building for a School of Music and concert hall, for the advancement of musical culture in Rochester, and their pride and satisfaction in Mr. Eastman's choice of the University to be the custodian of his gift; and also their readiness to cooperate with Mr. Eastman in perfecting the necessary plans for the organization and administration of the enterprise.[1]

---

[1]   Minutes, Seventh Meeting of the Executive Committee of the Board of Trustees of the University of Rochester, 28 February 1919. RRL.

Figure 6. The east side of Gibbs Street, November 1919, showing buildings existing prior to the construction of the Eastman School and Eastman Theatre.

Additionally, the executive committee authorized Rush Rhees "to make, execute, and deliver in the name of the University any and all agreements and contracts for the erection, equipment, and furnishing of buildings."

The full Board of Trustees, at a meeting on May 16, 1919, received a more detailed report from President Rhees, who explained that Eastman intended to erect a new music school with a large auditorium that would have a seating capacity of approximately three thousand and be used for "high class" motion pictures. Rhees also added that Eastman was committed not only to fully equip the buildings, but also to suitably endow the music school. Upon motion made by Rush Rhees, the Board expressed thanks to Eastman and conveyed to him their desire that he should consent to have the new school bear his name. The notion held by some commentators that Eastman was reluctant to have the school named after him is certainly not supported by the fact that he quickly responded to the trustees' request on June 2, 1919, indicating that he had no objection to calling it the Eastman School of Music.

The agreement between George Eastman and the University of Rochester was formalized in a Memorandum of Agreement, signed and dated on July 10, 1919.[2] The memorandum set forth Eastman's intention to provide the University with "a building or buildings for said college or school of music, a large concert and motion picture hall or auditorium, a smaller concert or recital hall, and a power plant" and "to properly equip the said buildings and plant and to endow the said college or school of music." Furthermore, the memorandum established that the school of music and "any other business or operation carried on in any way in said buildings" would be operated and maintained through a separate Board of Directors, nominated by Eastman himself but approved by the university's Board of Trustees. Future vacancies on this Board of Directors would be filled by the Board of Directors itself, with approval of the Trustees. The agreement further stipulated that if the University of Rochester ever wanted to move the music school, it could only do so if it constructed and equipped "similar buildings" at the new location. The memorandum also specifically prohibited using any income from the school's endowment to support the professional orchestra envisioned as part of the theater enterprise, adding that George Eastman did not intend to endow an

---

[2]   Memorandum of Agreement, 10 July 1919. SML.

orchestra nor did he wish to contribute to its maintenance "beyond any such proceeds as may be available . . . from the operation of the large concert and motion picture hall."

The D.K.G. Institute of Musical Art was not forgotten during all of these dramatic developments. On June 12, 1919, the university acquired the institute and its property from George Eastman for a price of $1.00, an action made possible by its amended charter. Rush Rhees informed Augustus Downing of this action on July 9, mentioning, perhaps prematurely, that the music school would "henceforth be known as the Eastman School of Music of the University of Rochester."[3] He added that new buildings and an "ample endowment" were being provided by Mr. Eastman, but that the present work of the school would proceed with "increased vigor" under the control of the university. Apparently, however, Rhees or someone else had second thoughts concerning the notion of putting Eastman's name on the music school's present structure. Therefore, the institute opened for its seventh year on September 8, 1919, with its catalogue-title reading "The University of Rochester Institute of Musical Art."

Among newer faculty members during these final years of the institute were Harold Gleason and Arthur Alexander, who both came to Rochester also to serve in musical roles at Eastman's house, the former as organist and the latter as coordinator of the Thursday evening and Sunday afternoon musicales. Bringing Arthur Alexander to Rochester in July 1918 was a bold and, in retrospect, curious move. Born in New Zealand in 1891 and educated in England, Alexander had made his reputation both as a pianist and as a singer, and he became known for presenting vocal recitals at which he served at the piano as his own accompanist. Eastman paid Alexander $10,000, a very generous amount, to direct the musical presentations in his home and also to teach voice at the institute. He had in mind, however, a much bigger role for Alexander, namely that of conductor of the symphony orchestra envisioned for the new theater.

It was Alexander who suggested to Eastman that he should hire Harold Gleason to replace George E. Fisher, who had been his organist for fourteen years. A student of Edwin Henry Lamare (1865–1934), W. Lynwood Farnam (1885–1930), and Joseph Bonnet (1884–1944), Gleason came to Rochester from Fifth Avenue Presbyterian Church in New York. His responsibilities at Eastman's

---

[3] Rush Rhees, Letter to Augustus Downing, 9 July 1919. RRL.

home included playing the organ at breakfast, a routine he later described in some detail:

> The breakfast hour was 7:30 o'clock on weekdays and 8:00 o'clock on Sundays. At exactly 7:30 his bedroom door opened, and I would begin to play as he came down the stairs to the music room. During my many years with him I was late only once, although I occasionally missed my breakfast. His only comment was a stern, "Mr. Gleason, I expect you to be on time." Breakfast was a favorite time for him to invite guests sometimes socially and at other times for serious discussions including some that might be called "top secret." Men and women from all walks of life appeared for breakfast. I sometimes thought that it gave him a peculiar pleasure to get them out at that hour, especially the musicians.[4]

In addition to his responsibilities at breakfast, Gleason was expected to play with the string quartet for the weekly dinners on Thursdays and Sundays. He performed a wide range of repertoire but was forced to respect Eastman's notorious dislike of the music of Bach. Eastman's initial salary offer was substantially lower than what Gleason was making at Fifth Avenue Presbyterian, and the organist had felt that he had to decline the position. However, Eastman was anxious to hire Gleason and increased the offer with the stipulation that he was also to teach at the Institute of Musical Art. Gleason's name appeared for the first time in the institute's 1919–20 catalogue, and he thus began a highly distinguished teaching career that would continue in Rochester for over three and a half decades.[5]

Including Gleason and Alexander, Klingenberg's faculty numbered twenty-three for the 1919–20 school year. There was no major expansion or change reflecting the fact that the institute was now owned by the university. For Rush Rhees, however, there were many new responsibilities. He met with the executive committee of his trustees on September 26, 1919, and reported that Eastman had deposited in the Alliance Bank one million dollars to meet construction costs for the new buildings, and had also deposited a sum

[4]   Harold Gleason, "Please Play My Funeral March," *The University of Rochester Library Bulletin* 26, no. 3 (Spring 1971): 113.
[5]   Harold Gleason was George Eastman's organist until 1930, when he felt the need to leave the position because of his increasing work load at the Eastman School of Music. His successor as organist at Eastman House was Elizabeth Vaughn, whose husband later became president of Eastman Kodak Company.

of $2,139,554.25 as an endowment for the school of music. The previous day Rhees had written another letter to Downing reminding him that the university was now the owner of the Institute and asking what steps might be necessary to secure recognition of the transfer of the institute to the university and its re-designation as the Eastman School of Music. Apparently, the situation was somewhat without precedent, for Downing did not reply until October 14; he began his letter by saying, "I have read your letter of September 25th before me and have read it pretty nearly every day since I received it."[6] He continued by suggesting that Rhees write a formal letter simply stating that the D.K.G. Institute of Musical Art no longer existed, its stock and property having come into the possession of the University of Rochester, which had organized a new Eastman School of Music. What appeared to be a stenographer's error in Downing's letter, however, caused Rhees to request a clarification in a letter dated October 20, 1919. (The stenographer's error was simply writing "Board of Trustees" rather than "Board of Regents.") His letter, however, was filed without reply for some reason, and this complicated question concerning recognition of the university's ownership and the relationship of the institute's charter to the new Eastman School of Music was not addressed again until three years later.

While Rhees was occupied by such matters, Eastman pursued the problems of planning for his great enterprise. Preliminary discussions were held with the Rochester architectural firm of Gordon and Kaelber. While the local firm would be in charge of providing the floor plans, Eastman also revealed that he intended to use a consulting architect who could assume responsibility for the design. The firm ultimately selected as consulting architects was McKim, Mead, and White of New York City, perhaps the leading architectural firm in America at the time, and the architect who would work on the Eastman project was Lawrence White. White was to be responsible for the exterior design of the building—both the school and the theater—as well as for designing the interior of the theater and the more important rooms of the school. In doing so, however, he was forced to utilize the basic floor plans developed by Gordon and Kaelber, an arrangement that produced a significant amount of tension and difficulty. Nonetheless, this arrangement was quite deliberate. Eastman feared putting the more practical decisions into the hands of White, who might approach the problem simply from

---

[6]   Augustus Downing, Letter to Rush Rhees, 14 October 1919. RRL.

an architectural standpoint. He considered the basic floor plan to be simply an "engineering proposition," and he felt more comfortable with having his local architects deal with these decisions.

While all of this was transpiring, Edwin S. Gordon began preliminary planning for the music school and theater. In April 1919 Eastman sent him on a tour of New York, Boston, Chicago, and New Haven to visit music buildings and to gather ideas for the new music school. The architect eventually visited eight schools of music, eight music halls, and thirty-five motion picture theaters. In addition, he studied the details of many other schools of music and theaters. In August of the same year Eastman made a down payment of $10,000 for architectural fees.

In selecting Gordon and Kaelber, Eastman passed over some other notable Rochester architects such as J. Foster Warner and Claude Bragdon. But Edwin Gordon's credentials were impressive: he had worked with both Warner and Bragdon in the 1890s, prior to forming partnerships first with William Madden and later with William Kaelber. His association with Kaelber, extending from 1919 to his death in 1932, produced such notable Rochester buildings as the University of Rochester River Campus complex, Cutler Union, the Rochester Gas and Electric Building, and the Hiram Sibley Building on East Avenue at Alexander Street. The problems confronting Edwin Gordon in 1919 were considerable, certainly complicated by the fact that the building lot for the school and theater was not rectangular in shape, since Main Street and Barrett Alley were not parallel. An unforeseen problem soon arose that further complicated the architectural plans when the owner of the large building on the corner of Main and Swan Streets demanded an exorbitant price for his property. Rather than yielding to an unreasonable demand, Eastman abandoned his efforts to acquire this particular parcel of property and ordered an architectural redesign to work around the corner building. This redesign meant that hopes for having the building's facade extend from Barrett Alley all around the corner along Main Street had to be altered. More important, the axis of the theater had to be repositioned so that it was no longer at a right angle to the facade, a situation that greatly troubled the New York architects.

When McKim, Mead, and White were consulted, the firm responded by submitting a new, alternate plan in August 1919, but Eastman answered in defense of existing plans by stating, "This plan has been worked out after about six months of hard work and consultation with the most experienced operating experts in the country, and embodies practically all their ideas, adapted to the shape of the lot which we have."[7] In the same letter he also responded directly to concerns that the New York architects had expressed concerning Edwin Gordon's design for an elliptical lobby:

> I cannot think that the relative angles of the elliptical lobby and the axis of the auditorium is a matter that will ever be noticed by the public, or, if it is, that it will make any difference in their impression of the place. I myself prefer the elliptical lobby to the circular one.

To his friend F. L. Babbott of New York he expressed his disappointment with the New York firm:

> The angles that McKim, Mead and White object to would never be discovered by anybody on entering the theater. They might discover it on leaving the theater, but if they did, it would not be of any importance in my estimation. We had a mighty nice interview, but I suppose right down in their hearts Messrs. Kendall and White think I am a pretty headstrong proposition, and I think that they are letting their art interfere with utility.
> . . . McKim, Mead and White are restive because the floor plans had been worked out practically to completion before the problem had been brought to them. This was my deliberate purpose, because I felt they would put the working-out of the floor plan layout into the hands of the designer, in this case Mr. White. He approached the problem purely from an architectural standpoint which is fundamentally wrong. A floor plan is an engineering proposition, and must take precedence over architecture in any commercial proposition.[8]

What should have been clear to everyone was the fact that George Eastman was going to be involved in every aspect of the planning and design of the school and theater. Years later Harold Gleason remarked that Eastman "knew exactly what he wanted," adding that "no matter what the architect said, if he didn't like it, he didn't get it."[9]

To Babbott fell the role of peacemaker with the New York architects. It was not until January of the following year that they agreed to come back to the theater project on Eastman's terms, but only

---

[7]   George Eastman, Letter to McKim, Mead, and White, 7 August 1919. GEH.
[8]   Ackerman, *George Eastman*, 424.
[9]   Harold Gleason, interviewed by the author. Tape recording of telephone conversation, 7 February 1978.

with the stipulation that all publicity would clearly state that they were not responsible for the floor plans. The architectural plan finally agreed upon called for the music school to occupy the land on the south side of the building site, with an adjoining theater sharing a common facade with the school and occupying the irregular north side of the site. The exterior was to be built of limestone in a modified Italian Renaissance style. The main theater entrance was designed to occupy the corner of Main and Gibbs and led in to an elliptical lobby of Botticine marble with black and gold marble columns. In fairness to Lawrence White's opinion on the matter, it is probably safe to say that the lobby is one of the few unsatisfactory aspects in the theater design. Although beautifully decorated, it is really too small a space to accommodate a large crowd of ticket holders. It was, however, what George Eastman wanted, and the New York architect had little choice other than to accept his judgment in the matter.

Eastman saw the theater as a means toward the broadest possible educational benefit of the community-at-large by using the popular medium of motion pictures as a vehicle for promoting the enjoyment of music. Therefore, he envisioned using his theater six days a week for the showing of motion pictures, reserving only Wednesday evenings for concerts and recitals. The large theaters of the day maintained orchestras for the accompaniment of the silent films then being produced, and presentation of films was often supplemented by instrumental or organ music, by vocal entertainment, and by dance. Eastman perhaps cannot be faulted for failing to anticipate the dramatic changes that were soon to occur in the motion picture industry and that would make the use of his theater as a "movie palace" relatively brief. In 1919 the plan seemed ingenious and far-reaching, and neither expense nor effort was spared in planning for a theater that would be second to none.

Rush Rhees was presented with a opportunity to discuss Eastman's vision when he addressed the third annual convention of the National Association of the Motion Picture Industry, which was meeting in Rochester in 1919:

> Mr. Eastman proposes to call in the aid of motion pictures in connection with his great enterprise for music education. The alliance between music and pictures is not new, having been worked out on an extensive scale in a number of metropolitan picture theaters. . . . The success of those theaters has demonstrated not only that the enjoyment of the best motion pictures is greatly enhanced when they are interpreted by carefully selected music, but also that the

people who are attracted to motion picture entertainments find interest and pleasure in music greatly enhanced. This fact indicates the possibility of greatly enlarging the number of persons in the community, who will know and value the satisfaction which good music has to offer by arranging to use the music hall in the new school for motion pictures of the best quality accompanied by music which will be furnished by a large orchestra.[10]

Meanwhile, preparations were being made to clear the construction site of its existing structures. A local contractor, Francis X. Yeoman, was paid $27,500 for the removal of existing buildings and for the initial excavation. At the southwest corner, where Barrett Alley enters Gibbs Street, stood an imposing brick building that served as the office of Dr. Edward W. Mulligan, George Eastman's physician and one of his closest friends. Associated in practice with Mulligan was Dr. Audley Durand Stewart, who became Eastman's doctor upon Mulligan's death a few years later. For some reason, the building that housed the office of these two physicians was spared demolition and moved to a parallel site on Swan Street, where it became for about the next half-dozen years the local office for the Burroughs Adding Machine Company. The rest of the structures on the building site, however, were demolished. Adjacent to Dr. Mulligan's office was a rooming house and a larger apartment building called "The Smithsonian." Closer to Main Street was the home of Mr. and Mrs. George Karl and Mary Rhines, who also had a dressmaking business at this location. On the corner of Main and Gibbs stood the lovely home of Anna London, owner of a lodging house next door at 431 East Main Street. In addition to the demolition of these buildings, several more along the west side of Swan Street needed to be cleared to make room for the new school and theater.

On the opposite side of Swan Street stood a row of wood-frame houses, both single and multi-family structures. The one closest to Barrett Alley was removed to make room for the brick building being moved there from Gibbs Street, and the adjacent three-family structure just to the north made way for the school and theater's central heating plant. This was to be a two-story brick structure set back from the street to provide space for the delivery of coal and providing over 200,000 cubic feet of space. The building, constructed at a cost of $208,149, would be equipped with four boilers, and heat

---

[10] Ackerman, *George Eastman*, 419–20.

and electricity would be supplied to the school and theater through a tunnel eight feet wide and ten feet high that ran beneath Swan Street. The boiler house building was constructed with a view that it might some day bear the weight of an eight-story dormitory to accommodate students from the music school "should the provision for such quarters become necessary in the future."[11]

With the school now under construction, Rush Rhees turned his attention to the problems of establishing a curriculum for the proposed bachelor of music degree. Awarding such a degree was, of course, a primary reason why the University had originally agreed to affiliate with Klingenberg's school. On March 23, 1920, Rhees wrote Augustus Downing to ask what institutions were registered with the Regents to confer music degrees. Downing replied on April 1 to the effect that only two institutions at the time were registered to confer the music degree, but he also included a study showing that a considerable number of schools offered the degree without asking to have it registered in Albany. More correspondence occurred during 1920, but it was not until December 4, 1922, that Rhees finally submitted his application for registration of the Bachelor of Music degree. As we will relate, the registration was approved in Albany on January 25, 1923, about seven months after the Eastman School of Music had already conferred its first baccalaureate degrees.

Even though there was yet no baccalaureate curriculum when the institute reopened in September, 1920, for its eighth year, the university claimed that the Prince Street school was already functioning as its music department. The 1920–21 catalogue, in its historical sketch of the University of Rochester, now contained the following information.

> In 1918 the institution [i.e., the University of Rochester] expanded its scope to include a University School of Music. By the liberality of Mr. George Eastman, it acquired the property and corporate rights of the Institute of Musical Art at 47 Prince Street opposite the Campus, and continued the Institute as the University School of Music under the able supervision of Mr. Alf Klingenberg as Director.[12]

The date of 1918 is, of course, incorrect, since the university did not acquire the Institute until the following year. Curiously, this

---

[11]   University of Rochester, *Building Progress Bulletin* 1, no. 3 [undated]. SML.
[12]   *The University of Rochester College of Arts and Science Annual Catalogue 1920–1921*, October 1920, 33.

inaccuracy persisted in many publications for years to come. Enrollment at the school was close to five hundred, including preparatory students, but there was expectation of major expansion once the new buildings were available, as evidenced by an Eastman letter dated January 5, 1920, that he addressed to Charles Lapworth of Goldwyn Pictures.

> The School of Music referred to is already in existence and has a registration of about 500. The new school building, which will adjoin and connect with the auditorium, will provide the most modern and complete accommodations for about 2,500 students.[13]

Figure 7. The Eastman School of Music under construction, 27 March 1921.

---

[13] George Eastman, Letter to Charles Lapworth, 5 January 1920. GEH.

Progress continued quite dramatically at the construction site. The music school building had been given priority over the theater so that it would be available for use the following September. By the end of 1920 the frame of the school building was nearing completion, and work progressed rapidly during the early months of 1921. A. W. Hopeman and Sons Co. was the general contractor, and the amount of work accomplished in a relatively short time was quite impressive. For the school itself, not including the theater, which had hardly begun, twelve hundred tons of steel were used along with close to a half million bricks, over twenty-five hundred tons of stone facing, and four thousand five hundred barrels of cement.

On June 4, 1921, the institute held its annual commencement, graduating three students from its Four Year Course and seven students from the Public School Music Course. The commencement ceremony brought to an effective end eight years of music education on Prince Street. These eight years had seen the opening of the Dossenbach-Klingenberg School in 1913, its reorganization as the D.K.G. Institute of Musical Art in 1914, its consolidation with the Rochester Conservatory in 1916, the sole directorship and ownership of Alf Klingenberg in 1917, the purchase by George Eastman in 1918, and the acquisition by the University of Rochester in 1919. The simple yet dramatic move to Gibbs Street, planned for September 1921, would so profoundly change music education in Rochester that the entire history of accomplishment on Prince Street would quickly recede from memory.

Chapter 4

1921–1922
The Opening of the Eastman
School of Music

While the new Eastman School buildings were still under construction, it became clear that the one-million-dollar construction fund provided by George Eastman would be insufficient to cover all costs. In accepting the fund from Eastman, the university had agreed to relieve him of any further obligation that might be incurred. His help was needed, however, and he generously gave the university 5,000 shares of Eastman Kodak stock on April 20, 1921, for use as collateral for borrowing money payable to the building fund, with income from the stock being used to pay the interest on such loans. This gift in April brought his total contribution to slightly more than three and a half million dollars, and by the completion of construction Eastman had increased support to a total of close to five and a half million dollars. This, in turn, grew with additional contributions to more than twelve million dollars within a few years, and the best estimate of Eastman's total cost for the school was an eventual figure of nearly seventeen and a half million dollars, about five times his original commitment to the project.

In a New York Times interview dating from the beginning of the construction period, Eastman had explained his motivation in this rather extraordinary endeavor:

> I am interested in music personally, and I am led thereby, merely to want to share my pleasure with others. For a great many years I have been connected with musical organizations in Rochester. I have helped to support a symphony orchestra. Recurrently, we have faced the fact that what was needed was a body of trained listeners quite as much as a body of competent performers. It is fairly easy to employ skillful musicians. It is impossible

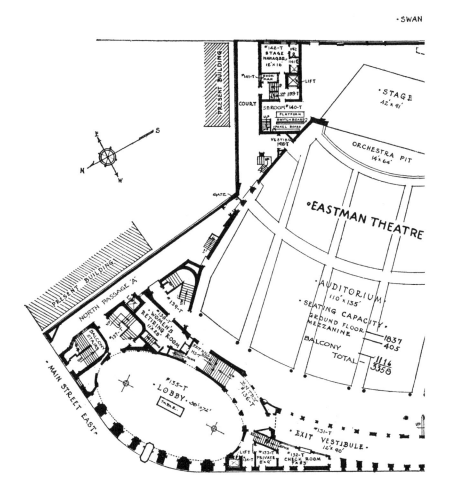

· FIRST FLOOR PLAN ·

Figure 8. First floor plan of the Eastman School and Eastman Theater. Note the angle of theater stage and seating in relation to entrance and lobby. (Collection of the author.)

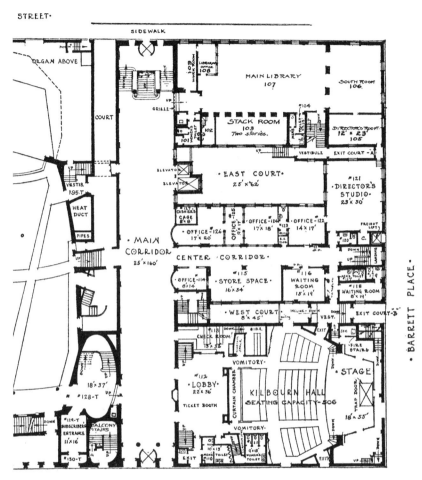

Figure 8. (continued)

Figure 9. The east side of Gibbs Street, 4 August 1921, showing the school and, beyond it, where the Eastman Theatre was being constructed. School would start just a month later.

to buy an appreciation of music. Yet, without appreciation, without a presence of a large body of people who
understand music and who get joy out of it, any attempt
to develop the musical resources of any city is doomed to
failure. Because, in Rochester, we realize this, we have
undertaken a scheme for building musical capacity on a
large scale from childhood.[1]

The scope of this undertaking was very broad. The school was to
function as a university department that would train candidates for
the bachelor of music degree and, in addition, serve as a community school offering instruction to both adults and children.
Furthermore, the theater was designed to provide a cultural exposure to the broadest possible segment of the community.

The anticipated completion of the school building for use in
September 1921 was eagerly awaited. An expansion in faculty was
planned, and Klingenberg was involved in recruitment for a considerable period of time. There was great hope that Jean Sibelius
(1865–1957) might accept an offer to teach composition.
Klingenberg had befriended him many years earlier when they
were both studying in Berlin. In September 1920, he was sent to
Finland to pursue the matter. Negotiations with Sibelius have led
to a persistent assertion that the great Finnish composer was
offered the director's position at the Eastman School of Music.
This story has been endlessly repeated, including by several of
Sibelius' biographers. In all probability, however, it is not true.
Sibelius was approached to teach theory and composition, not to
direct the school. Karl Ekman, in his 1936 biography of Sibelius,[2]
may have been the first to make the claim that the director's position had been offered to the Finnish composer. Since Ekman's
book was widely considered to be the "authorized biography" of
Sibelius, it was generally viewed as the indispensable source for
all later writers.

More than a half-century later Robert Layton was repeating the
same information,[3] and even the latest edition of the prestigious
New Grove Dictionary[4] repeats the assertion that Sibelius was

[1] "Philanthropy under a Bushel," *New York Times*, 21 March 1920. SML.

[2] Karl Ekman, *Sibelius* (London, Alan Wilmer, Ltd., 1936).

[3] Robert Layton, *Sibelius*, The Master Musicians, 4th ed. (London: J. M. Dent &
Sons, Ltd., 1992), 53.

[4] James Hepokoski. "Sibelius, Jean" in *The New Grove Dictionary of Music and
Musicians*, ed. Stanley Sadie, 2nd ed. (London: Macmillan Publishers, and New
York: Grove's Dictionaries, Inc., 1995), 23:336.

offered the director's position at Eastman. By contrast, Harold Johnson's well-researched biography of Sibelius relates quite a different story:

> One year prior to the grand opening of the Eastman School of Music, Klingenberg, who retained his title as director, toured Europe in search of a well-known faculty. In answer to a letter inquiring whether he would be interested in teaching theory and composition, Sibelius wrote that the proposition was "not disagreeable." . . . In September 1920, Klingenberg visited Järrenpää, where he was staggered to learn that Sibelius demanded a salary of $20,000 for nine months of teaching. . . . By January of the following year, all of the composer's demands had been met. . . . In April, however, the composer had a change of heart. . . .[5]

Johnson's account seems to be fully supported by existing documentary evidence, including a copy of a telegram from George Eastman to Alf Klingenberg during the period of negotiation with Sibelius, which authorized him to offer Sibelius $20,000 for teaching composition at the Eastman School of Music during 1921–22. The salary offer was two and a half times what Klingenberg was making as director of the school. The telegram made no mention of the director's position in connection with this offer. Besides, there is no evidence that George Eastman and Rush Rhees were seeking to replace Alf Klingenberg as director of the new school at that time. If they had that intention, they certainly would not have sent Klingenberg to negotiate with the Finnish composer. In any event, Sibelius had last-minute doubts concerning the move to America, and he ultimately declined the offer. He explained his reasons in a letter to Klingenberg:

> I see now that it is completely impossible for me to teach. It would be the greatest calamity for your conservatory to have me as a teacher. I can conduct my compositions tolerably well, but as a teacher—impossible. Furthermore, there are other reasons. Dear friend, act accordingly, and please understand me.[6]

This decision came so late that the initial bulletin issued by the Eastman School was already in print and included Sibelius' name

---

[5]   Harold Johnson, *Sibelius* (New York: Alfred Knopf, 1959), 185.
[6]   Ibid: 187.

in the listing of theory and composition faculty.[7] An insert announced that Christian Sinding (1856–1941), the eminent Norwegian composer, was going to replace Sibelius on the faculty.

Educated in Germany, Sinding was widely considered by the Norwegians to be their country's greatest composer since Grieg. His fame grew so rapidly that, at the age of thirty-four, he received a stipend from the Norwegian government that enabled him to devote himself entirely to composition. Although he wrote many works, he is chiefly remembered today as the composer of "Rustle of Spring," a rather insignificant little piano piece which, nonetheless, was a popular favorite with piano teachers and piano students for many years. In 1921, however, he was considered to be a serious and important figure in the compositional world, and his agreement to teach at the Eastman School was greeted with considerable enthusiasm. His work at Eastman was confined to the school's opening year, and his replacement on the Eastman faculty the following year was the Finnish composer Selim Palmgren (1878–1951).

In addition to hiring Sinding, Klingenberg also recruited a number of other prominent European musicians. Thomas Henry Yorke Trotter secured a leave of absence from his position as principal of the London Academy of Music to join the Eastman School theory department, and organist Joseph Bonnet agreed to come from France to join Harold Gleason on the organ teaching staff. Also from France came the distinguished pianist, Pierre Augieras, who had been a student of Antoine-François Marmontel (1816–1898), Charles Wilfrid de Bériot (1833–1914),[8] and Isidor Philipp (1863–1958) at the Paris Conservatory, and who had served as Philipp's assistant for four years. Augieras enjoyed a distinguished performing career before and after the First World War. During the war years, however, he joined the French aviation service and was wounded in battle on three occasions. For his bravery he was awarded the Croix de Guerre.

Closer to home, Raymond Wilson left Syracuse University to join the 1921 Eastman piano faculty, thereby beginning a career at the school that would span more than three decades and would see Wilson become assistant director, head of the piano faculty, director of the Preparatory Department, and director of the Summer Session. Wilson had studied with Ernest Hutcheson (1871–1951)

---

[7] Bulletin of Information No. 1. Undated, but presumably issued in the spring of 1921.
[8] Not to be confused with his father, Charles Auguste de Bériot, the famous violinist.

and Rudolph Ganz (1877–1972) and became a member of the faculty at Syracuse in 1914. Also new to the faculty was Adelin Fermin, who had been a voice teacher at the conservatory of music in The Hague before coming to the United States and joining the faculty of the Peabody Conservatory in Baltimore. He had an impressive record of recital tours in Europe and in America, and was also a rather successful composer.

Among faculty members preparing to make the transition from the Prince Street school to the new school on Gibbs Street were the four members of the Kilbourn Quartet, namely Arthur Hartmann, Gerald Kunz, Samuel Belov, and Gerald Maas. The most widely known member of the quartet was its first violinist, Arthur Hartmann. He had been recruited by Arthur Alexander in 1918 to be the principal violin teacher at the institute and the first violinist in a new string quartet that was to perform regularly at George Eastman's home. This generally involved playing at the small Thursday evening dinner parties and the larger social affairs on Sunday, which remained a regular feature of the millionaire's social life in Rochester. The new quartet replaced the group led by Hermann Dossenbach, which had been playing at Eastman's home for about fifteen years. A child prodigy, Arthur Hartmann began his career in 1887 when he was only six years old. Over the years he had attained an enviable reputation as a violinist through many concert tours in Europe, the United States, and Canada.

The cellist, Gerald Maas, also had rather impressive credentials. A graduate of the Paris Conservatory, Maas quickly established himself as a solo and chamber music player of the first rank. After teaching briefly at the Frankfurt Conservatory, he came to the United States and became cellist of the Letz Quartet before joining the institute faculty in 1920. Kunz and Belov also became faculty members in 1920. Born in Russia, Samuel Belov came from a family of musicians. After arriving in the United States, he became a member of the Philadelphia Orchestra and a teacher of violin and viola at the Philadelphia Conservatory of Music.[9] Gerald Kunz was born in Milwaukee and had studied with Franz Kneisel (1865–1926)[10] at the Institute of Musical Art in New York. It was on Kneisel's recommendation that he came to Rochester to be second violinist of the quartet.

---

[9] The Philadelphia Conservatory of Music is now part of the Philadelphia Colleges of the Arts.
[10] Franz Kneisel is best remembered for having organized the Kneisel Quartet in 1886, an ensemble that concertized extensively until it disbanded in 1917.

Among others preparing to transfer their teaching to the new school were singers Arthur Alexander, Frederick Benson, Lucy Lee Call, and Marian Weed. Joining them was Oscar Gareissen, who had severed his relationship with Klingenberg in 1918 but now returned as a member of the faculty. Hermann Dossenbach, who had also ended his connection with Klingenberg in 1918, did not return or have any subsequent role at the Eastman School of Music. However, his daughter, Hazel, began teaching violin at the institute in 1919 and continued as a faculty member at Eastman until 1926. In all there were almost three dozen faculty members in September 1921, providing instruction in theory and composition, music history, public school methods, piano, voice, organ, violin, viola, cello, and harp. The addition of faculty to teach woodwinds, brass, and percussion would have to wait for a few years.

Meanwhile, construction of the school had fallen behind schedule, and hopes for a completed building in time for the opening of the 1921–22 school year were not fulfilled. Nonetheless, two floors—the third and fourth—were ready for use by students and faculty in September 1921. Access to the third and fourth floors was through a temporary passageway leading from the Gibbs Street entrance directly to the elevators. The third floor contained an assembly room at the end of the building's east wing, eleven studios, and four classrooms for instructional purposes, while the fourth floor provided an additional assembly hall, lecture room, theory room, office, and nineteen studios, in addition to the organ department.

The organ department was situated in the west wing of the fourth floor, but the pipes for the practice and studio organs were located in chambers on the fifth floor above these rooms. The practice organs were all two-manual instruments with seven stops, while the studio or teaching organs had three manuals and seventeen stops. The cost of the two studio organs and seven practice organs was somewhat in excess of $30,000. The school was also initially equipped with thirty-eight pianos, including five concert grands, eight parlor grands, ten baby grands, and fifteen uprights. These were purchased from Steinway at a cost of about $50,000, and it was claimed that this was the largest single order ever received by an American piano manufacturer from a music school or conservatory.

Pierre Augieras is reported to have had the distinction of giving the first lesson in the new building, and Ella Mason was apparently the first student to receive instruction. Studios were designed to provide a generous amount of space for the faculty. They varied somewhat in size, but most of them were about 125 square feet. All of the studios, classrooms, and corridors had a cork tile floor. This flooring

Figure 10. Fourth floor lecture hall in the Eastman School, presently the site of Hanson Hall.

material survived for decades at the school until finally replaced by institutional carpeting. The presence of windows in the studio doors is a legacy of Alexandra Klingenberg's sense of propriety. The doors were originally solid wood, but the director's wife was quite horrified to think that young women would be taking lessons from male teachers behind closed doors. Therefore, it was at her insistence that the octangular windows were added to the doors at the last moment before the school opened.

The new school year saw more than one hundred students enrolled in George Barlow Penny's music history class, with a similarly high level of enrollment in Yorke Trotter's theory classes. Total enrollment of students during the year exceeded 1,200, of which only 38 were candidates for the bachelor of music degree. Tuition for the degree program was $200 for the year, except for voice students, for whom tuition was $250. Various scholarships were available, including some for full tuition. Prominent among the scholarships were those from the Molly Mulligan Fund, which had been established through a gift of $10,000 from George

Eastman's close friends, Dr. and Mrs. Edward W. Mulligan of Rochester. The fund that they endowed at the university was named for their young daughter, Molly, who later earned a bachelor's degree in piano from Eastman. Other prominent Rochesterians, such as Edward Bausch and Hiram W. Sibley, also provided scholarship assistance for deserving students.

Admission standards were relatively simple. All entering students were required to have completed fifteen units of high school work. Demonstrated proficiency on an instrument was almost at an intermediate level. For example, in piano the sample audition program included a Bach Two-Part Invention; Mozart's Sonata in G Major, K. 283; some selected studies such as Czerny; and one additional piece selected by the applicant's teacher. The first student recital was held on Wednesday afternoon, October 19, and featured Dorothy Dodd, Roslyn Weisberg, and George MacNabb, all of whom had come with Raymond Wilson from Syracuse University. MacNabb had already graduated from Syracuse and had been given a scholarship for post-graduate work, but he preferred to follow his teacher to Eastman. He was soon to join the piano faculty at the new school.

During all of these activities, construction continued. The noise, confusion, dirt, and debris were a source of concern and annoyance to everyone, and someone humorously volunteered the suggestion that a musical attachment be given to the riveters working on the theater so that they could at least "play in unison." The completion of the school building was marked by a formal opening to the public on Friday, March 3, 1922. A number of people have recalled that Eastman personally inspected the building to insure that everything was in order before the public was admitted. In addition to the third and fourth floors, already in use, the basement, main floor, mezzanine, and second floor were now ready.

On the main floor could be found the business office, bureau of publications, and director's office and studio. These were all located off the twenty-five foot wide main hall, which extends from the main entrance at Gibbs Street through to Swan Street on the other side of the building. The floor is of Tennessee marble, laid in squares with a black border. At the far end of the main hall, in the east wing, was the new home for the Sibley Music Library (later the student lounge and now room 120, a rehearsal room), which was moved there from the Prince Street campus. At the time the library's collection was said to have numbered about 9,000 volumes, although some sources have put the total as high as 15,000. Whatever the exact number, the collection was considered at the

Figure 11. Eastman School main lobby.

time to be a very significant one. Also located off the main hall is one of the architectural jewels of Rochester, Kilbourn Hall, a lovely recital hall in Italian Renaissance design, with seating for about 450. It was dedicated in memory of Eastman's mother, Maria Kilbourn Eastman. The scheme of the hall was planned by architect Lawrence White, who selected Thomas Wadelton to design the paneled ceiling.

Figure 12. Grand staircase, leading from the school's main hall to the second floor hall.

Wadelton had previously designed the beautiful dining room in George Eastman's house on East Avenue.

The mezzanine provided an office and other facilities, while the second floor contained an assembly hall and fifteen additional studios. The second floor hall was planned to be identical in size with the main hall, but its design was kept much simpler, with the intention of using the space for loaned art exhibits. The hall was also designed to serve as a promenade for patrons attending concerts and recitals in Kilbourn Hall or in the Eastman Theatre.

The basement of the school building provided seventeen practice rooms and other facilities, including a student locker room, a kitchenette and lunch room, and space for the superintendent's office and janitorial staff. High above, in the attic or fifth floor of the school

Figure 13. Bottom of the grand staircase, east end of the main hall.

building, could be found the operating equipment for the school's ventilating system. Also located there was the automatic exchange for the school's original telephone system, plus a master clock mechanism that controlled the clocks in all the rooms of the school.

The evening following the formal opening of the school was the occasion for the official dedication of Kilbourn Hall, an event that featured the Kilbourn Quartet with Alf Klingenberg as piano soloist. The program consisted of the Beethoven String Quartet in B-Flat Major, Op. 18, no. 6, and Christian Sinding's Piano Quintet. Also on the program was a dedicatory poem provided for the occasion by University of Rochester professor John Rothwell Slater:

> Here shall music have a home.
> Here shall many lovers come,

Figure 14. Eastman Theatre staircase, just off the school's main hall.

Seeking at her inner shrine
Meanings intimate, divine.
These four walls shall hear the strings
telling of immortal things.
Youth and age and music meet
Here beside the busy street.
Youth's allegro violin,
Love's adagio stealing in,
Joy's gay scherzo and caprice,
And the final chords of peace:
Life's sonata, played for all
In this dedicated hall,
All who know and all who care
For the fine things and the rare.
In this consummated whole
Rochester shall find a soul.

Figure 15. Kilbourn Hall.

Dreams of years take form at last;
Beauty rises from the past.
Mothers see more than children know:
Mothers of music, long ago.
Could you dream these marble halls

Figure 16. Eastman School second floor hall, showing doors to the Eastman Theatre balcony on the left and to Kilbourn Hall on the right.

Where the voice of beauty calls?
Could you hear the harmony
Still unuttered, still to be?
Are you waiting now to hear
Music of the future clear.
Happy mother, so to come
to your everlasting home.[11]

The opening of Kilbourn Hall also signalled the availability of its 90-rank Skinner pipe organ, which Joseph Bonnet began to use for his master classes. He declared the organ to be one of the finest ever constructed. Bonnet also highly praised the studio teaching organs and the practice organs that had been installed on the fourth floor, considering the equipment to be unsurpassed anywhere in the world. His enthusiasm was a tribute to Harold Gleason, who had been largely responsible for developing the plans for the organ department. Gleason had traveled widely to inspect organs in various parts of the country and had also visited organ manufacturers such as Austin, Moller, Skinner, and Wurlizter. In addition, he had hired several consultants to provide written opinions of the proposed specifications for both the Kilbourn Hall and Eastman Theatre instruments.

As the initial school year moved towards its conclusion, two events of importance occurred in April. An announcement was made on April 19 that the local newspapers, the *Democrat & Chronicle* and the *Times-Union*, had agreed to establish and maintain radio broadcasting equipment at the school. The operating room for this equipment was eventually located on the top floor of the school at the corner of the southwest wing. The license to operate the radio station—which was given the call letters WHAM—was authorized by the Secretary of Commerce on July 6, and the first broadcast, consisting of a piano recital by Raymond Wilson, was on July 11. The plan for the station called for broadcasting recitals from the school three times a day during the school year. WHAM was one of the earliest commercial radio stations, and its association with the Eastman School during the next several years would prove to be a significant and interesting experiment. The station still broadcasts (now at 1180 on the AM dial), though not from the Eastman School.

April also saw the final resolution of the issue involving the institute's charter. Walter Hubbell, attorney for the university, wrote

---

[11]   Program, Formal Opening of Kilbourn Hall, 3 March 1922. SML.

to Augustus Downing on April 26 suggesting that the University desired to surrender the charter of the Institute of Musical Art in view of the fact that the institute's property was now owned and used by the university in its Eastman School of Music. Downing replied on May 2, indicating that this procedure would be sufficient to close up the affairs of the D.K.G. Institute. Thus ended a long saga that had begun more than four years earlier with Rush Rhees's first letter to Downing on March 27, 1918.

As the initial school year approached its conclusion, there were announcements concerning some important changes to the faculty. The cellist, Gerald Maas, was leaving; he would be replaced by Joseph Press, who had previously been one of the leading teachers at the St. Petersburg Conservatory in Russia. Born in Lithuania, Press was trained at the Moscow Conservatory, which he entered in 1897. Soon after graduating from the conservatory's five-year program, he moved to Berlin and organized the Russian Trio with his brother as violinist and sister-in-law as pianist. The trio performed extensively throughout Europe during the prewar years. At the same time, Press was able to pursue his own solo career and appeared as soloist with orchestras under such distinguished conductors as Arthur Nikisch (1855–1922), Richard Strauss (1864–1949), Karl Muck (1859–1940), and Willem Mengelberg (1871–1951). The outbreak of the First World War, however, forced Press to leave Berlin and return to Russia, where he joined the faculty of the St. Petersburg Conservatory as head of the cello department. He remained there until the 1917 Russian Revolution, when he fled the country and resumed concertizing. It was following several concerts in America that he received a telegram from George Eastman inviting him to join the faculty at the Eastman School of Music.

Arthur Hartmann also resigned his faculty position at Eastman at the end of the 1921–22 school year. There is a story that he had displeased George Eastman by entering the millionaire's home by means of the front door each time he arrived to perform with the quartet.[12] (Musicians, like other employees, were expected to use the side entrance.) It is possible, therefore, that Hartmann's departure from Rochester was not entirely voluntary. It is more likely, however, that he simply wished to pursue his professional aspirations elsewhere. He was replaced by Vladimir Resnikoff, a much

---

[12] Another version of this story, however, suggests that Eastman admired Hartmann's assertiveness in using the front entrance. From what is known about George Eastman, this seems somewhat unlikely.

younger man who came to Eastman with the strong endorsement of Otakar Ševčik, with whom he had studied. An exceptionally talented violinist, Resnikoff had also studied with Leopold Auer.

At about the same time the school also announced that Max Landow would join the piano faculty in September. Landow had studied in Paris with Eduard Risler (1873–1929), a graduate of the Paris Conservatory. Risler was considered one of the best pianists in Europe, and he may have been the first French pianist to perform all of the Beethoven piano sonatas and the entire *Well-Tempered Clavier* of Bach.[13] Quite untypical of French-trained pianists of his generation, he had pursued additional training in Germany, studying there with Karl Klindworth (1830–1916), Bernard Stavenhagen, and Eugene d'Albert (1864–1932), all of them former students of Franz Liszt. It was probably due to Risler's recommendation that Landow also went to Germany to continue his piano studies with Klindworth. Thus his background as a pianist included both French and German training, which was rather unusual at that time. Landow came to Eastman from the Peabody Conservatory in Baltimore, where he had been a member of the faculty since 1914. Prior to his arrival in the United States at the outbreak of the First World War, he had been a teacher for eight years at the Stern Conservatory in Berlin.

Landow, like Resnikoff and Press, would begin his teaching responsibilities at Eastman in September. Meanwhile, the University of Rochester commencement exercises for 1922 included the first conferral of the new bachelor of music degree. Roslyn Weisberg, the young woman who had come to Eastman as a transfer student from Syracuse University, received her degree at the ceremony. Her graduation recital in Kilbourn Hall on June 14 included music of Bach, Paderewski, Chopin, and Grieg, the latter composer being represented by the A-Minor Piano Concerto, with Raymond Wilson providing the orchestral accompaniment at the second piano. She was a genuinely accomplished pianist and later married Jacob Robert Cominsky, a 1920 graduate of the University of Rochester who was to achieve national attention and praise for his work as publisher of *Saturday Review of Literature*. Also receiving a bachelor of music degree in 1922 was Marion Eccleston, who had the distinction of receiving a degree from the Eastman School of Music even though she apparently never studied at the Gibbs Street

---

[13] Risler was born in Baden-Baden of an Alsatian father and German mother. The family settled in Paris the year after his birth.

school. She had begun her work at the institute in 1917, completing the Four Year Course in 1921, for which she was granted her diploma. In September 1921 she enrolled for academic work at the university, and by combining this credit with her diploma at the institute, she qualified to receive the Eastman degree. When Hazel Dossenbach left the faculty in 1926, Marion Eccleston was offered a position and taught violin at the school until 1936.

The school's first summer session opened on June 26, 1922. It offered various courses for public school teachers of music, as well as private lessons in piano, voice, violin, organ, and harp. As the summer months drew to a close, there was much sense of anticipation in Rochester and throughout the country for the scheduled opening of the Eastman Theatre in September. George Eastman's vision for using the popular medium of motion pictures to elevate the cultural life of the community received much national attention, including an occasional note of skepticism as illustrated by the following comment from the Boston Sunday Post:

> [Rochester] will be sprayed with music and artistic movies beginning in September, in an effort by George Eastman, the Kodak millionaire, to raise the ethical standards of the nation by saturating the people with culture.[14]

Nonetheless, as opening day approached, everyone was anxious finally to see George Eastman's magnificent theater, which was nearing completion adjacent to the splendid new music school. They would not be disappointed by what they saw.

[14] *Boston Sunday Post*, Boston, Mass., 20 August 1922. SML.

Chapter 5

1922–1923
The Opening of the Eastman Theatre

The summer months of 1922 saw what was described as feverish work to complete the theater, which was designed with a seating capacity of slightly more than 3,300.[1] George Eastman acknowledged that such a large theater might be a little ahead of the times, but his great faith in the future of motion pictures led him to see a growing tendency towards theaters of this size. He had originally intended to have the theater named the "National Academy of Motion Pictures," and it was not until November 3, 1921, that Eastman finally yielded to the suggestions of his friends and agreed that the theater would bear his name.

At the time, Rochester was certainly not lacking in theaters. The city boasted eight theaters used primarily for legitimate theater and vaudeville, and over a dozen movie houses. Perhaps the most important of the theaters was the Lyceum, located on the east side of Clinton Avenue south of Main Street. With a seating capacity of 2,000, the Lyceum had opened in 1888 and featured the best theatrical productions as well as being occasionally used for concerts. Its interior decoration was described by one observer as "a gilded, rococo nightmare,"[2] but it had good acoustics and was probably the best facility in town.[3] The most frequent location for musical events, however, was Convention Hall on Washington Square. It was originally the State Armory building, providing facilities for the 54th Regiment from 1870 to 1907. During its relatively brief existence as a concert venue, many great artists appeared in Convention Hall,

---

[1] It now seats just under 3,100.
[2] John Rothwell Slater, "Rochester Forty Years Ago," in *Rochester Historical Society Publications*, vol. 20, compiled by Dexter Perkins (Rochester, 1942), 32.
[3] It has since been torn down.

Figure 17. The Eastman Theatre construction site, 25 April 1921.

including Enrico Caruso (1873–1921), Dame Nellie Melba (1861–1931), Jascha Heifetz (1901–87), and Ignace Paderewski (1860–1941).[4] But neither Convention Hall nor the Lyceum would be able to compete with the concert hall that George Eastman was constructing at the corner of Main and Gibbs.

The work that was being done at the Eastman Theatre during the summer months of 1922 included the final stages of installing the huge theater organ with its 10,000 pipes and 140 stops. Constructed at a cost of about $80,000 by the Austin Organ Company of Hartford, Connecticut, the instrument at the time was said to be the largest theater organ ever built. Many newspapers reported detailed account of its specifications:

> The eight divisions of the organ, all really separate organs, any one of which is larger than the average church or theater organ are: Great, Swell, Choir, Solo, Orchestral, Echo, String, and Pedal. . . . In addition to these eight divisions, the organ contains a complete percussion and trap department, including tympani, fire gongs, xylophone, glockenspiel, sleighbells, drums, deep bells, etc., all playable from the several manuals. . . . The organ speaks through the proscenium arch, instead of above or on either side, as is the case in most theaters, this arrangement contributing to its effectiveness in accompanying the orchestra. . . . The spectator hears the beautiful tones, but he does not see the wonderful mechanism that produces them. For this reason, it may be difficult for him to realize that the organ weighs 45 tons; that there are several thousand miles of electric wires used in the electrical circuits; that about 15 tons of metal was used in construction consisting of platinum, silver, brass, copper, lead, tin, zinc, steel, bronze, and aluminum; that upwards of 30,000 feet of lumber was used consisting of ebony, walnut, oak, birch, maple, whitewood, pine, and cherry; that the largest pipe is 32 feet in length and weighs over 400 pounds. . . . The console is mounted on an elevator and turnstile and can be moved from orchestra pit to stage as desired. . . . Ninety-one pistons are distributed between the manuals and over the pedal keys to bring in operation the various groups of stop keys. . . . [The console] controls and plays a grand piano by means of a movable player placed over the keys.[5]

[4]   It is now the home of thke Geva Theater Company.
[5]   *Post-Express*, Rochester, [?] August 1922. SML.

The Austin Organ

IN THE

EASTMAN THEATRE, ROCHESTER, N. Y.

The largest theatre organ ever built.

THE CONSOLE

AUSTIN ORGAN COMPANY

HARTFORD, CONN.

Figure 18. Console of the Eastman Theatre organ as designed by the Austin Organ Company. (Collection of the author.)

The new organ was not the only marvel to be admired in the theater. The switchboard, which controlled house and stage lights, was described as a "marvel of its kind" and "the only one built whereby all circuits of switches can be controlled by one operator,"[6] and was designed and built by Wheeler-Green Company of Rochester. Not all the equipment, however, was locally constructed, and the 1922 coal and railroad strikes created unanticipated difficulties in keeping the construction project on schedule. So as to not delay the theater's opening, arrangements were made to bring material to Rochester by truck rather than by railroad. This included, among other items, the four-ton dimmer bank built in Mount Vernon, New York, and the scenic investiture for the stage, which was constructed in New York City. A local firm, however, provided the forty carloads of marble used in the building's construction. The James C. Barry Co., founded in 1887, was responsible for this work and used Champlain black and French grey from Vermont quarries, McMullen grey from Tennessee, Grecian Tinos, Belgian Black, and three different varieties of marble from Italy. All of this was placed in the lobbies, stairways, auditorium foyer, mezzanine foyer, balconies, and general interior.

The entire color scheme of the interior was supervised by the noted American muralist, Ezra Winter (1886–1949). He also executed the paintings on the left of the stage, which represent festival, lyric, martial, and sylvan music. It is said that the artist used his friends as models for the various figures in the four murals. The corresponding decorations on the right were done by Barry Faulkner (1881–1966), and these represent religious, hunting, pastoral, and dramatic music. Both artists were paid the rather handsome fee of $32,500 for their work. All of the figures are painted against an Italian landscape background. The interior walls of the theater, which appear to be stone, are constructed of a composition board called Zenitherm. The material was used by the architects to create the illusion of the stone facing typical of a Florentine Renaissance palazzo. Ezra Winter and Barry Faulkner were also responsible for two circular panels on the ceiling of the lobby, where they also installed reproductions of the famous "Cupid and Psyche" decorations, based on drawings by Jacques-Louis David (1748–1825) and prepared by the French artist Lafitte for Napoleon Bonaparte. A set of these reproductions was also installed in the mezzanine. The mezzanine and lobby panels were all printed in fifty different shades of gray from the original wood blocks.

[6]   *Rochester Herald*, Rochester, undated news clipping. SML.

Figure 19. The noted American artist, Ezra Winter, at work in the Eastman Theatre.

Figure 20. Ezra Winter (center) and other workers at lunch in the Eastman Theatre.

Another artistic treasure was a painting by Maxfield Parrish (1870–1966). It was placed in the balcony foyer,[7] situated close to a fountain with a figure of a cupid and dolphin after an original by the Flemish artist Giovanni de Bologna (1529–1608), who worked for the Medici family in Florence. George Eastman was personally delighted with the Parrish work, which was entitled "Interlude" by the artist, and he wrote to Rush Rhees on August 17 when it arrived in Rochester:

> Parrish's picture has arrived. I went up to look at it with Lawrence White this morning in the room where it is stored in the Music School. White pronounced it a "peacherina" [*sic*] and I echo his sentiments. I hope you can translate this into real art language. It is very strong, simple, and forceful.[8]

[7] Because of concern for possible damage to the painting, it was later removed to the Memorial Art Gallery and replaced by a photographic reproduction.
[8] George Eastman. Letter to Rush Rhees, 17 August 1922. RRL.

Among the other works of art added to the new theater were double-life size busts of Bach and Beethoven. They had been modeled in plaster by Leo Friedlander (1890–1966), a noted American sculptor who had studied in Rome. Central to the theater, however, was its magnificent crystal chandelier, which measures fourteen feet in diameter and thirty-five feet in depth. Weighing two and a half tons, the chandelier contains 585 lights and 20,000 pieces of glass and crystal. It hangs from a beautiful gilded sunburst in the middle of a coffered domed ceiling. It was also decided to add two smaller chandeliers on either side of the rear of the hall, but they could not be procured in time for opening night. Therefore, lighting fixtures were improvised out of two galvanized washtubs. It is said that George Eastman was particularly amused by the presence of these improvised fixtures and refused to order permanent chandeliers. The washtub lights have never been replaced.

A more practical matter of construction was the heating and ventilation system. A mechanical engineering marvel for its time, the system utilized an immense fan in the attic over the stage dressing room section, which took in 122,000 cubic feet of air per minute, and then washed, humidified, and warmed it to a temperature of 70 degrees. After being forced through a tunnel under the basement, the air was brought under pressure control and flowed through mushroom ventilators under each seat at a velocity of only 150 feet per minute, and then rose to the ceiling where it was expelled by two exhaust fans in the attic.

The design of the theater also had to provide space for those who were to be responsible for its management and day-to-day operation, and this space was principally located in the front of the building in an area completely hidden from public view. The manager's office was on the mezzanine level above the theater lobby and accessible by an elevator or staircase, located behind a door on the right side of the lobby. Additional offices were located in the same area, providing space for the manager's secretary, a stenographer, a bookkeeper, and the treasurer. Immediately above these offices was the space occupied by the balcony men and women's lounges, and above these lounges could be found additional offices, workrooms, and the projection room for the screening of films. The actual projection booth for the theater was located on the next floor above, along with the publicity office, a studio for the poster artist, and an organ studio for the training of future theater organists. The basement level in the front of the theater provided space for electrical and carpenter shops, a room for the ushers (including an office for the head usher), a laundry room, a

Figure 21. Eastman Theatre chandelier, shown shortly after its installation in 1922.

Figure 22. Technicians operating the Eastman Theatre light panels.

Figure 23. Eastman Theatre movie projection room.

place for storage of uniforms, and a room for printing tickets and stationery.

Dressing rooms were separately located on several upper floors in the rear of the theater. The stage manager had his office on the ground floor below the dressing rooms, and the basement level provided locker rooms, a machinery room and electrical shop, a room for the stage hands, and toilet facilities for the musicians. All of this connected to a musicians' room measuring 30 by 37 feet, which was located in the basement level of the school just to the right of the staircase that led down from the main floor.[9] Directly across the corridor from the musicians' room was a 44 × 58 foot assembly and tuning room for the orchestra members. To the rear of this room was the orchestral library and office of the orchestral librarian. These areas in the front and rear of the theater—and extending into the basement of the adjoining school building—provided necessary space for the nearly 150 people, including musicians, who comprised the theater staff.

As the Eastman Theatre neared completion, many existing musical activities in Rochester were drawing to a close. Among the

[9]   In later years the musicians' room became an area for student lockers.

various impresarios who had been sponsoring musical events in Rochester (mainly at Convention Hall), there was a clear understanding that the new Eastman Theatre would most certainly change their professional activities. James Furlong was the preeminent local concert manager, and his expertise did not go unnoticed. When the Eastman Theatre opened, he was engaged to continue using his managerial talents as an official of the newly formed Eastman Theatre Subscribers' Association. Lesser Paley, another local impresario, similarly became associated with the Eastman enterprise. John D. Raymond and Arthur See, two latecomers to the concert managerial field, simply retired from the profession.

Hermann Dossenbach was among the other professional casualties associated with the opening of the Eastman Theater. He had disbanded his Rochester Orchestra in deference to plans associated with the new enterprise, plans that included the need for two orchestras: a fifty-member ensemble for the showing of movies and a larger ninety-member symphony orchestra. Dossenbach aspired to lead the symphony orchestra, but the decision had long since been reached that he was not the man for the job. Instead, the leadership of the symphony orchestra would go to Arthur Alexander, and Dossenbach would be offered the smaller movie orchestra, a position he declined. Therefore, it was to Alexander, not Dossenbach, that the task fell to hire an orchestra in preparation for the opening of the theater. Members for that orchestra were mainly recruited locally, most coming from the now-disbanded Rochester Orchestra. Victor Wagner was lured from his position as conductor at the Criterion Theatre in New York to serve as associate conductor. He was soon to be joined by the Russian conductor, Vladimir Shavitch. The orchestral library, said to be the third largest of its kind in the world, required a staff of five headed by Joseph Roeber, former manager of the orchestral department of G. Schirmer, the music publisher. Other theater personnel included Managing Director Charles H. Goulding, who selected Arthur Amm as house manager. As the month of September approached, all was in readiness for the long-awaited opening of Mr. Eastman's new theater.

The Eastman Theatre was scheduled to open on Labor Day, September 4, with continuous performances from 1:00 in the afternoon until 11:00 at night. To avoid any "class distinctions," tickets were sold on a first-come, first-served basis. Admission for afternoon shows ranged from twenty to fifty cents, while tickets for evening performances ranged from thirty-five cents to a dollar. One section of the mezzanine, however, was reserved for those who contributed

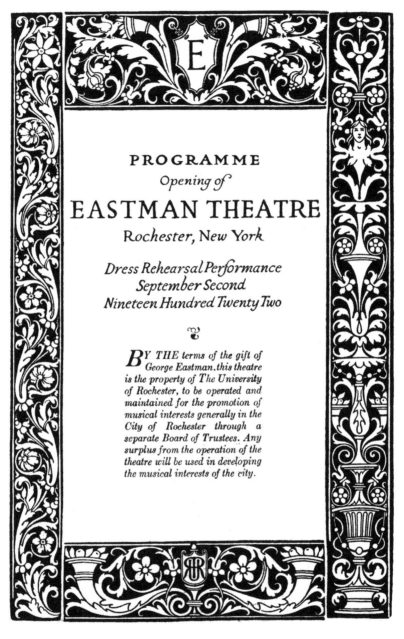

Figure 24. Program cover for the Eastman Theatre's opening dress rehearsal performance, 2 September 1922.

$150 a year in addition to the regular box office price, these being members of the Eastman Theatre Subscribers' Association.

Two days preceding the opening, there was a gathering of celebrities who had been invited to inspect the theater in the afternoon, and then to attend a special dress rehearsal of the opening show. For this privileged preview, George Eastman had personally sent several thousand invitations:

> The new Eastman Theatre will be opened to the public on September 4. In order to afford representatives of all branches of the motion picture industry, musical, theatrical, and educational interests generally and the press, an opportunity to inspect the theatre and its equipment, the institution will be open for that purpose throughout Saturday, September 2nd, after 3 P.M. For the benefit of those who wish to see the theatre in operation there will be a dress rehearsal of the opening programme in the evening about 8:30, but there will be no attempt to give formal entertainment. You are cordially invited to be present and I shall be very much pleased to see you on this occasion.[10]

Among those accepting invitations were Winfield Sheehan, financial director of Fox Films Co.; Charles L. O'Reilly, President of the Motion Picture Theater Owners of the State of New York; Florence French, editor of the *Musical Leader*; Charles L. Wagner, concert manager of John McCormack and others; Alexander Russell, concert director of Princeton University; R. Charles Rodda, news editor of *Musical America*; and many directors of movie theaters from such diverse areas of the country as Pennsylvania, Ohio, Florida, and Minnesota. Will H. Hayes, President of the Motion Pictures Producers and Distributors of America, was represented by Joseph J. O'Neill, his assistant, and was able to personally inspect the theater on a visit to Rochester about a week later.

From Monday, September 4, until October 16, the Eastman Theatre was scheduled to show motion pictures seven days a week. Then, commencing October 16, there was an entire week of opera performances, eight different productions presented in six days by the San Carlo Grand Opera Company. Operas presented that week were *Aida, Madama Butterfly, Tosca, Il Trovatore, La Bohème, Cavalleria Rusticana, Pagliacci,* and *Carmen*. Following the special week of opera, the Eastman Theatre was scheduled to show motion pictures

---

[10] George Eastman, Invitation to the Dress Rehearsal Performance, 4 September 1922. SML.

Figure 25. Rochesterians lining up at the box office on the Eastman Theatre's opening day, 4 September 1922.

six days a week, Wednesday evenings being reserved for concerts. The first scheduled concert was a recital by the noted Italian tenor Giovanni Martinelli (1885–1969).

The opening show for September 4 featured the showing of Rex Ingram's *The Prisoner of Zenda*. The program opened with a performance of the *1812 Overture* of Tchaikovsky with Arthur Alexander conducting the new Eastman Theatre Orchestra. This was followed by "Eastman Theatre Current Events," a one-reel film produced by Fox Films that showed various aspects of the new theater. Ester Gustafson, a well-known dancer hired for the occasion, then performed "Russia" to the music of Rachmaninoff's G-Minor Prelude, and "The South at Work" to Dvořák's *Humoresque in A Minor*, Op. 101, no. 5. Her dancing was followed by "Eastman Theatre Magazine," an interesting group of short pictures by the Eastman Theatre management, including for the first time portraits projected using the new Eastman Kodachrome process. The program continued with a vocal selection by Scotch-Canadian soprano, Marion Armstrong (b. 1869), who sang "The World is Waiting for the Sunrise" by Ernest Seitz. Next in the program was the showing of the feature film, *The Prisoner of Zenda*, accompanied by the Eastman Theatre Orchestra. Finally, at the end of the show, there was an organ "exit." Two organists had been hired to work at the Eastman Theatre, Deszo d'Antalffy, who came from the Capitol Theatre in New York, and John Hammond who came from the Strand Theatre in Brooklyn. This opening program was a clear indication of the kind of shows that were to continue in the new theater on a weekly basis throughout the year.

More than 10,000 people attended the shows on September 4, and total attendance for the first year of the theater's operation exceeded 1,800,000. A local newspaper commentary concerning the theater's first day of operation provides a fairly clear picture of the excitement and enthusiasm with which the opening was treated by the citizens of Rochester:

> The intersection of Gibbs Street and Main Street was the busiest corner in Rochester yesterday. Automobiles parked wherever the statutes of the city permitted, and pedestrians in numbers that taxed sidewalk capacity provided plenty of work for traffic officers. And about the busiest person in town was the young woman who presided over the selling of tickets at the Eastman Theatre, opened to the public for the first time yesterday afternoon.
>
> The line before the ticket office began to form at 9 o' clock in the morning, and when the doors were opened at

PROGRAMME

NOTICE: This Theatre, with every seat occupied, can be emptied in less than three minutes. Choose NOW the EXIT nearest to your seat, and in case of fire walk (do not run) to that EXIT.

HARRY J. BAREHAM, *Commissioner of Public Safety.*

EASTMAN THEATRE

Main Street East and Gibbs Street
Telephone, Main 7140

Performances De Luxe

At 2:15, 7:00 and 9:00 P. M.
Daily Performances continuous 1:00 to 11:00
Sundays 2:00 to 11:00

PROGRAMME

Week Beginning September 4th, 1922

A. OVERTURE "1812" . . . . by *Tschaikowsky*

EASTMAN THEATRE ORCHESTRA

ARTHUR ALEXANDER AND VICTOR WAGNER, *Conductors*

Written to commemorate the withdrawal of Napoleon from Moscow in 1812, when, after he had occupied the Kremlin, the inhabitants fired the city, and drove the French general out. Three easily recognized themes form the principal material of the overture, the first, in solemn harmony, being taken from the Russian hymn, "God Preserve Thy People," the second, the "Marseillaise," and the third, the Russian National Anthem.

(AT 2:15; 7:00 AND 9 P. M.)

B. EASTMAN THEATRE CURRENT EVENTS

C. MUSIC INTERPRETED THROUGH THE DANCE

(a) "Russia" . . . *Rachmaninoff* (G. Minor Prelude)
(b) "The South at Work" *Dvorak* (Humoresque in A. Minor)

ESTER GUSTAFSON

(AT 2:40; 7:30; AND 9:30 P. M.)

12

Figure 26. Program for the first week of Eastman Theatre performances, 4–10 September 1922. (Collection of the author.)

PROGRAMME

CONTINUED

D. EASTMAN THEATRE MAGAZINE

An interesting group of short pictures edited by THE EASTMAN THEATRE MANAGE-
MENT, including for the first time on any screen portraits in color by the EASTMAN
KODACHROME PROCESS. "Film Fun" from *The Literary Digest*, "Out of the Ink-
Well," the Smartest of Cartoon Comedies, Movie Chats, etc.

E. VOCAL SELECTION

"The World is Waiting for the Sunrise" .   .   . *Seitz*

MARION ARMSTRONG, *Scotch-Canadian Soprano*

(AT 3:00; 7:40; AND 9:40 P. M.)

F. Metro Pictures Corporation presents

THE PRISONER OF ZENDA

(precisely as now shown at $1.50 prices at Astor Theatre, New York.)

From the novel by ANTHONY HOPE
Featuring LEWIS STONE and ALICE TERRY
Produced by REX INGRAM
With an all-star cast including ROBERT EDESON

G. ORGAN EXIT

DEZSO D'ANTALFFY and JOHN HAMMOND.   . *Organists*

NOTE: The programme is subject to change at any time without notice, and the foregoing time schedules are approximate and intended
merely for the guidance of our patrons.

Prices

AFTERNOON—Orchestra, thirty cents; Mezzanine, fifty cents; Loges, forty
cents; Grand Balcony, twenty cents. No war tax.

EVENING—Orchestra, fifty cents; Mezzanine, $1.00; Loges, seventy-five
cents; Grand Balcony, thirty-five cents. No war tax.

Coming Next Week

First Public Showing of GEORGE ARLISS in
"THE MAN WHO PLAYED GOD"

13

Figure 26. (continued)

Figure 27. Eastman Theatre main lobby.

1 the string of prospective patrons extended along Main Street as far as Union Street. Until about 9 o'clock in the evening there was no time that people were not waiting to purchase tickets. . . .[11]

In spite of the enormous public enthusiasm for the newly opened Eastman Theatre, there was tension behind the scenes that led to the resignation on September 25 of Charles Goulding, the managing director. His sudden departure, only three weeks after opening day, was not unanticipated, as reported in the local newspapers:

Mr. Goulding's resignation does not come as a startling surprise to theatrical circles. For some time past it has been generally understood that everything was not so peaceful up in the new theater as it appeared on the surface. There were stories of constant friction between those men who had been brought on to Rochester and put in charge of certain departments and those Rochester people who were interested in the theater.[12]

[11] *Democrat & Chronicle*, Rochester, 5 September 1922. SML.
[12] *Rochester Journal*, Rochester, 25 September 1922. SML.

Goulding had been named the manager of the Eastman early in 1921 and for a year before coming to Rochester he devoted himself to a study of motion picture houses all over the country. He arrived here early in the summer and started the organization of house personnel. The theatre opened on Labor Day and less than a month after the opening he tendered his resignation. The general opinion is that the new Eastman is going to be more or less of a white elephant on the hands of the sponsors. . . ."[13]

An interesting observation concerning these news stories from 1922 is the fact that the Eastman Theatre was already being referred to as "the Eastman." That jargon persisted in Rochester for many years and often puzzled Eastman School faculty and students alike. But it is easily explained by the simple fact that the Eastman Theatre was originally a movie house and, therefore, identified in the minds of the general public as "the Eastman," in the same sense that they would say "the Regent" or "the Paramount."

The newly opened theater continued to attract large audiences for its lavish movie productions. As yet there was no available in-house musical entertainment other than the theater orchestra and the organ. Therefore, a wide variety of outside musicians and dancers were engaged by the theater management. For example, during the week of September 10, the musical portions of the theater show were provided by pianist Herma Menth, who performed the first movement of the Tchaikovsky Piano Concerto with the orchestra, and by Richard Bonelli, who sang "Because of You." The following week violinist Margel Gluck played two movements from Wieniawski's Concerto in D Minor, and lyric tenor J. Steel Jamison sang "At Dawning." The choice of musical material shows an obvious attempt to mix something "serious" with something else of a lighter nature.

In February 1923 Enid Knapp Botsford was asked to establish a ballet company, to be known as the Eastman Theatre Ballet. Botsford was given a place to teach in exchange for producing ballets for the shows. Her initial class consisted of only six young women, but the enterprise soon developed into something very significant. In the absence of a real ballet studio, Botsford's classes were held in the musician's assembly and tuning room in the school basement. Several years later she reflected on the beginnings of the ballet school:

> When I arrived here and found this magnificent theater devoted primarily to the development of a musical center

---

[13] Unidentified Rochester news clipping, 27 September 1922. SML.

PROGRAMME

Eastman Theatre

Wednesday Evening, January 24th, 1923

Special Recital by

JOSEPH BONNET

Marking the Formal Opening of the Eastman Theatre Organ

Assisted by

THE EASTMAN THEATRE ORCHESTRA

ARTHUR ALEXANDER, Conductor

PROGRAMME

1. FORERUNNERS OF BACH

    (a) VOLUNTARY .... *Henry Purcell*
    (1658—1695)

    (b) SOEUR MONIQUE .... *Francois Couperin le Grand*
    (1668—1733)

    (c) PRELUDE .... *Clerambault*
    (1676—1749)

    (d) FUGUE .... *Buxtehude*
    (1637—1707)

NOTICE: This Theatre, with every seat occupied, can be emptied in less than three minutes. Choose NOW the EXIT nearest to your seat, and in case of fire walk (do not run) to that EXIT.

HARRY J. BAREHAM, *Commissioner of Public Safety.*

Photoplays Every Day This Week Except Wednesday

Figure 28. Program for recital by Joseph Bonnet, 24 January 1923, marking the formal opening of the Eastman Theatre organ. (Collection of the author.)

PROGRAMME

PROGRAMME—*Continued*

2. (a) In dulci Jubilo .... *John Sebastian Bach*
    (1685—1750)

    (b) Fantasia and Fugue in G minor .... *John Sebastian Bach*

    In the Fantasia of a highly dramatic character, recitatives, entreaties, and the most audacious harmonic progressions, are opposed one to the other amidst a formidable unloosing of sonorous resources. The Fugue contrasts with the Fantasia by the uninterrupted flow of its virile good humor. The wonderfully clean-cut subject of this splendid piece was already famous some years before the Fugue appeared.

3. (a) Romance Sans Paroles .... *Joseph Bonnet*

    (b) Variations de Concert .... *Joseph Bonnet*

    Variations de Concert, classical in form, begins with a brilliant introduction, which leads to the theme itself. Four varations follow: the first in staccato with the pedal; the second presenting the theme in the bass; the third written in the form of a choral prelude; the last, a variation with cadence of the manual and of the pedal including arpeggios, thirds and chords for the feet alone. These variations were chosen as a test piece by the Royal College of Organists, London, and by the American Guild of Organists.

Intermission.

4. Choral in A minor .... *Cesar Franck*
    (1822—1890)

    The three Chorals for the organ by Cesar Franck, of which he corrected the proofs on his deathbed in 1890, are not only an artistic "last will and testament" of the master, but perhaps the most complete and highest expression of his genius. It is this work which evokes in the highest sense the evangelic words in the Beatitudes so well set to music by himself:

    "Blessed are the pure in heart, for they shall see God."

    The third Choral in A minor is built in the form which embraces an accessory theme between two expositions of the principal motif. This piece begins with a prelude somewhat agitated, establishing the harmonic atmosphere where appears the contrite and humble theme of the Choral.
    The second motif is of a melodious and suave character, never surpassed in the works of Franck. This mystical cantilena transfigures the Choral which reappears more quietly than joyously confident, and affirms a resolute serenity. To sum up: the Choral in A minor is composed in three parts bound together, the second including the admirable melodic variations. Music thus inspired is a revelation of the Infinite.

5. Concerto-Symphony in D Minor ...... *Alexandre Guilmant*
    (for organ and orchestra)

    (a) Introduction and Allegro
        (cadenza by Joseph Bonnet)

    (b) Pastorale

    (c) Finale

During the intermission the Grand Corridors of the Eastman School of Music will be thrown open to all patrons as promenades. Three entrances on ground floor and one from Grand Balcony foyer. Chimes will be sounded two minutes before performance is resumed.

Figure 28. (continued)

> in Rochester, I could not help but think what an ideal
> atmosphere this would be in which to develop a ballet
> and what a splendid opportunity it would give to young
> people who were desirous of becoming dancers.
>   I had long thought of the development of the ballet in
> America, since my observation of the American girl, as
> compared with the Italian, French, or Russian, was that
> she was more delicately beautiful, her coordination was
> superior, and her velocity was greater.[14]

The inaugural performance of the Eastman Theatre Ballet took place on April 8, featuring dancers Natalie Thomas, Maria Dolores, and Marget Tremaine, with choreography by Serge Oukrainsky. The production also included two Polish "obertas" danced by Clara Forova and George Kunowitch.

Following their debut, the ballet corps danced regularly at Eastman Theatre shows, two or three weeks each month on average. Among the dancers were Thelma Biracree, Ruth Denio, and Dorothy Denmead, all of whom had a long association with ballet in Rochester. All of this remained Botsford's private enterprise until June of 1924, when the ballet corps became an official part of the theater operation. By then she had over one hundred students. The establishment of the ballet corps was only a beginning, however. The future would include an opera company, a new building to support the growing theater enterprise, and even the brief existence of a drama and dance school, but these developments need to be related in their proper time.

In addition to the regular theater shows, the Wednesday evening concerts, which had commenced with Martinelli's recital continued with a recital by Ignace Paderewski on November 15. Contralto Carolina Lazzari (1891–1946)[15] and harpist Alberto Salvi (1893–1983) performed on November 22, followed by violinist Mischa Elman (1891–1967), who presented a recital on December 6. After the New Year, pianist Ignaz Friedman (1882–1948) and violinist Jacques Thibaud (1880–1953) appeared together on January 10. A week later, the theater was the scene of an English-language production of Mozart's *The Impresario.* Joseph Bonnet was featured on January 24, giving the formal dedicatory recital on the Eastman Theatre organ. Soprano Florence MacBeth (1891–1966) presented a

---

[14] *Journal,* Rochester, 4 January 1925. SML.
[15] After many years as a performer, including appearances at the Metropolitan Opera in New York, Lazzari settled into a life of teaching. Among her many students was the actress Judy Garland.

recital with baritone John Charles Thomas (1891–1960) on January 31, and contralto Louise Homer (1871–1947) appeared on February 7. The Ukrainian National Chorus sang on February 21, and Feodor Chaliapin (1873–1938) was featured in a recital on March 7. The noted French soprano Emma Calvé (1858–1942) and the Festival Chorus of Rochester completed the first season on March 21 and April 4 respectively. To have presented people such as Elman, Thibaud, Friedman, Chaliapin, and Martinelli in one season was an impressive accomplishment. Yet it was done at a cost, namely a deficit that totalled over $11,000 for the year. The theater management had incurred its biggest single loss with Feodor Chaliapin, and it had even lost money on the recitals presented by Paderewski and Elman. However, this was not totally unanticipated, and other theater revenue was sufficient to cover all such shortages.

The spring of 1923 also saw the inaugural concert of the Rochester Philharmonic Orchestra. It presented its first concert in the Eastman Theatre on March 28 with Arthur Alexander conducting. The program consisted of Beethoven's *Leonore* Overture No. 3, Tchaikovsky's Symphony No. 6, the Grieg Piano Concerto with Alf Klingenberg as soloist, "Siegfried's Death" from Wagner's *Die Götterdämmerung*, and Victor Herbert's *Irish Rhapsody*. Ironically, it was not only Alexander's first Philharmonic concert, it was also his last. From the very beginning it appears that Alexander had incurred the displeasure of George Eastman. As early as February 1920, the millionaire philanthropist had written of his dissatisfaction with Alexander's attitudes with respect to the musical programs at Eastman's home:

> You are being given the opportunity of your life to fulfill your ambition to become a great conductor, and yet you are continually "chewing the rag." As a pure matter of business such as the conductorship I could put up with this and laugh at your childishness, but as I have again and again tried to make you understand, the music at my house is a pure matter of pleasure and I do not feel inclined to submit it to needless annoyance.[16]

The situation must have continued to deteriorate over the next several years, and Alexander submitted his resignation in early March 1923. Eastman responded rather acrimoniously on the

---

[16] George Eastman, Letter to Arthur Alexander, 12 February 1920. RRL.

nineteenth of the month that, prior to receiving the resignation, he had already come to the conclusion not to renew Alexander's contract.[17] The very next day Eastman sent a cable to Eugene Goossens in England inquiring if he would be willing to consider a proposition to join the Eastman School enterprise as head of orchestral activities at both the school and theater. As a successful businessman, George Eastman was wasting no time. Three days later, he once again wrote to Arthur Alexander:

> I am sorry to have hurt your feelings again. Lack of cooperation from you is the chief reason for my conviction that it is impossible to have you in the organization. I am afraid that you do not understand what the word cooperation really means. The enterprise as a whole cannot succeed unless it has a thoroughly cooperative staff. You have been occupying one of the key positions which requires breadth of vision, unselfishness, and cooperation to a high degree. You have lamentably failed in all of these. Whether you have the other qualifications which would enable you to organize and train an orchestra up to the highest pitch of musical delivery I still have an open mind; but inasmuch as you have failed in the other fundamentals I consider it hopeless to have you experiment further.[18]

Thus ended the turbulent and strange career of Arthur Alexander in Rochester.

As the 1922–23 season drew to a close, there was much evidence to indicate that the Eastman Theatre had been a grand success, notwithstanding the resignations of Charles Goulding and Arthur Alexander. The movie presentations had attracted a huge audience, the Wednesday evening concerts had presented some of the world's finest artists, and the new orchestra had made an auspicious debut. Among those lavishing praise on the new Eastman Theatre was the noted New York theater director Samuel L. Rothafel, who

---

[17] Harold Gleason related that Alexander's resignation followed an argument with George Eastman, who wished to consult with Samuel L. Rothafel, the managing director of the Roxy Theatre in New York. Alexander was opposed to inviting Rothafel to Rochester and threatened to quit if the invitation was made. Eastman supposedly replied, "I accept your resignation, Arthur." This argument may indeed have taken place, but there was a much larger history of problems between Eastman and Alexander of which Gleason was apparently unaware. (See Gleason, "Please Play My Funeral March.")

[18] George Eastman, Letter to Arthur Alexander, 15 February 1923. GEH.

visited Rochester in February despite the opposition of Arthur Alexander:

> I am thoroughly acquainted with every motion picture house of importance in both this country and Europe, and without exception, the Eastman Theater [sic], in point of beauty, good taste, refinement and artistic appointments, leads them all; in fact, there is nothing like it in the world.[19]

"Nothing like it in all the world." The thousands of people who attended that opening show during the week of September 4 entered a theater upon whose facade was inscribed "For the Enrichment of Community Life," appropriate words selected by Rush Rhees. As donor of the theater, George Eastman wished to develop within the community a deep appreciation for the art of music. "Incidentally, in the pursuance of that ideal," Eastman added:

> I should like to see Rochester become a great musical center, known throughout the world. There is no reason to prevent this city from getting the sort of fame which comes from the possession of institutions which are foremost in developing gifted musicians and which are distinguished in the stimulation of the musical appreciation of the great body of citizens.[20]

[19] *Times-Union*, Rochester, 28 February 1923. SML.
[20] *Exhibitors Herald*, Chicago, 16 September 1922. SML.

Chapter 6

1922–1923
A Change in Leadership at the School

The Eastman School of Music began its second year of operation somewhat in the shadow of the excitement generated by the opening of the Eastman Theatre. Enrollment for this second year showed substantial increases when compared with the previous school year. The number of preparatory and special (i.e., non-collegiate) students had risen from 1,205 to an impressive total of 1,524. Even more gratifying was the increase in collegiate enrollment from 104 to 196.[1] These totals included 84 students studying for the bachelor of music degree and 112 enrolled in the certificate program. The latter program was basically a continuation of the institute's "Four Year Course," and it was offered to students who felt that they could not devote the necessary time to complete the non-musical content of the curriculum that led to the bachelor's degree. Therefore, their program of study included all of the musical work done by the degree students, but excluded the academic courses. In piano, for example, those academic courses included a year of English, two years of a language, a year of psychology, plus two years of physical education. With such a small difference between the two curricula, it is difficult to understand why students continued to enroll in the certificate program. Yet it persisted into the 1930s, but as the years passed, more and more students enrolled for the bachelor's degree, and fewer and fewer for the certificate.

Several developments of importance occurred during the late fall of 1922. In November it was announced that George Eastman

---

[1] Enrollment figures are based on the *Reports of the President and Treasurer 1922–1923* (RRL). The *Annual Catalogue of the Eastman School of Music of the University of Rochester* (SML) gives slightly lower figures for 1922–23: 181 collegiate students and 1,524 preparatory and special students.

had purchased 426 musical instruments at a cost of $28,775, which he presented to the Rochester city schools. By means of this gift, the Board of Education was then able to lend the instruments to qualified students. All of this was in keeping with a philosophy that envisioned the necessity of cooperation between all organizations and institutions involved in musical education in Rochester. George Eastman's great scheme for "building musical capacity on a large scale from childhood" would not be limited to the buildings at Main and Gibbs, but would extend into the entire public school system of the city. The consequences of Eastman's gift of these instruments were enthusiastically described by Stewart Sabin in a 1932 essay for the Rochester Historical Society:

> These instruments, to the number of which additions were made in generous amount each year, were loaned without cost to the Rochester Board of Education for use by pupils of high schools, junior high schools and upper elementary grades. This it was that made possible the development of Rochester public school band and orchestral music, which has reached a status and importance in school and community musical interest exceeding that reached in any city of this country of the population, or approximating the population, of Rochester. This is written with confidence because it has been incorporated in the documents published by the National Teachers' Association and of the National Board of Music Supervisors. Along with the expansion in instrumental music instruction has gone the development of chorus instruction and of class teaching of voice in high schools. The result is to be found in the annual festivals given by the senior high school orchestras and choruses; by the junior high school orchestras, bands, and choruses, and by the participation in public events by the Inter-High School Orchestra and the Inter-High School Chorus.[2]

The other development of note in the late fall was the submitting of the application to register the bachelor of music degree with the Department of Education in Albany. Klingenberg and Rhees were somewhat tardy in doing so, in view of the fact that they had already awarded two degrees the preceding June. As we recall, correspondence concerning registering the degree had commenced in the spring of 1920. For whatever reason, the actual application was not submitted to Augustus Downing in Albany until December

[2]   Sabin, "A Retrospect of Music in Rochester," 73–74.

1922. Rhees listed the total value of the school's property at $3,000,000 (surely an understatement), and reported that annual receipts had been $239,278 the preceding year, as compared with $196,562 in expenses. The application listed thirteen "professors and instructors devoting their entire time to instruction."

Pierre Augieras	Piano
Lucy Lee Call	Voice
Adelin Fermin	Voice
Oscar Gareissen	Voice
Alf Klingenberg	Director/Piano
Max Landow	Piano
Selim Palmgren	Composition
George Barlow Penny	History/Appreciation
Olive Puttick	Piano/Teaching Methods
Hazel Stanton	Psychologist
Thomas Henry Yorke Trotter	Composition/Teaching Methods
Raymond Wilson	Piano
Jeanne Woolford	Voice

Absent from this list were twenty-four other teachers at Eastman, presumably excluded because their responsibilities may have been somewhat part-time or because their contracts included responsibilities other than teaching. The four principal string teachers, who formed the Kilbourn Quartet, would probably be in the latter category.

The application to register the bachelor of music degree with the State Education Department also provides an interesting glimpse at faculty compensation in these earliest days at the Eastman School of Music. Salaries ranged from $2,500 per year up to $10,000 per year, the latter figure being the salary of Thomas Henry Yorke Trotter. Klingenberg's salary was $8,000, Selim Palmgren was paid $7,500, and Max Landow $6,500. At the lower end of the scale were George Barlow Penny, Lucy Lee Call, Jeanne Woolford, and Hazel Stanton, who were all paid $3,000 per year, and at the bottom was Olive Puttick, whose annual salary was set at $2,500. Several years earlier the University of Rochester had established what they called "normal maximum" salaries of $3,500 for professors, $3,000 for junior (i.e., associate) professors, and $2,500 for assistant professors. Although these levels had probably risen since 1919–20, it is probably safe to conclude that the upper-level Eastman salaries in 1922 were really quite generous. These salary figures also help us to appreciate more fully the $20,000 salary that was offered to Sibelius in 1921.

The Board of Regents acted quickly in approving the application to register the Eastman School degree, and this information was conveyed to Rush Rhees by Augustus Downing in a short, one-sentence letter dated January 30, 1923:

> I have the pleasure in advising you that the Board of Regents, at a meeting held January 25, 1923, formally registered the Eastman School of Music, The University of Rochester, under section 404 of Regents Rules, in its course leading to the degree of Bachelor of Music (B.M.).[3]

At about the same time, another important issue arose that would occupy Rush Rhees for a considerable period of time, namely the tax status of the Eastman Theatre. On January 23, the local Department of Taxation and Assessment announced that the assessed value of the theater was $2,500,000 and the school $1,250,000. The City Assessor decided that the school was exempt from property taxes, but suggested that the school should pay a tax on the Eastman Theatre and on Kilbourn Hall since admission was charged for concerts and movies. This was potentially a very serious development, something that might jeopardize the entire mission of the Eastman Theatre. Fears were eased in March, however, with a decision that the Eastman Theatre would not be taxed because "the theater, as well as Kilbourn Hall, is a part of the University of Rochester, a corporation in the city of Rochester for more than fifty years and entitled to tax exemption under state laws affecting the property of education institutions."[4]

The matter might have ended with this announcement except for the efforts of various local interests who sought to have the courts intervene and rule that the Eastman Theater and Eastman School of Music were not legally exempt from city taxation. At the forefront of these efforts were several local labor leaders who had been dissatisfied with the conditions under which the school and theater had been built and who regarded any exemption from taxes as evidence of favoritism. Legal maneuvering would continue for a long while before the issue was finally resolved. In the meantime, the university's Board of Trustees authorized George Eastman and Rochester industrialist George Todd[5] to act on behalf of the university

---

[3] Rush Rhees, Letter to Augustus Downing, 30 January 1923. RRL.
[4] *Democrat & Chronicle*, Rochester, 11 March 1923. SML.
[5] George Todd (1860–1938) founded the Todd Protectograph Company in 1890 with his brother Libanus Todd. The company's business was the protection of the

with respect to any and all contracts and legal agreements necessary for the proper management of the Eastman Theatre.

Meanwhile, the educational process continued uninterrupted at the school. A growing student body, a faculty of ability and prestige, incomparable facilities, an endowment of sizeable proportions, and a budget where receipts would once again exceed expenditures would all seem to indicate that the Eastman School of Music was not only thriving but also under very capable management. At least these were the outward signs as the school's second year drew to a close. On June 18 the University of Rochester held its commencement ceremony in the Eastman Theatre. The bachelor of music degree was awarded to George Frederick McKay and to Cora Laila Skinner,[6] and certificates were presented to six other students. Four days later Alf Klingenberg received a letter from George Eastman requesting his resignation:

> Dr. Rhees has told me about your conference with him and how anxious you and Mrs. Klingenberg are in respect to arrangements for the coming year and my attitude toward you, so I am writing this at the earliest opportunity that you may not rest in any uncertainty.
>
> As you have doubtless inferred from some of my recent interviews with you, I am no longer favorable to your continued administration. This attitude has been arrived at through personal observation of your reaction to various problems that have come up and in the last few weeks it has become so fixed that I do not think there would be any good in temporizing with the situation.
>
> My high personal regard for you and Mrs. Klingenberg has not changed, and I am fully appreciative of the fine work that you have done and the important influence you have had in the organization of our School. But I have come to the conviction, which of course may be a mistaken one, that our enterprise has reached a stage in its development which indicates that a change in administration will be advantageous for all concerned.
>
> I therefore propose that you be given a year's leave of absence at full salary, from July 1st, 1923, with the understanding between you and me that you will place your resignation in our hands, to take effect at the pleasure of the Board.

integrity of bank checks. In 1955 the company merged with Burroughs Corporation (now Unisys).

[6]   Cora Laila Skinner later taught at the Eastman School; she was then known as Laila Skinner.

> The only publicity which needs to be given at this time
> would be the announcement that you have been granted
> the leave of absence, unless you should prefer to make
> another announcement.
>   My feelings for you and Mrs. Klingenberg make it very
> difficult for me to say this and at the same time make it
> imperative to be frank with you.[7]

Klingenberg's contract, signed in 1918 when he sold the institute to George Eastman, had been for a term of five years, but there is no evidence to suggest that he was not anticipating a renewal of his appointment as director. Public announcement of the director's resignation was accompanied by a statement that irreconcilable differences had arisen between Klingenberg and the school's Board of Managers (which consisted of Klingenberg, Rush Rhees, George Eastman, and George Todd).

It is, of course, highly significant that the request for Klingenberg's resignation came from Eastman rather than from the university president. The differences alluded to must have evolved gradually through many private conversations and meetings of which no record has been kept. Klingenberg's training had been very much confined to the European conservatory system. Perhaps it was felt he was reluctant to see the importance of the school as a university department. Yet, his earlier work in Kansas would certainly suggest that he was open to the academic side of music training. A clue to the reasons behind Klingenberg's departure might be contained in a letter that Eastman wrote on July 9 to the English conductor Albert Coates, who had visited Rochester on June 16 to inspect the school and theater:

> Since you left we have lost the Director of our School,
> who has resigned. It was in the air when you were
> here but not in shape to talk about. Mr. Klingenberg
> has many admirable qualities but he was not big enough
> to swing the job. What we want is a young man and
> our Trustees think that he must be an American or
> Englishman.[8]

---

[7] George Eastman, Letter to Alf Klingenberg, 22 June 1923. GEH. The original letter is presumably lost; the text quoted above is from a copy in the George Eastman Collection. Various markings on the copy suggest that perhaps the opening phrase of the third paragraph was not included in the final version of the letter sent to Klingenberg.

[8] George Eastman, Letter to Albert Coates, 9 July 1923. GEH.

Whatever the complete story might have been, Alf Klingenberg was forced to leave the Eastman School of Music after having served as its director for only two years. On June 28, 1923, Rush Rhees announced to the faculty that Arthur See, Secretary of the Eastman School, would be "in administrative charge" pending appointment of a new director, but in September this was superseded by an announcement that Raymond Wilson would serve as acting director. Prior to their departure from Rochester, the Klingenbergs were given a series of farewell entertainments, and he was given a watch by President Rhees on behalf of the Eastman School faculty. Then, on the evening of October 5, 1923, Alf and Alexandra Klingenberg left Rochester for New York City, and from there they embarked on the long voyage back to Norway.

In later life Alf Klingenberg lived mostly in France during the winter and in Norway for the summer months, where he had a beautiful home near Oslo. He led a modest and quiet life, occasionally giving concerts, but his leisure time was increasingly spent with painting and sculpture, for which he had considerable talent. He also composed music, but with undue modesty burned most his works prior to his death. Eleven years after leaving Rochester, Alf and Alexandra Klingenberg returned for a four-month stay in the United States, including a visit to Rochester, where they were warmly greeted by their many friends. Alf Klingenberg died after a long illness in Vestre Gausdal, Norway, during the winter of 1944.

Alexandra Klingenberg outlived her husband by several years, during which time she destroyed most of his papers and correspondence. Little remains in Rochester or in Norway, therefore, to document fully the contributions made by her husband towards the establishment of the Eastman School of Music. What can be said, however, is that the rich accomplishments of his successors were possible only because of the vision and dedication of Alf Klingenberg. By founding the Institute of Musical Art, he gave Rochester a music school of sufficient distinction to attract the interest and support of many important citizens of the city. By professionally associating himself with people such as George Barlow Penny, he prepared his school for the important transition from a conservatory to a music school belonging to a university, and elicited the interest and support of Rush Rhees towards that goal. Together with Rhees and other like-minded colleagues, he and his wife secured George Eastman's participation in their dream, without which the music school project never would have succeeded. He helped plan and prepare for the new building on Gibbs Street and was responsible for the selection of the initial

Eastman School faculty, many of whom continued at the school with great distinction for many years. Finally, Klingenberg helped to develop the initial baccalaureate program and to award the first bachelor of music degrees conferred by the Eastman School of Music. These were significant accomplishments for which the school's first director deserves much more credit than he is customarily given.

Klingenberg's resignation did nothing to slow the pace of events at the school and theater. On June 24 it was announced that a ballet studio would be constructed on top of the center wing of the Eastman School, making the building six stories in height. The school had originally been constructed to bear the weight of any such addition, should the provision for expanding the facilities become necessary in the future. In August, however, a bolder plan for the ballet studio was set forth with an announcement that a five-story annex to the Eastman Theatre would be constructed on the east side of Swan Street, connecting with the theater by means of a bridge extending across the street. The proposed building would provide for the ballet studio, as well as space for the design and construction of scenery.

Another factor contributing to the decision to build the annex was the announcement on July 18 that the Eastman School was going to open an opera department. Such a department would also need space for the construction and painting of scenery. The vision of providing operatic training at the Eastman School brought the Russian tenor Vladimir Rosing to Rochester. Rosing was born in Odessa, but he was living at the time in London, where he had established quite a reputation as a singer. He profited from a wide-spread interest and fascination with Russian culture and quickly became a very popular and charismatic recitalist. His highly personalized style has been vividly described by Nicolas Slonimsky.

> When he performed Mussorgsky's *Songs of Death*, he became death itself, demonstrating this transformation by drawing in his cheeks, screwing up his bony facial structure, and letting his long nose protrude from his countenance. In the next song he was the village idiot, dropping his jaw to convey an image of imbecility. For Mussorgsky's *Song of the Flea*, Rosing scratched himself all over as if being actually bitten by a flea.[9]

---

[9] Nicholas Slonimsky, *Perfect Pitch: A Life Story* (New York: Oxford University Press, 1988), 81.

The public was enamored with this style of singing, and Rosing was highly regarded and praised by people such as George Bernard Shaw and Ezra Pound. Rosing was also greatly interested in opera; he favored the idea of eliminating the big chorus scenes from operatic performances and creating "simplified" productions that would be sung in English and accompanied by a small ensemble rather than a full symphony orchestra. These ideas were quite revolutionary and gained many adherents.

In 1923 Rosing made a tour of America, giving successful recitals in Boston, New York, Chicago, and Washington, D.C., and also visiting the Metropolitan Opera and the Chicago Opera. On his return to England on board the S.S. Paris, he met A.J. ("Jack") Warner, who was also on his way to London.[10] This encounter might never have taken place because Rosing had originally booked passage on the S.S. Homeric, but he had changed his reservations upon discovering that the French liner was leaving New York two days earlier and would get him back to London in time for a scheduled recital. Jack Warner was suitably impressed with Rosing's enthusiasm for opera and cabled George Eastman about this interesting Russian tenor. Four weeks later, Rosing was invited to Rochester to talk with Eastman, and the Eastman opera department was born.

Rosing was able to launch his new department with an announcement that twelve scholarships were to be awarded, each providing full tuition plus a $1,000 allowance for living expenses. Applicants were required to be American citizens and to have voices deemed suitable for operatic work. Auditions were held in New York, Boston, Chicago, Cleveland, and New Orleans, as well as in Rochester, and ten singers were soon selected for the new department. The subsequent story of that department—and of the opera company that would emerge from it—is one of the most fascinating chapters in the history of the Eastman School, a story that unfolded very dramatically over the next several years.

While all of this was transpiring, progress continued in filling the conducting position for the Rochester Philharmonic. A month prior to his March 20 telegram to Eugene Goossens inquiring about his possible interest in the conducting position in Rochester, George

---

[10] There is considerable confusion concerning whom it was that Rosing met on board ship. Nicholas Slonimsky has written that it was George Eastman himself (Slonimsky, *Perfect Pitch*, 81) Others have suggested that it was George Todd. But both Vladimir Rosing and Ruth Glean Rosing confirmed that it was Warner.

Eastman had written Albert Coates, inviting him to come for a visit the next time he was in America. The conductor's visit in June was in response to that invitation, and it was obvious that the millionaire philanthropist was seriously considering both Goossens and Coates as potential leaders of the orchestra. Coates was the older of the two. He was born April 23, 1882, in St. Petersburg, the son of an English father and Russian mother. Following his general education in England, Coates had studied piano, cello, and conducting at the Leipzig Conservatory, where his conducting training was under the famous Arthur Nikisch (1855–1922). After conducting in Elberfeld, Dresden, and Mannheim, he was appointed to the Imperial Opera in St. Petersburg. He later appeared with much success as a conductor of Wagner at Covent Garden in England and also as guest conductor of the New York Symphony.

Eugene Goossens, born in London on May 26, 1893, was eleven years younger the Coates. He came from a family of musicians of Belgian descent and was educated at the Bruges Conservatory. Returning to England in 1906, Goossens pursued further study at

Figure 29. Eugene Goossens, conductor of the Rochester Philharmonic Orchestra and member of the Eastman School faculty. (Photograph by Alexander Leventon. Used by permission.)

Liverpool College and at the Royal College of Music before becoming associated with Thomas Beecham (1879–1961), who would later become one of England's most popular and distinguished orchestral leaders. Goossens and Coates were excellent candidates for the Rochester position, but George Eastman had one more Englishman in mind, namely Adrian Boult.

Born in Chester on April 8, 1889, Boult was educated at Westminster School and Christ Church, Oxford, before going to Germany to study conducting with Nikisch and composition with Max Reger (1873–1916). He made his debut as an orchestral conductor in 1918 and was then appointed instructor of conducting at the Royal College of Music. Boult's interest in Rochester, New York, has not been widely documented, not even deserving mention in his own autobiography.[11] His candidacy failed principally because he asked for too much. He not only wanted to be conductor of the Rochester Philharmonic and to have complete control over the Eastman Theatre, but he also wanted the now vacant position of director of the Eastman School of Music. George Eastman let it be known that he would not give that much power and authority to anyone. Therefore, the decision was made initially to divide the conducting responsibilities and hire both Goossens and Coates. The former would conduct four concerts in October and November, and the latter was scheduled to lead the orchestra in eleven concerts during the first four months of 1924.

The degree to which George Eastman was personally involved in all of these dealings during the spring and summer of 1923 is quite fascinating. He derived enormous satisfaction from this involvement, admitting to friends and acquaintances that the music school project had given him more enjoyment than anything he had ever previously attempted. He thought that it was quite humorous for someone to be in charge of such a significant musical enterprise without having any particular musical talent or aptitude. Less fun for George Eastman, however, was the continual question of the theater's tax exemption. The legal maneuvering, which had begun in January, continued into the summer months. Eastman now felt compelled to address the problem and issued a detailed statement that was printed on July 24 in the local newspapers:

> As to the effects of taxation, they would probably be something like this: During the year just closing the theater has

---

[11] Adrian Cedric Boult, *My Own Trumpet* (London: Hamish Hamilton, 1973).

just about managed to carry itself without charging anything for interest or depreciation on the real estate. There may be a little surplus at the end of the year but nowhere near enough to pay taxes. Therefore, if taxes are imposed the admission fee will have to be increased. The effect of this would of course be to distribute the tax right back to the citizens of Rochester. I cannot see that anybody would gain anything by this. There might, however, come about a very disastrous effect from increasing the price of admission. That would be to reduce the attendance. To meet that the first thing that would have to be done would be to cut down the expenses, by first reducing the size of the orchestra which now receives about 43 percent of the present income. This cutting down of the orchestra, however, would deprive the citizens of Rochester of that main thing for which the theater was built. The lessening of the orchestra might still further lessen the attendance, in which case there would still be a deficit. The University has no income to pay such a deficit and it would then be obliged to rent the theater to one of the big companies which operate such theaters the country over. There is no question whatever but what the theater could be rented for a commercial enterprise for a sum that would pay all the taxes and leave the University with a net income which it could devote to other purposes. That, however, would of course completely change the purpose and effect of the theater.[12]

Although all of this reasoning might seem quite logical, even George Eastman could not produce a quick resolution of this issue. The taxation question would be around for a while longer. But it was now time to turn everyone's energies to the immediate problem of selecting a new director for the Eastman School of Music.

[12] *Times-Union*, Rochester, 24 July 1923. SML.

Chapter 7

1923–1924
The Search for a New Director

The 1923–24 school year opened in September, with enrollment once again showing impressive gains. There were 231 students in the degree and certificate programs, an increase of twenty-five over the previous year. Preparatory and special students numbered 1,695, the highest enrollment of such students that the school would perhaps ever see. Raymond Wilson was now the acting director of the Eastman School of Music, and on September 10 he sent the following letter to his faculty colleagues:

> From Dr. Rhees you have no doubt heard that I have been invited to serve as Acting Director of the Eastman School for this season, by the end of which it is expected a permanent Director will have been secured.
>
> After very careful consideration and with hesitation, I decided to undertake this work realizing, as I am confident you do, the manifold duties of the Director's office and the grave importance of their proper execution.
>
> As a member of our faculty, I want to assure you that you may expect my hearty cooperation in your work, and I am so certain of your loyalty to the school that I desire to thank you now for your support which we in the administrative offices will so much need and believe you will give.
>
> This magnificent institution, with its matchless equipment and possibilities which Mr. Eastman has so generously given, must not in any way be allowed to suffer in the development which should rapidly place it in an exalted position among music schools of the world. Therefore, as we assemble for work this fall, let us be firmly united in our efforts to not only retain our present standards, but if possible to press forward to a higher level of attainments.
>
> May we earnestly strive throughout these few months to maintain such a healthy school spirit that we as a unit

may be able to properly welcome our new leader when
he comes.[1]

Wilson was a meticulous, dedicated, and hard-working man, and
he took his new responsibilities with the utmost seriousness.
Nonetheless, those responsibilities were most certainly very routine
and limited to the basic day-to-day operations. No one could have
doubted that Rush Rhees and George Eastman were really fully in
charge of the school's future direction.

New to the educational program in September 1923 was the
Eastman School Chorus, organized and directed by Oscar
Gareissen. An orchestra had been established the previous year
under the direction of Selim Palmgren, but it would not present its
first concert until the spring of 1924. One of the first actions of the
faculty was to select a committee of seven to select an appropriate
gift for Alf Klingenberg, for whom there was much sympathy and
affection. His resignation had come as a surprise to students and
faculty alike. One of his former students, Marie Erhart—later to
serve on the school's piano faculty for forty-eight years—recalled
learning of the resignation from Klingenberg himself:

> He said: "How would you like to study with Mr. Vas next
> year?" I said, "I would like to study with you." He said, "I
> won't be here." There was no elaboration. The only thing
> I can say is that all of a sudden Mr. Klingenberg was gone.[2]

Sandor Vas was new to the faculty this third year and became
one of school's most successful and outstanding piano teachers
during a long career at Eastman. Born in Arad, Hungary, Vas pursued his professional studies at the Leipzig Conservatory, where his
piano teacher was the famous student of Franz Liszt, Alfred
Reisenauer (1863–1907). A multi-talented musician, he also studied
conducting with Nikisch in Leipzig, being a classmate of Albert
Coates. Additionally, Vas was a serious composer and an excellent
cellist, but he soon began to direct all his energies towards the
piano. After studying with Terresa Carreño (1853–1917), he began
concertizing in 1908, appearing throughout Europe and making
two very successful tours of the United States. At the outbreak of

---

[1] Raymond Wilson, Letter to the Eastman School of Music faculty, 10 September
1923. Personal collection of the author.
[2] Marie Erhart Pearson, interviewed by the author. Tape recording, Rochester, 30
November 1977.

Figure 30. Sandor Vas, pianist, Eastman School faculty 1923–54. (Photograph by Alexander Leventon. Used by permission.)

the First World War, Vas was a professor at the Lodz Conservatory in Poland, and following the war he began teaching at the Fodor Conservatory in Budapest. He first appeared in Rochester in March 1923 for a recital in Kilbourn Hall, after which he was offered a faculty position at the Eastman School. His previous connection with Albert Coates suggests that it may have been the English conductor who recommended him to Rush Rhees and George Eastman.

Also new to the faculty in 1923 was the French organist, Abel Marie Decaux, who was hired to specifically represent the French organ tradition at Eastman. Although Decaux was not quite in the same class as Joseph Bonnet, who had conducted two series of master classes during the school's opening year, he was an organist and teacher of considerable reputation. Born in the northwestern part of France, he had been trained by Charles-Marie Widor (1844–1937) and had attracted the attention and support of Alexandre-Félix Guilmant (1837–1911). As the former organist of Sacré-Coeur in Paris, his presence on the Eastman faculty was a clear indication that the school attached great importance to its organ department.

The growing prominence of the faculty and the school's willingness to engage the world's finest musicians for appearances in

Rochester made this a time of unimaginable opportunities to hear great music. Many fine concerts were presented in Kilbourn Hall, adding to the incredibly rich musical experience provided by the Eastman Theatre concert series. French pianist Alfred Cortot (1877–1962) and English pianist Myra Hess (1890–1965) were among the recitalists who had appeared in Kilbourn during the preceding season. Cortot had accomplished the impressive feat of performing two completely different recital programs in one day. In the morning of November 7 he played music of Vivaldi, Chopin, Saint-Saëns, Debussy, Albeniz, and Liszt in a recital in Kilbourn Hall sponsored by a local organization, the Tuesday Musicale. He then returned to Kilbourn Hall in the evening for an Eastman-sponsored program, which consisted of the Franck *Prelude, Chorale, and Fugue*, all twenty-four Etudes of Chopin, Schumann's *Carnaval*, and three pieces of Liszt, including the Hungarian Rhapsody No. 11.

Among the luminaries appearing in Kilbourn Hall during 1923–24 was Frederic Lamond (1868–1948), the famous Scottish pianist who was considered at the time to be the finest interpreter of the music of Beethoven. His Kilbourn Hall recital on the evening of October 22 included both books of the Brahms *Paganini Variations*, Beethoven's "Appassionata" Sonata, the Chopin B-Minor Sonata, plus five shorter works of Chopin, Glazunov, and Liszt. This kind of herculean program was quite typical of a Lamond piano recital, although the pianist was already in his mid-fifties. Lamond, who had studied not only with Franz Liszt but also with Hans von Bülow and Anton Rubinstein, was also engaged by the Eastman School to teach a special course for advanced piano students and to give a series of ten lecture recitals in Kilbourn Hall. The special course for advanced piano students consisted of one-hour weekly lessons for ten weeks. The lessons were conducted as public events to which all members of the Eastman community were invited. Lamond's lecture-recitals were held on Mondays at 4:30 in the afternoon. The first, on November 19, was devoted to three popular Beethoven sonatas—the "Pathetique," "Moonlight," and "Waldstein"—which Lamond discussed and performed for the audience. This format was repeated nine more times, covering a wide range of the piano repertoire. Only a pianist with an enormous repertoire could have attempted such a series of lecture-recitals.

Other artists who performed in Kilbourn Hall included several faculty members. On November 19 Vladimir Rosing presented a vocal recital consisting mainly of Russian repertoire. Sandor Vas and Vladimir Resnikoff presented a program on January 22, and Harold Gleason and Joseph Press shared a recital in Kilbourn Hall on February 1. The Kilbourn Quartet—whose members at the time were Vladimir Resnikoff, Gerald Kunz, Samuel Belov, and Joseph Press—gave performances both semesters during the school year, and visiting quartets included the London String Quartet and the Flonzaley Quartet, two of the most widely known and admired chamber groups at that time. A very special event during the season occurred on January 14 when Marcel Dupré (1886–1971), organist at Notre Dame in Paris, presented a recital on the Skinner organ in Kilbourn Hall. Dupré had recently given a series of recitals in Montreal, in which he had played all the works of Bach by memory. One of the highlights of his Rochester recital was when the organist used themes provided by local musicians and improvised a four-movement sonata, the last movement being a fugue.

Meanwhile, the Eastman Theatre management was presenting eighteen concerts during the 1923–24 season, divided into three different series. In December the San Carlo Opera Company returned for another "opera week" in the theater, presenting *Rigoletto*, *The Barber of Seville*, *Cavalleria Rusticana*, *Pagliacci*, *La Traviata*, *Faust*, and *Aida* in four evening performances and three matinees. None of the performances found favor with Vladimir Rosing, since they represented absolutely everything he wished to change in opera productions. Rosing's own opera department had begun to make itself known in late November by staging Act 3 of Verdi's *Rigoletto* (sung in English). The following month plans were announced for two opera department presentations each month in connection with Eastman Theatre shows, one being a musical sketch and the other an act or scene from the opera repertoire. Eastman opera students began their studies each morning at 9:00 with a class in "mental training," which was part of their dramatic instruction. Each morning Rosing would challenge the students by reciting, "Every day in every way we are getting better and better." He was a believer in autosuggestion, and in his students he found many willing converts to his way of teaching. Their *Rigoletto* performance in November was only a first and hesitant step toward much more ambitious and successful undertakings in the future.

These opera events, however, served only as a prelude to a much anticipated visit of the Metropolitan Opera Company later in the year, this being the first of what became a series of annual Metropolitan Opera presentations in the Eastman Theatre. On May 5, a Monday evening, the company presented Gounod's *Faust*, with Feodor Chaliapin as Mefistofeles and Frances Alda (1883–1952) as Marguerite. The following evening Rochester audiences were treated to a performance of Puccini's *La Bohème*, featuring Lucrezia

Bori (1887–1960) as Mimi, Giovanni Martinelli as Rodolfo, and Giuseppe De Luca (1876–1950) as Marcello. Having Metropolitan Opera productions in the Eastman Theatre strongly suggested the progress that had been made in so short a time towards establishing Rochester as a major musical center in America, with Mr. Eastman's new theater as the centerpiece of this accomplishment.

In early January, however, the specter of taxing the theater once again reappeared when the State Tax Commission notified George S. Taylor, chairman of the Board of Assessors, that the Eastman School of Music should be put on the city assessment rolls, pending a conference between members of the commission and the Board of Assessors. A hearing was held at the end of February, at which George Eastman personally testified. On March 20 the State Tax Commissioner, Mark Graves, finally announced that the Eastman Theatre would be exempt from municipal, county, and state taxation. George Eastman issued a statement the following day, declaring that he could not see how they could have reached any other conclusion. Yet the issue was far from over, as appeals and legal maneuvering continued into the summer and fall months.

The most important issue of 1923–24, however, was the process that would lead to the appointment of a new director for the Eastman School of Music. Rush Rhees quickly decided on four basic qualifications. The new director should be American, preferably someone who could make the school a factor in the development of American music. He should be a man with an excellent general education as well as appropriate music credentials. He should be someone with previous administrative experience. He should be someone with wide general musical interests rather than someone prominent in one particular branch of music.

One of the first candidates considered for the position, however, was not American born. There was considerable interest in the noted composer Ernest Bloch (1880–1959), who was then the director of the Cleveland Institute of Music and who had previously taught at the David Mannes School in New York City. Among those suggesting Bloch for the Eastman position was the English pianist Harold Bauer. When Rochester music critic A.J. ("Jack") Warner met Bauer in November, he sent George Eastman a letter on the sixteenth of the month, conveying Bauer's enthusiastic (perhaps overly enthusiastic) remarks concerning Bloch:

> In all probability Ernest Bloch, who is at present director
> of the Cleveland Institute of Music, will resign his post at
> the end of the year. If Mr. Eastman could secure him, it is

my firm conviction that the Eastman Conservatory [*sic*]
would very shortly become one of the finest institutions
in the world.

These words may seem extravagant but I employ them
deliberately with all they imply. Bloch is not only one of
the greatest (if not the greatest) of composers alive today;
he is a man of the most profound culture, a pedagogue of
the highest attainments, and an administrator of remarkable ability. His insight and sympathies are of the clearest
and keenest, he is respected as a genius and regarded
with affection as a man by all with whom he comes in
contact, in short a personality who stands at the pinnacle
in the music world of today and a man in a million.[3]

Bloch, however, disappointed those who advocated his candidacy
for the Eastman directorship, writing to George Eastman on
February 28, 1924: "I do not want to apply for the directorship.
I have just resigned as Director of the [Cleveland] Institute for many
reasons, chiefly because I do not want to hold a high position nor be
bothered by a large salary."[4]

Another composer emerged as a possible candidate for the
Eastman position. Albert Coates, upon whom George Eastman was
increasingly relying for advice concerning the school and the
theater, suggested a young American composer who had been
awarded the Prix de Rome three years earlier. His name was
Howard Hanson, and they had met in Rome when Coates was
serving as guest conductor of the Augusteo Orchestra. An invitation was extended for Hanson to come quietly to Rochester in
January for a meeting with Rush Rhees and George Eastman.
Many years later, Hanson recalled the details of that first
encounter:

On meeting my two future mentors it became quickly
apparent that this was not a social, courtesy call. President
Rhees did most of the talking, generally in the form of
questions. Did I think that it was possible to build a first-
rate professional music school under the "umbrella" of a
university? Could the worlds of the artist, the performer,
and the scholar co-exist in administrative as well as tonal
harmony? What part should "general education" play in
the training of professional musicians? As a graduate of

---

3   A.J. Warner, Letter to George Eastman, 16 November 1923. GEH.
4   Ernst Bloch, Letter to George Eastman, 28 February 1924. GEH.

> both schools, did I prefer the administrative organization
> of New York's Institute of Musical Art—now the Juilliard
> School of Music—or the School of Music at Northwestern
> University? What was my impression of the famous for-
> eign conservatories that I had visited? What was my reac-
> tion to the music departments of America's "ivy league"
> universities, for example, Harvard?
>
> Although, as I have said, President Rhees did most of
> the questioning, Mr. Eastman entered the discussion
> briefly from time to time. He disclaimed any knowledge
> of either education or music but his questions were mod-
> els of clarity and incisiveness. His ability to search out the
> heart of a problem with a minimum of words was both
> impressive and a little frightening.[5]

At the conclusion of the meeting Rhees asked Hanson to put
into writing some of his personal views and opinions concerning
the development of a professional music school within the context
of an American university. In response to that request, he sent the
university president a four-page typewritten letter dated January
26. The letter contained a very strong endorsement of the thought
that it was vital to select an American for the position of director:

> The position of Director is one of great importance and
> I can easily understand why you are moving carefully in
> the matter. It is imperative that the Director shall have
> four qualities; good, practical (not merely academic)
> musicianship; tremendous enthusiasm for American
> music; proven ability in organization; tact in handling
> men, both the members of the faculty and student body.
> I would add to that one further qualification, that he
> should be an American, in full sympathy with American
> ideals and possessing a full understanding of and love for
> the American student.[6]

Included in the same letter was the following remark concerning
the responsibility of the man ultimately selected to direct the school:

> It will take the life of some man to do it. It is not a physi-
> cal task but a spiritual one. The Director of your school
> will have to breath fire into a great machine and endow it
> with his own enthusiasm for a great cause. Rochester is

[5]   Howard Hanson. "Music Was a Spiritual Necessity." *The University of Rochester Library Bulletin* 26, no. 3 (Spring 1971): 82–83.
[6]   Howard Hanson, Letter to Rush Rhees, 26 January 1924. SML.

Figure 31. Howard Hanson, second director of the Eastman School of Music. (Photograph by Alexander Leventon. Used by permission.)

not a music center and for it to become a music center a great thought would have to be born there which by its very bigness and idealism would attract to it all those who believed in the same things.

These were certainly bold and prophetic words, especially from a man who had just turned twenty-seven years old the previous October 28.

Howard Hanson was born in Wahoo, Nebraska, in 1896. He earned a diploma from Luther College in Wahoo when he was only fifteen years old, then continuing his studies at the University of Nebraska's Lincoln School of Music and at the Institute of Musical Art (later the Juilliard School) in New York. His teacher at the Institute was Percy Goetschius. Then he completed his bachelor's degree at Northwestern University in 1916, also serving as an assistant teacher of music theory. The following year Hanson was hired by the College of the Pacific in San José, California, becoming dean of the department of music in 1919. Hanson gained considerable attention as a promising young American composer, and was awarded the Prix de Rome in 1921 for two of his early works, *California Forest Play* (Op. 16) and *Before the Dawn* (Op. 17). The first of these works was written in 1919 for soprano and baritone solo voices, SATB chorus, dancers, and orchestra. Hanson conducted its first performance in July 1920, with the Anita Peters Wright Dancers, various vocalists, and instrumentalists from the San Francisco and Oakland orchestras. *Before the Dawn*, an orchestral work, was written during 1919 and 1920, and was premiered by the Los Angeles Philharmonic, Walter Henry Rothwell conducting. As a result of his 1921 Prix de Rome, Hanson became a Fellow of the American Academy in Rome for the next three years, where he was able to study for a while with Ottorino Respighi (1879–1936).

When Rush Rhees became interested in Howard Hanson as a possible candidate for the director's position, he made some discrete inquiries about the young American composer. He received nothing but favorable and enthusiastic responses, including from John Seaton, who had been president of the College of the Pacific when Hanson was appointed to the faculty, and from Eugene Noble, secretary of the Juilliard Musical Foundation. Especially encouraging was a letter from Tully Knowles from the College of the Pacific, who reassured Rhees that Hanson's youth should not be considered an impediment to his candidacy for the Eastman leadership.[7]

---

[7]   These letters are in the Rush Rhees Papers at Rush Rhees Library, University of Rochester. The letter from Tully Knowles is dated 28 January 1924.

Hanson returned to Rochester on March 19, 1924, responding to an invitation from Albert Coates to conduct his "Nordic" Symphony with the Rochester Philharmonic. On April 16 Rush Rhees sent a two-page letter to Hanson offering him the position of director of the Eastman School of Music. Included in that letter were the following paragraphs:

> If it had been possible for me to talk with you face to face it would have been simpler for you and for me to give the kind of thoughtful consideration which is necessary to our problem here. There are so many indications that you have the experience and equipment which would enable you to assume the direction of the Eastman School of Music that I should have been glad of an opportunity to discuss somewhat intimately with you several aspects of our problem.
>
> Inasmuch as such discussion is not possible, we have decided to ask you whether you will accept appointment as Director of the Eastman School of Music for the next academic year, with the understanding (which is usual in all of our appointments) that at the end of the year either party to the relation will be at liberty in respect of a renewal of the appointment.[8]

The reason Rhees could not speak directly with Hanson was that he had been in Europe and was returning to America at precisely the same time as Hanson was making the voyage back to Italy. They literally passed one another at sea. It is interesting to note that Rhees addressed his letter to "Harold" Hanson. At this point in time, Hanson evidently preferred to be called Harold, which was his middle name, but that preference was apparently dropped soon after his appointment as director of the Eastman School of Music.

Hanson immediately responded to Rush Rhees's offer with a three-word cable from Rome, which simply said, "Accept position/ Writing."[9] He then sent a letter on May 10 with a more detailed reply, which included the following statement: "I am deeply interested in your plans and assure you that I shall come to you with every energy bent on doing what I can to help in the realization of the limitless possibilities of the Eastman School of Music."[10] In the same letter he also commented on the salary offer, which was

8   Rush Rhees, Letter to Howard Hanson, 16 April 1924. RRL.
9   Howard Hanson, Telegram to Rush Rhees, 9 May 1924. RRL.
10   Howard Hanson, Letter to Rush Rhees, 10 May 1924. RRL.

several thousands of dollars less than what Klingenberg had been making as director:

> I am not questioning your decision regarding salary as I am far more interested in the tremendous possibilities which the Eastman School of Music offers towards the development of music in America. It is understood, of course, that, if at the end of one year you are satisfied with my work and I am happy in Rochester, my contract for the second year shall not be established on the basis of my first year's contract as precedent.

Rush Rhees received this letter on May 26 and responded the same day. He agreed with Hanson's comments concerning the salary figure[11] and also replied to a concern that Hanson had raised in his same letter:

> Referring to your opinion that it would be unfortunate for you to have your time so filled by details that you would have to give up your own productive work, you may count on my complete agreement and support in so arranging matters as to avoid that danger.[12]

On a more practical level the university president suggested that Hanson take the time while in Europe to acquaint himself with the curricula and organization of the more important schools and conservatories.

Three days following his letter to Howard Hanson, Rush Rhees addressed the following note to the Eastman School faculty:

> Saturday morning's papers will announce the appointment of Mr. Harold Hanson to be Director of this school. Mr. Hanson is an American of cosmopolitan musical training and experience, who has also had important and successful experience as teacher and administrator in a school of music associated with other college departments. He will begin his service with the next school year in September.
>
> Had it not been for the holiday on May 30th [i.e., Memorial Day], I should have asked you to meet me personally so that I could speak with you more at length

---

[11] Hanson's salary of $5,000 for his first year as director was raised to $8,000 the following year and to $10,000 two years later.
[12] Rush Rhees, Letter to Howard Hanson, 26 May 1924. RRL.

> concerning this very important decision before its public
> announcement. I hope I may meet you in a few days for
> a more intimate conference on this matter.
>   I feel very confident of Mr. Hanson's success in his new
> work, even as we count very confidently on your loyal
> cooperation with him.[13]

On May 31 all the local Rochester newspapers carried the announcement that "Harold" Hanson had been chosen as the new director of the Eastman School of Music. The Eastman School faculty met with Rush Rhees on June 4, 1924, at which time the university president discussed the selection of Hanson as director. All of this was in anticipation of official approval of the appointment at the forthcoming meeting of the Board of Trustees. The trustees met on June 14, and Howard Harold Hanson was officially confirmed in his new position.

The University of Rochester held its commencement in the Eastman Theatre on June 16. The exercises began with the sounds of the great theater organ, Robert Berentsen performing Rollo F. Maitland's Concert Overture in A Major, followed by Felix Borowski's *Marche solennelle*, which served as the processional. After an opening prayer the Eastman Theatre Orchestra played Richard Wagner's Overture to *Rienzi*. Then came the commencement address, which was offered by Edwin Holt Hughes, Bishop of the Methodist Episcopal Church. The announcement of prizes and honors followed the Bishop's remarks, the ceremony then continuing with the conferral of degrees and certificates. Nine of the graduates were awarded the bachelor of music degree, including Ernestine Marie Klinzing, who was already a member of the Eastman School piano faculty. Three of her classmates in 1924 now joined her on the school's faculty, Lyndon Croxford and Florence Ruby Alexander as members of the piano department and Ruth Northrup in the theory department. Five students also graduated from the Eastman School's certificate program.

The ceremonies continued with an address by Rush Rhees, followed by a performance of "Elizabeth's Prayer" and the "Pilgrim's Chorus" from Wagner's *Tannhäuser*, sung by several students from the new opera department at Eastman. The conferral of honorary degrees led to the singing of the commencement hymn and the offering of a benediction. Robert Berentsen then returned to the

---

[13] Rush Rhees, Memorandum to the Eastman School of Music Faculty, 29 May 1924. RRL.

Eastman Theatre organ, performing the finale from Mark Andrews' Sonata in A Minor as a recessional.

Howard Hanson was not yet on the scene. Nonetheless, he was busily studying the Eastman School catalogue and wrote to Rush Rhees on June 18:

> I have been studying the catalogues. Many points concerning the administration of the School of Music please me greatly. With your approval I may make some changes in the courses of the theory department, however. I should like to make this department one of the strongest in America inasmuch as it is a most important part of the work for degree candidates. . . .[14]

He added that he wished to teach some courses so that he would have personal contact with the students, hoping to "divert their attention" toward the degree curricula. This remark plainly indicates that the old certificate program would not find an advocate in Howard Hanson.

---

[14]   Howard Hanson, Letter to Rush Rhees, 18 June 1924. RRL.

Interlude

Chapter 8

1924–1930
The Rochester American
Opera Company

When Vladimir Rosing came to Rochester in September 1923 to teach at the Eastman School of Music, he most assuredly had more in mind than simply heading up an opera department for the school. From the very beginning it is obvious that Rosing's real aspiration was to start an opera company, more specifically an opera company that would be distinctly American. He came to his first meeting with George Eastman in the late spring of 1923 with a clear understanding that it was absolutely necessary to secure Eastman's support if his dreams were to be realized. Therefore, he carefully presented his proposal to the millionaire philanthropist:

> I therefore propose that Rochester's Eastman Music School [*sic*] and Theatre form an American national opera company composed entirely of American singers who will sing in English, using beautiful English translations; that English diction will be on a par with the dramatic theatre; and that singers will be actors who will look the part of the roles they sing. I propose two years to train a company of twenty-five to thirty singers in my style of realistic and rhythmical action, blending music and drama as one entity. Instead of a bastard art built of compromise, opera could and should be the greatest artistic expression because of the blending of all its artistic components.[1]

George Eastman was suitably impressed but gave him only two days to prepare a budget for the next four years. He assured Rosing that, if the budget was acceptable, all expenses involved with the

---

[1]   Ruth Glean Rosing, *Val Rosing: Musical Genius, an Intimate Biography* (Manhattan, Kans.: Sunflower University Press, 1993), 107.

Figure 32. Vladimir Rosing, founder of the Rochester American Opera Company. (Photograph by Alexander Leventon. Used by permission.)

development of an opera company would be covered. Rosing worked feverishly for the next two days, assisted by the secretary of the Eastman School, Arthur See, and was able to present the millionaire philanthropist with an acceptable plan and budget.

To help him fulfill this dream, Rosing quickly assembled a rather amazing cast of characters. Perhaps the most notable was Rouben Mamoulian, later to achieve fame as a producer and director on Broadway and in Hollywood. Mamoulian was born on October 8, 1898, in Tiflis (Tbilisi), Georgia. His father, an ethnic Armenian, was a successful banker, but he was also very much interested in local theatrical organizations. As a young man, the elder Mamoulian had even appeared in various amateur stage productions. Mamoulian's mother was heavily involved with Armenian drama and theater. She was not only a wonderful actress but also an excellent painter and pianist. The family lived for a while in Paris, where the young Rouben began his education, but they then returned to Russia, where he continued his studies and graduated in law from the University of Moscow, also working with the Vakhtangov Studio of the Moscow Art Theatre. He then returned to Tiflis, where he became involved as a producer and as a teacher of drama. In 1921 Mamoulian went to London to work with a Russian drama company, and while there he met Rosing at a chorus rehearsal that involved a group of Russian refugees. Mamoulian was about to go to Paris to accept a contract with the Théâtre des Champs-Élysées, but Rosing invited him to come to Rochester instead. He readily accepted the invitation.

Another Rosing recruit was Nicolas Slonimsky, who was also destined to make a big name for himself in the future. Born in Russia in 1894, Slonimsky received his first piano lesson from his maternal aunt, Isabelle Vengerova (1877–1956),[2] and later attended the St. Petersburg Conservatory. After leaving Russia he toured with Rosing in 1921 and 1922, serving as his accompanist in France, Belgium, and Spain. The following year Rosing offered him a salary of $3,000 a year (a truly impressive sum at the time) for serving as an accompanist and coach at Eastman. The poor man spoke practically no English at all when he stepped off the train in Rochester, but he spent two wonderful years at Eastman. He left in 1925 to become Serge Koussevitzky's personal secretary and, in time, a major proponent of modern American music and a brilliant author and editor.

Other coaches who eventually joined Rosing's team included Emanuel Balaban and Guy Fraser Harrison. Both enjoyed long careers in Rochester, the former as director of the opera department and the latter as conductor of the Rochester Civic Orchestra and teacher of conducting at the school. Balaban was a New Yorker and had studied at the Institute of Musical Art before spending four years in Germany, principally in Dresden, where he was assistant conductor of the Dresden Opera. As a pianist he gained favorable attention by serving as an accompanist for Efrem Zimbalist (1889–1985) and Mischa Elman. Harrison was English by birth and had received his early musical training in the choir school of Christ Church Oxford. An accomplished organist, he came to Rochester in 1920 to become organist at St. Paul's Episcopal Church on East Avenue, joining the Eastman School faculty the following year.

Two other coaches recruited by Rosing were Ernst Bacon and Otto Luening. Bacon's training had been at Northwestern University and at the University of Chicago. He spent three years in Rochester

---

[2] Vengerova, a student of Annette Essipova (1857–1914), later became famous in America as the teacher of Leonard Bernstein (1918–90), Lucas Foss (b. 1922), Gary Graffman (b. 1928), and Leonard Pennario (b. 1924).

before leaving for a position at the San Francisco Conservatory. Bacon later taught at Converse College in South Carolina and then became director of the music school at Syracuse University, a position he held from 1945 until 1963. The German-born Otto Luening studied in Munich and then in Zurich, Switzerland. He also spent three years in Rochester before going on to a highly successful career that included two Guggenheim Fellowships. He is perhaps best remembered as the co-director of the Columbia-Princeton Electronic Music Center, a position he held from 1959 until 1980.

Rosing also hired a young man named Paul Horgan as stage designer. Born in 1903, Horgan came to Rochester with hopes of studying voice with Arthur Alexander and also working for one of the local newspapers. When he arrived, however, he discovered that Alexander had left town and the newspaper had been sold to new owners. Now uncertain about his immediate future, Horgan suddenly became aware of a meeting scheduled at the Eastman School at which a Russian by the name of Vladimir Rosing would discuss exciting new plans for establishing an opera company in Rochester. Deciding to attend the meeting, Horgan listened with growing enthusiasm to the charismatic Rosing, but it occurred to him that Rosing had not yet considered the important question of stage design. Although Horgan had practically no experience at all in this line of work, he decided to become stage designer for Rosing. Therefore, he quickly drew and painted some scenes from operas and showed his work to Rosing the following morning. He was hired on the spot.

Horgan, Mamoulian, and Slonimsky became close friends, sharing a wonderful sense of humor and a definite enjoyment of mischief. They even formalized their friendship by establishing what they called a "Society of Unrecognized Geniuses." Slonimsky was president, Mamoulian was vice-president, and Horgan secretary, but they voted against including Rosing, whom they deemed a bit too serious for the group. The three comrades, all in their twenties, especially enjoyed marching around in public pretending to be Germans. Their mischievous behavior undoubtedly attracted a lot of attention, some perhaps negative, in a town that was noted for its basic conservatism.

Slonimsky later admitted that the three young men all shared a passion for Lucile Johnson Bigelow, the harpist of the Rochester Philharmonic and harp teacher at the Eastman School. Whenever she returned home to visit her family in Buffalo, they would accompany her to the railroad station, clicking their heels, wearing monocles, and speaking in what they hoped people would assume to be German. It was an act that created curiosity and probably a degree of disapproval among the onlookers, but one in which the three young men took much pleasure. Sixty years later Slonimsky recalled an incident when their quest for fun and merriment got slightly out of hand:

> In honour of Lucile's birthday, we staged a party in a Rochester coffee shop. We placed a boxful of matches inside the birthday cake; I lit the candles, and as they melted, the matches ignited under the icing and the cake blew up with an impressive bang. We were asked to leave.[3]

The cast of characters for the great opera enterprise in Rochester was completed by four conductors: Eugene Goossens and Albert Coates, who were just then beginning to share the leadership of the Rochester Philharmonic Orchestra, and Vladimir Shavitch and Victor Wagner, who were the leaders of the Eastman Theatre Orchestra. Shavitch, however, left in the spring of 1924 to do some conducting in London and Paris before returning to America to become the conductor of the nearby Syracuse Symphony. His replacement on the conducting staff at the theater was Frank Waller, a young American who had been assistant conductor at the Boston Opera, and who had also spent two seasons with the Chicago Opera.

Several of the people associated with the new opera enterprise received invitations to become members of the Corner Club. Located in an eight-room house on the southwest corner of Grove Place and Windsor Street, the club had been founded in 1921 for men and women who shared an interest in the arts. Its membership was limited to one hundred and included many people from the local artistic community, especially musicians. But the club could also boast a healthy representation from Rochester's most socially prominent families. The building that housed the Corner Club was maintained by a live-in caretaker whom everyone knew as "Mrs. Thompson." She was responsible for the upkeep of the premises, as well as for preparing meals. Afternoon tea was available to members without notice, and lunch or dinner could be ordered if Mrs. Thompson was notified by 11:00 in the morning. A light lunch consisting of soup, salad, and dessert cost forty cents. Adding the "plat du jour" increased the price to sixty cents. Rosing and Mamoulian joined the Corner Club in January 1924, and Paul Horgan

---

[3] Nicolas Slonimsky, *Perfect Pitch: A Life Story* (New York: Oxford University Press, 1988), 87.

was admitted the following year. It was at the club that Horgan befriended Helen Rochester Rogers, who was the great-grand-daughter of Nathaniel Rochester, one of founders of the city. She was then serving as secretary of the Corner Club, a position later held for many years by Barbara Duncan, the Eastman School librarian.[4]

There is no telling how much time Rosing spent at the Corner Club, but his membership probably provided him with many relaxing moments as well as opportunities to interact with people who greatly valued his efforts to bring opera to the people of Rochester. Rosing had assembled an impressive group of people for the first year of Eastman's new opera department, and they were all busy at work, inaugurating the work of the department and dreaming of the eventual opera company that George Eastman had promised to finance. Among the ten students chosen as the recipients of scholarships for the first year were soprano Cecile Sherman from Birmingham, Alabama, tenor Charles Hedley from Rochester, and bass George Fleming Houston from New York City. During the year it was announced that four additional scholarships would be awarded for 1924–25. The productions during the department's first year were only a preparation for larger plans that lay in the immediate future.

The training of Rosing's young American singers had been underway for a year when, on November 8, 1924, the Eastman School of Music announced the formation of the Rochester American Opera Company. Rosing would be director, and the Eastman students who had displayed special abilities would become members of the company. All of the company members would be American, and all of their performances would be sung in English in an effort to reach a vast new audience for opera. The first performance of the new opera company took place on November 20, 1924, in the Eastman Theatre, the program consisting of two scenes from *Boris Godounoff* with Eugene Goossens conducting, and *Pagliacci* with Frank Waller conducting. George Fleming Houston sang the role of Boris, and Charles Hedley the role of Canio. A review in *Musical America* declared that the performances had been a brilliant success.[5]

---

[4]   The Corner Club disbanded in the early 1950s and, through the courtesy of Barbara Duncan, donated an interesting collection of memorabilia to the University of Rochester.

[5]   *Musical America* byline, 22 November 1924. SML.

On January 17, 1925, the company presented its first complete performance of a lengthy opera. Gounod's *Faust* was given in the Eastman Theatre for an audience of 2,700, with George Fleming Houston appearing as Mephistopheles. Several nights before the performance Rosing was in an uncharacteristically light-hearted mood and suggested to Mamoulian and Horgan that they should attend a séance that was being held that evening. The three men gathered in the small downtown apartment of Peggy Williamson (with whom Rosing was romantically involved at the time). Guy Fraser Harrison, by that time one of the conductors of the Eastman Theatre Orchestra, was also present, as were cast members George Houston, Mary Bell, and Cecile Sherman. During their séance they imagined that they had conjured up Dr. Faustus himself, who promised to reappear on Thursday afternoon at precisely the time when the company would be presenting the opera in the Eastman Theatre.

At a point during that performance, a cross of light highlighted soprano Cecile Sherman as she was kneeling on the stage preparing to sing. Unexpectedly the light began to move all around the stage, causing Sherman to miss her cue. The light continued to move erratically over the stage for several moments and then finally quieted itself. The performance continued without further incident. Sherman was so rattled by the experience that she almost fainted backstage. The unexplained event provided much merriment for Rosing and his friends, and they all decided that the only possible explanation for the strange behavior of the light on stage was that the spirit of Dr. Faustus had kept his promise and appeared during the opera performance.[6]

The production of *Faust* was so enthusiastically received that a return engagement was presented two weeks later. *Musical America* made note of the performance by declaring, "Rochester Opera Company gains new success with Gounod's 'Faust,'"[7] and one of the local Rochester papers noted that the production "justified the hopes and faith of the backers of this experiment."[8] The performance of *Faust* was followed by a production of Bizet's *Carmen* on March 26, with Waller conducting.

[6] Paul Horgan later wrote a highly entertaining account of the "séance" and its consequences in the April 1936 issue of *Harpers Magazine*. His article was entitled "How Dr. Faustus Came to Rochester."
[7] *Musical America* byline, 17 January 1925. SML.
[8] *Rochester Herald*, Rochester, N.Y., 16 January 1925. SML.

Figure 33. Cast picture of student production of *Carmen* in 1925. In the center, row 1: Nicholas Slonimsky; row 2: Vladimir Rosing, Rouben Mamoulian; row 3: Perhaps Frank Waller, the conductor of the production.

Various changes, however, were to occur the following month. On April 18, 1925, Eastman School Director Howard Hanson announced that Rosing would henceforth concentrate entirely on opera productions:

> Vladimir Rosing, for two years director of the operatic department of the Eastman School of Music and producing director of the Rochester American Opera Company, which is an outgrowth of that department, will relinquish his executive work in connection with the Eastman School department at the close of this school year, so that he may devote his full time to production of the operas which will be given in the Eastman Theater and in Kilbourn Hall next season. . . .[9]

Rouben Mamoulian remained with the school's department as its "dramatic instructor," although significant new responsibilities and authority were soon to be conferred on him. By contrast, Rosing would be concerned only with producing operas, principally those of the Rochester American Opera Company but also any by the opera training program at the school. This meant that Rosing was slowly pulling away from the school and concentrating his energies on the professional company. And it also meant that the team of Rosing and Mamoulian was going in different directions.

Three days later it was announced that conductor Frank Waller was also leaving the Eastman opera department at the close of the school year. Feeling that opportunities to conduct operas were simply too limited, Waller decided to seek those opportunities elsewhere. In response to his departure, the school announced that Eugene Goossens would be the general director of its operatic training program, with Emanuel Balaban serving as his assistant. Taken together, these developments all indicated that a separation was gradually occurring between the educational aspects of opera training at the Eastman School and the professional productions of Rosing's Rochester American Opera Company.

The second season of the Rochester American Opera Company opened with a performance of Flotow's *Martha*. The company presented five performances, which took place in Kilbourn Hall on October 14, 15, and 16, 1925, with Emanuel Balaban conducting. The opera was then repeated on October 20 in nearby Geneseo, New York, the first out-of-town presentation by the new opera

---

[9]   *Times-Union*, Rochester, N.Y., 18 April 1925. SML.

company. Marking the second anniversary of the founding of the Eastman School opera department—and the first anniversary of the founding of the Rochester American Opera Company—a dinner and dance was held on November 20, 1925, presided over by Vladimir Rosing and attended by George Eastman, Rush Rhees, Howard Hanson, and many others.

On December 2, 1925, the Rochester American Opera Company presented *Madama Butterfly* in Kilbourn Hall, with Eugene Goossens conducting. The following month Rosing led various members of the company on a tour of several western Canadian cities, including Vancouver, Victoria, Calgary, Saskatoon, and Winnipeg. They gave a total of seventeen performances, including four complete operas plus scenes from a half-dozen others. Reviews were rather mixed, including some very negative comments. One Canadian critic even suggested that the performances were nothing more than a rather cleverly disguised advertisement for the Eastman School of Music. A newspaper in Vancouver came to the conclusion that "the tour of the visiting organization was ill-advised."[10] Back in Rochester, however, Rosing's Canadian tour was seen as a grand success.

Following their return to Rochester, the Rochester American Opera Company made its first radio broadcast on February 10, 1926, with a studio performance of Gounod's *Faust*. For this WHAM broadcast they were accompanied by members of the Rochester Philharmonic Orchestra. The school's opera department was also active at this time. On February 12 and 13 Rouben Mamoulian presented scenes from *Carmen, Samson and Delilah,* and *Fidelio,* with Otto Luening conducting the singers and with Herman Genhart and Ernst Bacon at the piano. More opera scenes were forthcoming from the Eastman School opera department on March 5 and 6, and again on May 21 and 22. While public attention seemed more and more focused on Rosing and his young professional company, the people in charge of the opera department at the school were patiently developing a program that would flourish under Emanuel Balaban's direction long after Rosing's dream had ended.

But the dream was still very much alive. In early April 1926 the Rochester American Opera Company presented a week-long opera festival. *The Marriage of Figaro* was performed on Monday, Wednesday, and Thursday evenings, and there was also a matinee

---

[10] *Vancouver Sunday Province,* 24 January 1926. SML.

performance on Saturday. *Cavalleria Rusticana* and *Pagliacci* were presented together on Tuesday, Friday, and Saturday evenings. During the summer months the company performed *Martha* in Chautauqua, New York, its first outdoor presentation. While preparing for that presentation, news was received that Rouben Mamoulian was unexpectedly leaving the Eastman School to seek new career opportunities in New York.

Rosing and his young opera company began its third season with great expectations and hopes for the future. During the first six days of November 1926 they presented *The Abduction from the Seraglio* and *Martha* in a series of Kilbourn Hall performances, and this was followed in early December with productions of Howard Hanson's "Prelude" and "Ballet," Gilbert and Sullivan's *The Pirates of Penzance*, Charles Wakefield Cadman's one-act operatic cantata *The Sunset Trail*, and Leoncavallo's *Pagliacci*. On February 7, 1927, the company presented a performance of *Carmen* in Kilbourn Hall, with the famous soprano Mary Garden (1874–1967) appearing as guest artist in the lead role. When she came to Rochester to appear in the Eastman Theatre for a recital the previous October, she had toured the school and heard members of the young opera company rehearsing. Greatly impressed, she agreed to return in February to sing the role of Carmen with them, traveling to Rochester on three consecutive weekends for rehearsals prior to the February 7 performance.

But big changes were occurring that would have profound consequences on the fortunes of Rosing and his singers. At the end of March, an announcement was made that the Rochester American Opera Company, which was preparing for its New York City debut at the Guild Theater on April 4, 1927, would become an independent professional opera company. George Eastman had reached the end of his willingness to finance Rosing's dream, and the fault in this probably rested entirely with Rosing himself, as was later suggested by Slonimsky:

> Poor Rosing! He failed miserably as administrator of the American Opera Company in Rochester and ran through Eastman's money long before he could stage any opera that would possibly bring in some returns for the investment. George Eastman, a good businessman, refused to pour more funds into Rosing's undertaking, and the American Opera Company, as it was proudly named, expired ingloriously.[11]

---

[11] Slonimsky, *Perfect Pitch*, 85.

The company, however, was not quite ready to expire. Rosing's venture now became the American Opera Company, dropping the word "Rochester" from its title, and it would be supported by a national committee with a board of directors who were committed to making it a nationally successful institution. The company's advisory council included George W. Chadwick (1854–1931), the noted American composer and long-time director of the New England Conservatory; Walter Damrosch (1862–1950), the famous American conductor and educator; Deems Taylor (1885–1966), the well-known American composer and writer; and Howard Hanson. Among the singers were Cecile Sherman, Brownie Peebles, Charles Hedley, and George Fleming Houston, who had been among Rosing's "stars" almost from the beginning of his Rochester venture. After leaving Rochester, the group moved to an old, abandoned luxury hotel in Magnolia, Massachusetts, just south of Gloucester. For the next three summers Magnolia would serve as the location for preparing repertoire for their forthcoming productions, which would include several Gilbert and Sullivan productions as well as standard classic operas.

As Rosing's now independent company embarked on its 1927–28 season, back in Rochester Howard Hanson sought to clarify the school's position concerning the recent events.

> Now that the company [i.e., Rosing's American Opera Company] is on an assured professional basis, the opera department of the Eastman School will return to its work of training students for opera, organizing courses on the basis of a school rather than of a company. The curriculum will correspond to the junior, senior, and post-graduate years of the voice department, and intensive training will be given not only in subjects related directly to operatic singing and acting, but also to securing of sound musicianship by its students. With the happy agreement which has been reached whereby Vladimir Rosing, director of the American Opera Company, will retain his connection with the Eastman School as producing director of the opera department productions, a close relation between the American Opera Company and the Eastman School is assured. The opera department will be to a certain extent the training ground for the development of singers for the company.
>
> Eugene Goossens, conductor of the Rochester Philharmonic Orchestra, who acted as musical director of the company in its New York debut last April, will continue as director of the opera department of the Eastman School of Music, while Emanuel Balaban, who conducted

several New York performances as assistant conductor,
will remain with the Eastman School as assistant director
of the opera department. Otto Luening continues as exec-
utive director of the department. The other members of
the faculty include Herman Genhart, chorus master;
Adelin Fermin and T. Austin Ball, voice instructors; Miss
Marion Weed, dramatic instructor and German diction;
Miss Theodora Cummins, French diction; Mrs. Hilda
May and Miss Majorie Barnett, dance instructors; Mark
Johnson, stage manager.[12]

In short, Hanson sought to emphasize that the Eastman School,
while retaining some form of association with Rosing's American
Opera Company, was quite capable and quite prepared to provide
appropriate training to its own students.

For Rosing and his young singers, there were many performances during the next several seasons, perhaps the most important
of which was their debut in Washington, D.C., in December 1927.
The company chose to present *Faust* during their three-day engagement in the nation's capital, and among those who greeted their
performance with great enthusiasm was President Calvin Coolidge.
The Washington performances were followed by the opening of
their first season in New York City on January 10, 1928, at the new
Gallo Theater. In the early months of 1929, the American Opera
Company came under the management of Arthur Judson, Inc., of
New York, with plans for a national tour during the 1929–30 season,
including its first appearances in several southern cities. But the
worsening economic conditions in America finally sealed their fate.
In January of 1930, following a final performance in Richmond,
Virginia, Rosing was forced to call a halt to the rest of the season
because of the country's financial woes. There was great hope for a
revival of the company in 1930–31 "if the ensemble can be held
together, if its influential friends can be kept interested and . . . if
public demand returns to former levels,"[13] but the truth of the
matter was that Rosing and his opera dream had come to the end of
the road.

At about the same time, the original cast of characters whom
Rosing had assembled during his first year at the Eastman School
of Music found themselves thinly disguised as characters in a novel
being published by Harper & Brothers in 1933. Originally entitled

[12] *Democrat & Chronicle*, Rochester, 9 October 1927. SML.
[13] *Democrat & Chronicle*, Rochester, 26 June 1930. SML.

Winter Warm, it was accepted for publication in 1932 and appeared the following year under the title *The Fault of Angels*, winning the Harper Prize for 1933–34. The Harper Prize Novel Contest had been established in 1922 and was held every other year to recognize the work of an author who had not yet achieved a wide reputation in the literary world. The judges who had selected *The Fault of Angels* as the recipient of this award were Sinclair Lewis, Harry Hansen, and Dorothy Canfield, and the author of the prize-winning novel was none other than Paul Horgan.

Horgan's story takes place in the fictitious city of Dorchester, where the millionaire Henry Ganson ("Mr. Westman" in Horgan's earlier draft) has opened the fabulous new Ganson School of Music and Ganson Theatre. All four of Rochester's conductors appear in the story. Vladimir Shavitch, Eugene Goossens, and Alfred Coates are all easily recognizable as Vladimir Arenkoff, Hubert Regis, and Freddie Banner. (Coates spoke with a slight lisp, and Horgan even gives Freddie Banner the same kind of small speech impediment.) Victor Wagner is less easily identified in Horgan's story, but he is probably portrayed as the opportunistic George Doore. Nicolas Slonimsky appears in the book not too cleverly disguised as Nicolai ("Colya") Savinsky, and the character John O'Shaughnessy is probably Horgan himself. Then there is Lydia, someone obviously inspired by Lucile Johnson Bigelow. The need for a villain is supplied by the evil Mrs. Kane, whom Horgan apparently patterned after a certain socially prominent woman who lived near George Eastman on East Avenue. Horgan originally called her Mrs. Vates in his book, but this was changed because "Vates" was said to be a little too close to her real name.

A much more likable character in the book is Blanche Badger, obviously inspired by Helen Rochester Rogers, who was reportedly quite flattered to find herself in a prize-winning novel. The two female voice teachers at the Eastman School of Music provided the inspiration for the character Julie Rale, and Eastman Theatre Manager Eric Clark is only thinly disguised as Cyril Derek. But the central character in Horgan's novel is Nina, who is the wife of the conductor Vladimir Arenkoff in the story. She is depicted as a fascinating and captivating Russian, even attracting the attention of the aging Henry Ganson. The inspiration for this character, however, was not Vladimir Shavitch's wife (the pianist Tina Lerner) but rather the first wife of Emanuel Balaban. Of all the characters associated with the Rochester opera company, the only important ones not appearing in Horgan's book, strange as it may seem, are Vladimir Rosing and Rouben Mamoulian.

Prior to the publication of his novel, Paul Horgan received news of George Eastman's death by suicide. About a month and a half later he wrote to his old friend Helen Rochester Rogers, commenting on that event and on his novel, which had yet to be published:

> My Mr. Westman did not commit suicide, thank God, for if I had so fictionally forecast the end of George Eastman, no more should sleep have lain upon my lids from folk-fear. And his name has been changed to Henry Ganson, for the sake of decency and modesty. Other characters, too, are taken from physical models; but incident and episode, and inner motives are all imaginary . . . the only direct shameless steal is Nina's name: which I have kept: using a different last name, of course; and putting her through a history that touches her's in externals only. The background, of course, is frankly Rochester and the Eastman Theatre. Though they appear as Dorchester and Ganson Theatre.[14]

When Horgan's novel was published in 1933, it created quite a sensation in Rochester, with local readers immediately recognizing the novel's various characters. Three quarters of a century later, it reads like a very dated and not very well-paced story, unless, of course, the reader knows the history behind Horgan's book—and knows the *real* identity of the various characters. With that background *The Fault of Angels* can still provide a fascinating and entertaining glimpse of Rochester and the Eastman Theatre in the 1920s.

---

[14] Paul Horgan, Letter to Helen Rochester Rogers, 2 June 1932. RRL (Papers of Helen Rochester Rogers).

Chapter 9

1925–1926
The Eastman School of Dance and Dramatic Action

George Eastman's great experiment to bring culture to the masses fired the imagination of many young, talented, and ambitious men. Opportunities such as those being presented in Rochester were not to be found everywhere, especially since George Eastman was not only able but also apparently quite willing to provide the funds to make every man's dream a reality. Rouben Mamoulian came to Rochester not necessarily because of his own dream but because of Vladimir Rosing's. But Rosing's Rochester American Opera Company had been established in November 1924, and now it was time for Rouben Mamoulian to turn his dream hopefully into a reality. Since he was an enormously talented man, it was probably unthinkable that he would stand forever in Rosing's shadow. As a matter of fact he eventually achieved the kind of widespread fame and success that always seemed to elude the Russian singer.

During the summer months of 1925, Rochester newspapers carried the announcement that a new Eastman School of Dance and Dramatic Action would be opened in September, with Rouben Mamoulian serving as its artistic director and administrator. The new school would consolidate activities that had formerly been divided between the Eastman Theatre and the Eastman School of Music. Ballet training had been a function of the theater staff, while dramatic art and dramatic action had been taught in the opera department of the school. It was now envisioned that all of this would be combined in a new school headed by Mamoulian.

The location of this new enterprise would be the theater annex building that had been constructed on the east side of Swan Street, a building that in later years would simply be called Annex I (or Annex A). The building had opened in the spring of 1924, providing essential space for preparing the theater shows. It would now also serve the needs of Mamoulian's new school. Built at a cost of about $155,000, the annex was five floors high and provided over a half million cubic feet of space. The first floor was designed to serve as a garage for the more important school and theater administrators, while the second floor was devoted to the construction and painting of scenery for the theater shows as well as for the opera and ballet productions. The painting of the scenery was done on a huge frame measuring seventy square feet, which was manipulated on a slot moving up and down between the second and the third floor. The office of the theater's art and scenic director was on the third floor of the annex. His facilities included a miniature model of the Eastman Theatre, complete in every detail (even to the chandelier), which was used in planning scenic designs for the theater. The third floor was also the location of the dye room and one of the ballet studios. The fourth floor contained space for wardrobe storage, dressing rooms, offices, a property room, a dark room, and a color studio. The top floor contained a ballet studio and dressing rooms, and also a dressmaking room.

On July 23 Mamoulian announced that Ester Gustafson, who had danced at the opening of the Eastman Theatre in 1922, had been hired to head the dance department. Then on August 2 a further announcement was made that Martha Graham was coming to Rochester to share the teaching responsibilities with Gustafson. Mamoulian was very clever in his choice of these two dancers because their styles were so very different. Gustafson was heavily influenced by the flowing movements of Isadora Duncan, while Graham was a much more dramatic performer. In reflecting back on her time in Rochester, Martha Graham made note of this difference in style:

> Ester Gustafson, the teacher who preceded me in Rochester, was what was then called a nature dancer, emphasizing all that was natural in movement, in clothes, very restrained and proper, no makeup to speak of. She gave the impression that she thought eyeliner was an instrument of the devil.
>
> I entered my first class in clinging red silk kimono, with a long slit up each leg, in full makeup, my hair pulled back severely but dramatically. The students, who were used to their Swedish teacher's more down-to-earth approach, were in a state of shock after the class.[1]

---

[1] Martha Graham, *Blood Memory / Martha Graham* (New York: Doubleday, 1991), 106.

Graham's memory may be slightly inaccurate as to the chronology of events, since she and Gustafson both started teaching for Mamoulian at about the same time. At this early date the students were probably not accustomed to the style of either of the teachers, but the differences between the two dancers were very obvious and certainly did not go unnoticed.

An apparent casualty in Mamoulian's plans for dance instruction was Enid Knapp Botsford, the founder of the Eastman Theatre Ballet. It is unclear whether she was excluded from Mamoulian's plans or simply declined an offer to join the new enterprise. Whatever the reason, Botsford's days at the Eastman Theatre were drawing to a close. Her Eastman Theatre Ballet made its farewell appearance in the theater during the week of August 16, and local newspapers noted the occasion:

> The Eastman Theater Ballet will make its farewell appearance this week. After September 14th it will be absorbed by the Dance Department of the new Eastman School of Dance and Dramatic Action and will no longer be known as a Ballet. Future dance presentations on the Eastman stage will probably be under the name of Eastman Theater Dancers or some such title. The word ballet is being dropped because the new dance training will be of a much broader scope, comprising all forms of the dance.[2]

Several members of the Eastman Theatre Ballet, among them Thelma Biracree and Olive McCue, associated themselves with the new school and continued to appear in Eastman Theatre productions. Enid Knapp Botsford opened her own ballet studio, first on East Avenue near the school and theater, then on Gibbs Street, and eventually further out East Avenue. She continued to be a prominent and highly influential figure in the local dance community for many years.

The Eastman School of Dance and Dramatic Action opened for instruction on September 14, 1925, with three main aims:

> To firmly establish and deeply insert into the life of communities the arts of Dance and Dramatic Action as a valuable and essential part of the education of young and old.
> To advance the cause of the true art of the Theatre by giving a complete training in both the Dance and

---

[2]   *Democrat & Chronicle*, Rochester, N.Y., 16 August 1925. SML.

Dramatic Action to performers on the stage and to aspi-
rants to stage performance.

To recognize anew the close kinship of the arts of the
Dance and Drama and to develop a new form of theatrical art—Dramatic Action to Music—in which drama and
dance linked with music will combine into an inseparable
unity.[3]

The dance department of the new school offered children's classes,
junior classes, senior classes, Saturday evening classes, evening
classes, health education classes, and private instruction in all
forms of the dance. Similar programs were offered to the community by the drama department, including instruction in deportment,
children's classes, beginner's classes, an advanced class, a class in
stage makeup, and a class in diction. Enrollment apparently
exceeded three hundred students.

More important to Mamoulian's mission, however, were the professional courses offered by both departments. There was much in
common between the two curricula. Students in both dance and
drama took instruction in the theory and practice of dramatic art, pan-
tomime, dramatic action to music, makeup, diction, history of the theater, and history of the dance. Those enrolled in the dance department
were also given full instruction in dance technique and all forms of the
dance (interpretive, character, and ballet), while students in the drama
department were given full instruction in dramatic action. All students worked and rehearsed daily for stage presentations and professional stage experience to be gained through appearances in regular
performances in the Eastman Theatre and in Kilbourn Hall. An additional requirement for all students was the opportunity to work before
motion picture cameras. Tuition for the professional course was $500
for the year, not an inconsequential sum by any means. Instruction in
drama was provided by Mamoulian and his assistants. Dance training was given by Graham and Gustafson, with the assistance of
Thelma Biracree, who specialized in toe dancing.

Rouben Mamoulian assumed full direction of the various acts
and sketches that were presented as part of the Eastman Theatre
shows. Soon, however, theater programs listed him as being in
charge of "stage presentations." This may have been somewhat
of a cosmetic change in terminology, since "stage presentations"
seemed to indicate something a little more artistic and sophisticated

---

[3]   From a twelve-page "announcement bulletin" published in connection with the
opening of the Eastman School of Dance and Dramatic Action. SML.

than "acts and sketches." In early November the Eastman Theatre management officially announced that Mamoulian would now be in charge of all stage productions for what were known as the "deluxe programs." These programs were presented three times each day, at mid-afternoon and twice in the evening, and they featured the Eastman Theatre Orchestra and rather lavish stage presentations. By contrast, the early and late afternoon shows featured one of the theater organists, who would accompany the silent film and provide the musical entertainment. Mamoulian's involvement with the stage presentations at the "deluxe programs" was a natural outgrowth of his work as director of the new Eastman School of Dance and Dramatic Action. His students needed the professional experience that the theater shows could provide. The needs of these students presented the theater management with a seemingly inexhaustible supply of dancers and actors for its programs. In theory at least, the collaboration between the school and theater was equally beneficial to both parties. It seemed to be an ideal partnership.

The kind of presentations that Mamoulian provided for the theater shows varied greatly from week to week, and no two shows were exactly alike. The choice of material probably depended upon many different factors, including the nature and length of the feature film. An example of a typical Eastman Theatre show might be the one that was presented during the week of October 18, 1925. The "deluxe" program at 3:00 in the afternoon and at 7:00 and 9:00 in the evening opened with a performance by the Eastman Theatre Orchestra of Wagner's Overture to *Rienzi*. This was followed by "Eastman Theatre Current Events" and then by an elaborate dance production entitled "A Pompeian Afternoon," arranged by Martha Graham and Ester Gustafson. This dance routine consisted of three different scenes: "The Lady of the Garden," "Dancers of the Garden," and "Youths of the Garden," each featuring students from the Eastman School of Dance and Dramatic Action. "A Pompeian Afternoon" was featured Monday through Saturday,[4] but it was replaced by a vocal solo on Sunday. The vocalist for this particular show was soprano Mary Silveira, a student from the Eastman opera department, who sang "The Kiss Waltz" by Arditi. The live stage production then led to the feature film presentation, *Little Annie Roonie*, starring Mary Pickford, and the show ended with a short comedy film entitled *Mixing in Mexico*.

[4]   Although motion pictures were scheduled at these times, they were sometimes replaced by concerts.

The two other shows at 1:00 and 5:00 in the afternoon, as previously noted, were less elaborate productions at which one of the theater organists provided all of the music. Central to each and every theater show, however, was the silent feature film that required a musical score performed either by one of the theater organists or by the Eastman Theatre Orchestra. But the mission of the Eastman Theatre was not simply to show popular movies. It was to educate the public culturally by presenting those movies within the context of a program that would expose the audience to serious cultural entertainment. The Eastman Theatre Orchestra certainly had a central role in that mission, especially through its performance of an overture at the beginning of the deluxe presentations. The overtures varied from serious concert repertoire to light classics and operettas. During the 1925–26 season, for example, Wagner and Harrison conducted overtures as diverse as Rossini's *William Tell*, Wagner's *Die Meistersinger*, Weber's *Der Freischütz*, and Friml's *The Vagabond King*, as well as Sir Arthur Sullivan's *Overture di Ballo*.

Mamoulian, however, had the more important role in elevating the cultural tastes of the movie audiences. With the Eastman School of Music and his own Eastman School of Dance and Dramatic Action, he had at his disposal a wonderful variety of resources from which he could design his stage presentations for the theater. His dancers had a central role in the productions. After a while, Gustafson's name ceased to be noted on the programs, and Martha Graham apparently became the sole planner of dance routines for the theater shows. Sometimes these were relatively simple, such as when Thelma Biracree and Marion Tefft appeared during the week of December 13, 1925, in a number entitled "Charleston." Others were more elaborate, such as the production entitled "The Flute of Krishna," which Graham produced to music of Cyril Scott for the shows that started on May 9, 1926.

Mamoulian also made use of singers from the Eastman Opera Department, several of whom were also involved with the Rochester American Opera Company. Martha Atwell, Francis DeWitt Babcock, Allan Burt, Harold Conkling, Charles Hedley, Marion Keeler, and Brownie Peebles were among the Eastman singers who appeared in theater productions. The most important and elaborate acts produced by Mamoulian involved both singers and dancers, such as the production for the week of February 7, 1926. This was entitled *A Summer Night* and involved music of Offenbach and Tchaikovsky, performed by singers Francis DeWitt Babcock and Brownie Peebles, assisted by dancers Susan Vacanti and Harold Kolb.

Not all the theater shows, however, featured students from Mamoulian's school or from the opera department of the music school. Eastman faculty member Sandor Vas was recruited to perform Liszt's *Hungarian Rhapsody No. 13* during the week of November 25, 1925. It is unclear why a pianist of his stature would agree to play during the movie shows, but his appearances on the Eastman Theatre stage must have been among the highlights of the season. Performing the Liszt work three times each day for six days not only demonstrated stamina but also a degree of courage. On a few occasions the shows featured visiting performers, such as the Albertina Rasch Solo Dancers, who appeared during the week of February 14, 1926, and the Royal Welsh Choir, which sang for the shows presented during the week of March 14, 1926.

On other occasions the musical entertainment was supplied by instrumentalists, principally drawn from the Eastman Theatre Orchestra. For example, William and Stanley Street from the orchestra's percussion section performed on marimba, vibraphone, and xylophone during the week of April 4, 1926. Music was provided the following week by an "Eastman Theatre Jazz Ensemble." Two weeks later, the orchestra's harpist, Lucile Johnson Bigelow, was joined by concertmaster Alexander Leventon in accompanying soprano Maxine Kisor in a performance of Schubert's "Ave Maria." (Joining Bigelow for these performances was her young student from the Eastman School, Eileen Malone, later to become one of Eastman's truly legendary teachers.) The variety of musical entertainment, therefore, was very great, but the main responsibility fell on Mamoulian and his students from the Eastman School of Dance and Dramatic Action.

Appearances by Mamoulian's students were not limited to the theater shows. On January 15 and 16, 1926, the School of Dance and Dramatic Action presented *Sister Beatrice*, a three-act play by Maurice Maeterlinck, in Kilbourn Hall. This was designed to serve as a demonstration of a new form of theatrical art conceived and developed by Mamoulian, which he called "rhythmic drama to music." The production was directed by Mamoulian, with a musical score written by Otto Leuning and performed at the Kilbourn organ by Guy Fraser Harrison. The translation of Maeterlinck's play was done by Paul Horgan.

At least one member of Mamoulian's staff, however, was becoming restive. Martha Graham later recalled that the people of Rochester simply did not understand that dance was going to develop into an art form and not remain simply an entertainment. Moreover, as a teacher she had to provide dance instruction to students of widely mixed levels of ability, since Mamoulian's philosophy was that everyone in the school—dancers, singers, and actors—had to learn to do everything. Even Mamoulian did not seem to understand that Graham was interested in creating dances that were not simply a part of a mixed entertainment program. Fortunately for Graham, some of the dancers understood and shared her vision. Therefore, when she came to establish her own company of dancers, it was with several of her Rochester dancers.

The Rochester community finally had the opportunity to see Martha Graham as a dancer rather than a producer of popular entertainment when she presented a dance recital in Kilbourn Hall on the evening of May 27. Accompanied by pianist Louis Horst, she danced to the music of Bernheim, Brahms, Debussy, de Falla, Franck, Gluck, Goossens, Horst, Rachmaninoff, Ravel, Satie, Schubert, Scriabin, and Wolf-Ferrari. For several of the dances she was assisted by Thelma Biracree, Evelyn Sabin, and Betty MacDonald, with whom she was soon to form her own dance company. Other dancers appearing on the program included Jean Hurvitz, Robert Ross, Harold Kolb, Harold Conkling, and Henry Riebeselle, all presumably Graham's students from the Eastman School of Dance and Dramatic Action.

At about the same time, Martha Graham was confronted with having to make a decision concerning her immediate future when she was asked to sign a contract to renew her contract for another year:

> As I walked into the huge room, I thought I was ruining myself just for the money. I approached the desk, picked up the fountain pen, and started to sign my name. I got as far as the M., then put the pen back down on the desk.[5]

A somewhat different version of the story was related by Rochester composer David Diamond (b. 1915), who knew Martha Graham very well. According to Diamond, Graham's decision to leave Rochester followed a heated argument with Howard Hanson, during which she had thrown the local phone book at the school's young director, apparently striking him on the forehead just above his left eye.[6] One way or another, Martha Graham had made her

---

[5] Graham, *Blood Memory*, 108.
[6] David Diamond, interviewed by the author. Rochester, 26 June 2002.

decision, and she left Rochester to begin one of the most fabled careers in the history of dance.

An even more shocking departure from Rochester was announced at the end of June. Rouben Mamoulian had resigned his position as the head of the new Eastman School of Dance and Dramatic Action and his position as director of stage presentations at the Eastman Theatre. His pending departure from Rochester was apparently the result of a dispute concerning his salary for the next season. As a result of his resignation, the school that Mamoulian had founded just a year earlier was not being continued. A reorganization would take place, and some of the activities would be absorbed into the curriculum of the Eastman School of Music. Mamoulian would be succeeded as director of stage presentations at the Eastman Theatre by Benjamin Webster.

Mamoulian went on to achieve fame as a Hollywood director. In a career that spanned more than a quarter century, his many films included *Dr. Jekyll and Mr. Hyde* (1932) with Frederic March; the unforgettable *Queen Christina* (1933) with Greta Garbo; *Blood and Sand* (1941) with Tyrone Power, Rita Hayworth, and Linda Darnell; *Summer Holiday* (1947) with Mickey Rooney and Gloria DeHaven; and the classic Fred Astaire film, *Silk Stockings* (1957), with Astaire and Cyd Charisse. He was also associated with the highly successful stage production of George Gershwin's *Porgy and Bess* and with stage productions of *Oklahoma* and *Carousel* by Rodgers and Hammerstein. These include 2,248 consecutive performances of *Oklahoma* in New York City.

The closing of the Eastman School of Dance and Dramatic Action signaled a return to the original concept of the school and theater. Although the Eastman Theatre's mission was educational in the broadest sense of the term, its function was to present entertainment ranging from popular films to concerts, recitals, and opera performances. On the other hand, the Eastman School's function was clearly educational, serving the needs of the general community as well as training future professional musicians—performers, composers, scholars, and teachers. While there was an obvious working relationship between the school and the theater, their administration, budget, and operation were separate.

Mamoulian's school was a bold attempt to create an institution that shared the functions of school and theater, creating a bridge between the two. His successor at the Eastman Theatre, Benjamin Webster, was responsible for simply assembling a company of dancers and singers who could provide appropriate acts for the theater shows. All of the educational functions—unfortunately not including dance—returned to the control of the Eastman School. It is difficult to guess what might have happened if Mamoulian had remained in Rochester in charge of a school devoted to dance and drama. Within a few years, however, the Eastman Theatre's life as a movie palace with lavish stage productions would come to an end. The Eastman School of Dance and Dramatic Action, therefore, would have lost its role of training and supplying people for those productions. Whether it might have survived solely as an educational institution is a question for which there is no real answer, only speculation.

The closing of the Eastman School of Dance and Dramatic Action was the first of several disappointments for those who envisioned Rochester as a major cultural center in the United States. Such thinking was not uncommon during the exciting days of the early to mid-1920s. Robert M. Searle, president of Rochester Gas and Electric Company and one of the more important business leaders of the city, was among those Rochesterians who were predicting great things for the future:

> The Eastman School of Music will be the musical center of the world in 1935, Rochester will have a grand opera theater of its own, and all the great musical artists of the world will broadcast their concerts and programs from Rochester.[7]

A few years earlier George Eastman had spoken in similar terms, expressing his wish that Rochester would become a great musical center, known throughout the world.

None of this seemed unreasonable at the time. The city could boast of a theater that was arguably the most beautiful and well equipped in the country, an auditorium that contained one of the world's largest theater organs. Conductors such as Albert Coates and Eugene Goossens had been secured to develop the Eastman Theatre Orchestra, properly augmented to full symphony size, into a serious and creditable ensemble. The facilities of the Eastman School of Music were also regarded as the finest anywhere, and the school's faculty and growing student body suggested an institution that was quickly assuming a leadership position in American music education. High-class entertainment was consistently available in the Eastman Theatre, with performers being trained not only at the

---

7   *Democrat & Chronicle*, Rochester, 19 January 1926. SML.

Eastman School of Music but also at a new and exciting school for dance and drama. The greatest international artists were appearing in concerts and recitals held in the Eastman Theatre and in Kilbourn Hall. A young and exciting opera company, led by a charismatic and visionary Russian tenor, was attracting valuable attention and support. And all of this was happening in Rochester, New York.

But Mamoulian and Graham now left, and with their departure the dream of a dance and drama school ended. In less than a year George Eastman ceased his funding of Rosing's opera company, the first step on the downward slope that would see the end of Rosing's dream in just a few more years. In addition, the next several years would present serious challenges to the continued operation of the Eastman Theatre, a development that would even threaten the future of the Rochester Philharmonic Orchestra. What had gone wrong? In truth the euphoria of the 1920s, so well articulated by Robert M. Searl, was a reflection of the money that George Eastman was pouring into the cultural life of Rochester. But even George Eastman's money was not inexhaustible, and a city of Rochester's size simply could not afford to continue to fund all these cultural and educational initiatives. Moreover, all of these efforts tended to diffuse the effectiveness of George Eastman's support. Too much money was perhaps being spent on too many projects.

It may be safe to assume that Howard Hanson was not terribly unhappy to see Mamoulian and Graham leave Rochester, or to see the closing of Mamoulian's school after only a year of operation. Some might even suggest that he deliberately sought an end to their presence and influence in Rochester, but this would probably be an unfair accusation. The young director of the Eastman School of Music was certainly in no position at this point in his career to make that kind of decision independent of Rush Rhees and George Eastman. Hanson may have also been relieved to witness the end of George Eastman's support of Vladimir Rosing the following spring. His responsibilities were centered around the school of music, and he surely would have wanted to consolidate under his own control all of the musical resources, instead of sharing respon-sibility with others. Similarly, he would not have wanted to com-pete with Mamoulian and Rosing for George Eastman's generosity and support.

Rush Rhees must have had similar feelings. With these distrac-tions now gone, Eastman's local philanthropy could finally be totally focused on the University of Rochester. It was no longer just a question of the Eastman School of Music. In 1920 Eastman had contributed an initial $4,000,000 towards a fund for a new medical school at the University of Rochester. The first class of medical students entered this new School of Medicine and Dentistry in September 1925, coincidentally the same year that saw the opening of the Eastman School of Dance and Dramatic Action. Rush Rhees had additionally announced plans for a new campus for the Men's College, a campus that would open in 1930 on the site of what had been the Oak Hill golf course. By 1930 Rush Rhees had built a music school, a music theater, a medical school, and a new campus, accomplishing all of this in slightly more than a decade. It was a monumental accomplishment, one that transformed the University of Rochester from a small, regional school into an institution of national prominence. Rhees clearly had priorities in mind for George Eastman's financial support, priorities that realistically may not have included the dreams of people such as Rouben Mamoulian, Martha Graham, and Vladimir Rosing.

Chapter 10

1923–1930
The Eastman Theatre amid
Changing Times

The Eastman Theatre celebrated its second anniversary in September 1924 and boasted that about 4 million people had attended movies, concerts, and recitals over the two-year period since the grand opening in 1922. Admittedly, the vast majority of these people had come to the theater for its movie presentations, but it is quite remarkable that the average daily attendance had been well in excess of 5,000. As previously noted, the theater was used for motion pictures six days a week, with five shows each day, three in the afternoon and two in the evening.

Wednesdays, however, were reserved for concerts and recitals.[1] During the 1923–24 season, there were twenty different concert dates, starting in mid-October and extending into the beginning of April (not including the special Metropolitan Opera performances in early May). There were often two concerts on a Wednesday, with a Rochester Philharmonic Orchestra matinee performance in the afternoon and an "artist" event in the evening. There were eighteen artist events during the 1923–24 season, divided into three different series. Series A presented the famous contralto Ernestine Schumann-Heink (1861–1936), dancers Ruth St. Denis (1879–1968) and Ted Shawn (1891–1972), the Rochester Philharmonic Orchestra with Frederic Lamond as soloist, tenor Tito Schipa (1889–1965), and the Cleveland Orchestra with Selim Palmgren as soloist. Series B included the legendary piano virtuoso Josef Hofmann (1876–1957), the New York Symphony with Walter Damrosch conducting, contralto Marguerite D'Alvarez (1886–1953) and tenor Richard Crooks (1900–1972), baritone

---

[1] Because of conflicts with Wednesday evening prayer meetings and choir rehearsals, the scheduling of Eastman Theatre concerts was transferred to Thursdays at the end of the 1923–24 season.

Figure 34. Eastman Theatre stage, set for a recital performance.

Figure 35. Eastman Theatre stage, set for the showing of motion pictures.

Figure 36. Eastman Theatre Orchestra on stage for a movie presentation.

Reinald Werrenrath and violinist Paul Kochanski (1887–1934), a one-act opera and concert presented by Florence Macbeth and Company, and the Rochester Philharmonic Orchestra with Joseph Press as soloist. Series C included the incomparable ballerina Anna Pavlova (1885–1931), the noted American baritone John Charles Thomas (1891–1960), the Detroit Symphony, the Rochester Philharmonic Orchestra with Vladimir Resnikoff as soloist, the noted contralto Sigrid Onegin (1889–1943), and the sensational young violinist Jascha Heifetz. Tickets were priced from $5 to $10 for each series of six concerts, but tickets in the mezzanine were $12.50.

The Rochester Philharmonic Orchestra, which had given only one performance during the theater's opening year, presented fifteen regularly scheduled concerts during the theater's second year. Twelve of these were matinees, and three were included among the official Wednesday evening programs. George Eastman took an active interest in promoting the success of the orchestra, keeping a close eye on attendance figures and quietly distributing complimentary tickets for each of the evening performances to create the impression of a well-attended event. He also vetoed a suggestion from Albert Coates for including well-known soloists, commenting in a letter dated December 13 that by doing so "we would never know whether the people are coming to hear the soloists or to hear the orchestra."[2]

Eugene Goossens and Albert Coates shared the conducting responsibilities, Goossens being on the podium for four concerts at the beginning of the year, and Coates leading the orchestra from mid-January to the end of the season. In addition, Vladimir Shavitch conducted two of the concerts, one on December 12, 1923, and the other on January 9, 1924. The December program featured his wife, the Russian-trained pianist Tina Lerner, who performed the Tchaikovsky Concerto, while Sandor Vas appeared on the January program, performing the Franck *Symphonic Variations*. Using Rochester-based musicians as soloists apparently met with no opposition from George Eastman.

The concertmaster of the Eastman Theatre Orchestra at this time was Alexander Leventon, who arrived in town in August 1923. Like several other Rochester musicians, Leventon was a Russian, having received his training at the Imperial Conservatory in Moscow and then studying with Ševčik in Vienna. He was a student in Austria at the outbreak of the First World War. Since Austria was at war with Russia, Leventon was placed in an internment camp, where one of

---

[2]   George Eastman, Letter to Albert Coates, 13 December 1923. GEH.

his fellow prisoners was Vladimir Resnikoff. It was undoubtedly through Resnikoff's recommendation that Leventon came to Rochester. He brought amazing skills to his new position at the Eastman Theatre and earned the admiration and respect of his colleagues in the orchestra and at the school. But he is chiefly remembered for his wonderful talent as a photographer, a talent that received widespread notice, including awards in competitions in Dublin, London, Canada, and at least a half-dozen American cities. Among his prize-winning photographs was a study of his first wife, entitled "En Noir," which was named one of the winning prints in an international competition conducted by the prestigious magazine *American Photography*. Leventon generally specialized in portrait photography, and his work included pictures of many Rochester musicians. But he was especially noted for his photographs of many of the great artists who visited Rochester to perform in the Eastman Theatre.[3] George Eastman was among Leventon's many admirers and agreed to pose for the photographer. He considered the portrait taken by Leventon to be one of his favorites, and had it framed and displayed in his East Avenue home.

The highlight of Leventon's first season as concertmaster was a concert given by the Rochester Philharmonic Orchestra under the direction of Albert Coates in Carnegie Hall on April 7, 1924. The orchestra performed the *Suite ancienne* written by its conductor, Respighi's *Fountains of Rome*, the Leo Sowerby *Ballad* for Two Pianos, and the *London Symphony* of Ralph Vaughan Williams. Soloists for the Sowerby Ballad were Guy Maier (1892–1956) and Lee Pattison (1890–1966). There was widespread curiosity about the Rochester experiment of augmenting a theater orchestra to form a symphony orchestra. The day before the New York performance, Olin Downes wrote an article in the New York Times that questioned "whether a symphony orchestra of real artistic quality can be created when the men play a large part of the time in the theater."[4] His review following the concert was fairly generous in his appreciation of the performance:

> The orchestra showed immediately that it could play
> the notes of complicated symphonic scores, play them

---

[3]   A fine collection of Leventon photographs was donated to the Eastman School of Music by his widow, Gladys Leventon. A listing of the Alexander Leventon Collection (Ruth T. Watanabe Special Collections, Sibley Music Library, Eastman School of Music, University of Rochester) can be found at http://sibley.esm.rochester.edu:8080/specialc/findaids/leventon.htm.

[4]   *New York Times*, 6 April 1924. SML.

confidently and with rhythmic swing. These players are
not inexperienced amateurs. Furthermore, there are good
men at the first desks. The thing that the tone lacks at
present . . . is fineness of balance and of shading, supple-
ness of phrase, variety of color—a condition inevitable
and to be expected under the circumstances.[5]

Back in Rochester, the orchestra played a special Eastman
Theatre concert on the evening of April 9, not repeating any of the
repertoire from their New York performance two days earlier.
Their program in Rochester consisted of Rimsky-Korsakov's
Scheherazade, Scriabin's *Le Poème de l'Extase*, and the Saint-Saëns
Cello Concerto with Joseph Press as soloist. At the conclusion of
the program, Rush Rhees appeared on the stage of the Eastman
Theatre to announce that Coates would return the following sea-
son, and then he presented the conductor with what was described
as a "gorgeous baton" in commemoration of the orchestra's New
York debut.

A few weeks after the orchestra's final appearance for the season, the Eastman Theatre management announced that a major
improvement were going to be made to the theater stage by the
addition of two movable sections, each sixty feet long and eleven
feet wide, which would extend the stage out to the edge of the
orchestra pit. For symphonic concerts, both sections would be
raised, giving the largest possible stage area for the musicians. For
opera or other events requiring a large orchestra in the "pit," one
section would be raised to provide more stage room. Both sections
would be lowered during motion picture presentations, which
required the least amount of stage space. The musicians would
enter the orchestra pit from the basement level and take their
places. At the start of the overture, the two sections would be
mechanically raised to stage level, bringing the orchestra into view.
Following the overture, the musicians would be lowered back to the
pit level. This new stage mechanism would be available by the start
of the new season.

The 1924–25 concert season once again featured fifteen events
divided into three series. Tickets for each series of five concerts
were priced at $8.50 and $7.50 for orchestra seats; $8.50 for the
loges; $6.50, $5.00, and $4.50 for seats in the grand balcony; and
$10.50 for the mezzanine. The Rochester Philharmonic Orchestra
was to perform thirteen times during the year, four concerts

[5]   *New York Times*, 8 April 1924. SML.

directed by Goossens and nine by Coates. The scheduling of these concerts, however, changed from Wednesdays to Thursdays at the request of many local church leaders, who complained that the concert schedule conflicted with Wednesday evening services and choir rehearsals. Although the majority of the scheduled recitals were given by vocalists—such as Mary Garden, Frieda Hempel (1885–1955), Florence MacBeth, and Richard Crooks—the season also included recitals presented by Jascha Heifetz and Mischa Elman.

The end of the concert season brought the unexpected and disappointing news that Albert Coates would not be returning the following year because of a "disagreement" with George Eastman concerning future policy.

> Referring to the statement made in New York Saturday by Albert Coates that he was not expecting to return to Rochester next season, and stating as the reason that it was owing to a disagreement on matters of policy, George Eastman said that unfortunately this is true and the fact that Mr. Coates is not coming back next season is to be doubly regretted because the Eastman School organization will lose the benefit of his services in other matters than just the direction of the orchestra; that Mr. Coates had been of great assistance in many ways during the formative years of the organization, having given the school the benefit of his wide experience without stint.[6]

There is no clear understanding of what the "disagreement on matters of policy" might have been. However, a month earlier George Eastman had privately indicated that Goossens and Coates were both equally satisfactory to the school and theater management, and that it would be financially advantageous to only retain one of the conductors. Since Coates was older and more experienced, he was deemed the more expensive and was, therefore, expendable. It was simply a matter of good business management.[7]

The financial considerations that contributed to the departure of Albert Coates may have been connected with an announcement in early May that the Eastman Theatre concerts had shown a loss of $50,924 during the 1924–25 season. George Eastman had specifically

---

[6]   *Democrat & Chronicle*. Rochester, 13 April 1925. SML.
[7]   George Eastman, Letter to Albert Eastwood, 11 May 1925. GEH.

planned that any surplus from the movie shows was to be used to underwrite the cost of the concerts. Additional support was available through the Eastman Theatre Subscribers' Association, which consisted of increasing numbers of people who were interested in the cultural life of their city and willing to make annual contributions in support of that cultural life. It was this organization that provided the funds to cover the $50,924 deficit.

Prior to the announcement of the deficit, the theater management had announced that the number of daily movie presentations would be increased from five to six (except on Sundays). Effective April 4, 1925, weekday shows would be at 1:00, 2:30, and 4:30 in the afternoon, and at 6:00, 7:30, and 9:30 in the evening. The "deluxe" presentations with the Eastman Theatre Orchestra would be the mid-afternoon and final two shows each day. The decision to expand the movie schedule must have been taken with an expectation of increasing theater revenue.

In spite of the deficit the previous season, the 1925–26 concert series in the Eastman Theatre again consisted of fifteen events offered in three series of five concerts each. As in the previous year, there were many vocal recitals including programs featuring Tito Schipa, Amelita Galli-Curci (1882–1963), John McCormack, Roland Hayes (1887–1977), Ernestine Schumann-Heink, and Sigrid Onegin. Tito Schipa shared a recital program with the pianist Ossip Gabrilowitsch (1878–1936), who was not only a noted piano virtuoso but also the conductor of the Detroit Symphony. Schipa's accompanist, however, was not Gabrilowitsch but the young, Cuban-born pianist, José Echaniz, who joined the Eastman piano faculty about twenty years later. Among instrumentalists offering Eastman Theatre concerts were violinist Mischa Elman, returning for the third time in four years, and Josef Hofmann, considered by many to be the greatest pianist in the world. Perhaps the most interesting choice for the Eastman Theatre concert series was an appearance by Paul Whiteman (1890–1967) and his Orchestra on December 3, 1925. Whiteman's program included a performance of Grofé's *Mississippi—A Tone Journey*, four adaptations of standard selections to dance rhythm; five current popular songs; and *Circus Days* by Deems Taylor.

The Rochester Philharmonic Orchestra, now conducted solely by Eugene Goossens, had its customary series of matinee concerts during the 1925–26 season, and also performed three evening programs in the theater. Goossens relinquished his baton to Howard Hanson for the eighth matinee concert, which included Hanson's symphonic poem *Exaltation*. Soloists with the orchestra included several Eastman faculty members—among them Gustave Tinlot,

Vladimir Rosing, Selim Palmgren, Max Landow, and Sandor Vas—and various members of the Rochester American Opera Company. Eastman School graduate Rosalyn Weisberg returned to her alma mater on December 10, 1925, to perform the Grieg Piano Concerto with Goossens and the orchestra. Her playing was warmly greeted by the audience and praised by the local music critics: "Back in 1921 she played well; in 1923 she played better. She comes back with professional beginnings made, and she plays still better."[8]

Perhaps the most interesting and highly anticipated symphonic program of the season was the fifth matinee concert, which featured Willem Mengelberg as guest conductor. The leader of the famed Concertgebouw Orchestra of Amsterdam, Mengelberg had been a frequent guest conductor for many of the most notable European orchestras and first appeared in the United States in 1905 for a concert with the New York Philharmonic. Throughout the 1920s he regularly appeared in America and was awarded an honorary doctorate by Columbia University in 1928. Mengelberg's program in Rochester consisted of Weber's Overture to *Der Freischütz*, Beethoven's Symphony No. 7, *Romeo and Juliet* of Tchaikovsky, and *Les Préludes* of Liszt. Mengelberg was lavish in his praise of the Eastman School of Music:

> The most unique institution of its kind in the world. This school has the atmosphere of quiet and repose essential to the serious study of music. Its situation apart from the turmoil of life in the large cities is conducive to concentration. Furthermore, the school offers facilities through its large endowment which are present in none of the purely commercial institutions for music learning. It seems almost inevitable that Rochester will produce musicians who will eventually achieve a notable place in the musical life of the world.[9]

The 1925–26 season ended with a return of the Metropolitan Opera, which presented *Rigoletto* on May 6 with Giuseppe De Luca in the title role, and *Tosca* on May 7. The Puccini work featured Florence Easton (1884–1955) as Floria Tosca, Giovanni Martinelli as Mario Cavaradossi, and Antonio Scotti (1866–1936) as Baron Scarpia. Both performances were conducted by Tullio Serafin

---

[8]   *Democrat & Chronicle*, Rochester, 11 December 1925. SML.
[9]   *Herald*, Rochester, 13 January 1926. SML.

(1878–1968), the former principal conductor at La Scala in Milan who was now in his second year as conductor at the Metropolitan Opera in New York.

The Eastman Theatre celebrated its fourth anniversary during the week of September 5, 1926. Eric Clarke, the general manager, could once again boast that attendance for all events the previous year approached two million people. Clarke claimed that approximately one-eighth of the total population of Rochester was attracted each week to the theater's various presentations. In addition to the general manager, the professional staff that made all of this possible included conductors Victor Wagner and Guy Fraser Harrison, organists Harold O. Smith and Robert Berentsen, house manager John O'Neill, projection engineer Lewis Townsend, art director Norman Edwards, publicity director Arthur Kelly, poster artist Batiste Madalena, maintenance supervisor Clarence Livingston, and Frank Smith, who served as treasurer. The poster art of Madalena, created while he worked at the Eastman Theatre, became highly appreciated and valued in later years.

Eastman Theatre concerts for 1926–27 once again consisted of fifteen Thursday evening events. Series A offered performances by tenor Beniamino Gigli (1890–1957) and violinist Paul Kochanski, Mikhail Mordkin and his Russian Ballet, contralto Louise Homer (1871–1947) and pianist Alfred Cortot, baritone John Charles Thomas and soprano Florence MacBeth, and the Rochester Philharmonic Orchestra. Series B offered audiences the opportunity to attend performances featuring soprano Mary Garden, pianist Josef Hofmann, dancers Ruth St. Denis and Ted Shawn, the Rochester Philharmonic Orchestra, and tenor Giovanni Martinelli. Finally, Series C featured concerts by the Boston Symphony Orchestra, tenor Tito Schipa and violinist Toscha Seidel (1899–1962), tenor Roland Hayes, contralto Sigrid Onegin and baritone Emilio De Gogorza (1874–1949), and the Rochester Philharmonic Orchestra. The practice of having two artists share a recital program was quite typical of the times, and was viewed as an opportunity to increase the size of the paying audience. A highlight of the year was the concert by the Boston Symphony under the direction of Serge Koussevitzky (1874–1951). Their program consisted of Mozart's *Eine kleine Nachtmusik*, Debussy's "Nuages" and "Fêtes" from his *Images* for orchestra, the Suite from Prokofiev's ballet *Chout*, and Tchaikovsky's Fourth Symphony.

The Rochester Philharmonic Orchestra contributed three programs to the Thursday evening concerts, plus its usual Thursday matinee appearances. One of the highlights of the season was their matinee concert on March 10, 1927, which featured Cecile Genhart—recently appointed to the Eastman piano faculty—in performances of the Franck *Symphonic Variations* and Richard Strauss's *Burlesque*. The Strauss, an especially difficult work, won widespread praise from the audience as well as from local music commentators. Other Eastman faculty members appearing as soloists with the orchestra during the season included violinist Gustave Tinlot, pianist Sandor Vas, organist Harold Gleason, pianist Raymond Wilson, and pianist George MacNabb. Gleason's performance involved the world premiere of Howard Hanson's Concerto for Organ and Orchestra, Op. 27. A.J. Warner reported that the audience responded in a highly favorable manner, and that "there was a prolonged outburst of applause for Mr. Goossens, Mr. Gleason, Dr. Hanson, and the orchestra."[10]

The month of April saw the inauguration of a new weekly feature at the Eastman Theatre movie shows. Each Sunday, beginning on April 24, the Eastman Theatre Orchestra would present a short "Popular Concert" between 3:30 and 4:00 in the afternoon. People who attended the 2:00 movie show could remain for the concert, and those planning to attend the 4:00 movie show could come early to enjoy the music. Victor Wagner and Guy Fraser Harrison conducted on alternate weeks. Wagner was on the podium for the first of these events and led the orchestra in music of Tchaikovsky, Johann Strauss, Schumann, Mendelssohn, and Bizet. The concert season ended, as usual, with performances presented by the Metropolitan Opera. Rosa Ponselle and Giuseppe De Luca had the lead roles in Verdi's *La Forza del Destino* on May 9, and Lucrezia Bori and Laurence Tibbett appeared in Offenbach's *Les Contes d'Hoffmann* the following evening.

One amusing episode involving the Eastman Theatre during the 1926–27 season was the accusation leveled at the theater management that they were showing morally inappropriate films. Several letters had been sent complaining about the showing of "sex pictures," one of them prompting a letter on February 27 from George Eastman to Rush Rhees's secretary, Carl Lauterbach:

> I saw this picture Saturday afternoon and examined it critically in view of the complaints. Of course all of these so called sex pictures are objectionable but I saw nothing in this picture that was unusually so, or that could be cut

---

[10] *Times-Union*, Rochester, 7 January 1927. SML.

out of it, except perhaps the kissing which I thought was
unduly prolonged.[11]

The picture in question was *Flesh and the Devil*, starring Greta Garbo
and John Gilbert.

The 1927–28 season would prove to be the last year the Eastman
Theatre would enjoy before experiencing a major crisis that threat-
ened not only the annual concert series but also the future of the
Rochester Philharmonic. An indication that there were continuing
financial problems in the theater's operation was the decision to
reduce the Thursday night concerts from fifteen events to twelve.
There were now only two series, each with six concerts. Those con-
certs still featured internationally known artists, such as Jascha
Heifetz, Ignace Paderewski, Amelita Galli-Curci, and Josef Hofmann.
However, there were no visiting orchestras, perhaps due to the
expensive nature of booking an ensemble such as the Boston
Symphony.

Hofmann's recital in November was a spectacular success with
the local audience, A.J. Warner commenting in his review that "the
listener was left breathless in the whirlwind of Mr. Hofmann's
genius.[12] He went on the describe the pianist's performance of
Liszt's *La Campanella* as being the "impossible . . . accomplished in
the way of digital dexterity." Jascha Heifetz appeared in January
12, 1928, opening his program with the Vitali *Chaconne* and then
continuing with Lalo's *Symphonie Espagnole*. After intermission, he
played a group of shorter works and then closed with the
Paganini-Auer Caprice No. 24. The local press reported that every
seat in the Eastman Theatre had been sold, including extra seating
on the stage. Rochester turned out in equal numbers for
Paderewski's recital on March 29, at which time he presented
an all-Chopin program that included the *Fantasie* in F Minor, the
B-Flat-Minor Sonata, and the Fourth Ballade. This was his first
appearance in Rochester in five years, and it came amid rumors of
his pending retirement, rumors that must have increased interest
in attending the recital.

The Rochester Philharmonic Orchestra opened its season with
a matinee performance on November 10, 1927 featuring an all-
Wagner program. Cecile Genhart appeared with the orchestra for
the second time in an all-Tchaikovsky concert on January 5, 1928.

---

[11]   George Eastman, Letter to Carl Lauterbach, 27 February 1927. RRL.
[12]   *Times Union*, Rochester, 17 November 1927. SML.

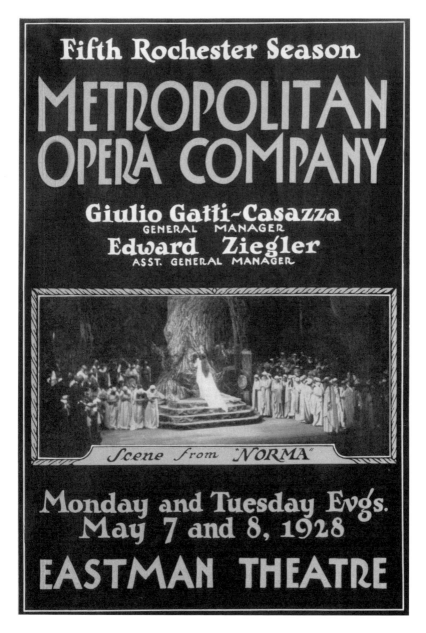

Figure 37. Announcement for the fifth annual Eastman Theatre performances by the Metropolitan Opera Company, 7 and 8 May, 1928. (Collection of the author.)

The Philharmonic season ended on March 1, 1928, when the orchestra appeared with the Rochester Festival Chorus and the Eastman School Chorus in a program highlighted by a performance of Howard Hanson's *The Lament for Beowulf*. Goossens generally selected very interesting and varied repertoire for his concerts, balancing the familiar and unfamiliar with commendable skill. While his programs throughout his tenure in Rochester included a generous amount of Wagner and Tchaikovsky, he also introduced Rochester audiences to various works by composers such Arnold Bax, Gustav Holst, Arthur Honegger, Maurice Ravel, Alexander Scriabin, and Richard Strauss.

The Metropolitan Opera performances in May began with a production of *La Bohème*, with Giovanni Martinelli as Rodolfo, Lucrezia Bori as Mimi, and Giuseppe De Luca as Marcello. The following evening, the company presented Bellini's *Norma* with Rosa Ponselle (1897–1981) in the lead role.

When the 1928–29 season was announced, Rochester audiences were delighted to note that the Thursday evening concerts had been increased to fourteen in number. In addition, two orchestras—the New York Philharmonic and the Boston Symphony—were included in the schedule. While the return of Koussevitzky and his Boston players was eagerly awaited, there was even greater excitement at the prospect of hearing the New York Philharmonic playing under Arturo Toscanini (1867–1957). The Italian conductor had chosen a wonderful program for his Rochester debut, consisting of Mozart's Symphony in D Major, K. 385, Respighi's *Feste Romane*, *Ibéria* of Debussy, and the Overture to *Tannhäuser* by Wagner.

In the midst of the enthusiasm created by the new concert season, however, there were rather ominous signs of problems at the Eastman Theatre. First of all came the resignation of Eric Clarke as general manager, and immediately afterwards much discussion in the news media about the new "talking pictures" being produced in Hollywood. Bowing to the inevitable, the Eastman Theatre installed photophone equipment for the showing of such movies, but the management also quickly denied that this installation would result in the orchestra being reduced in size. Just before Thanksgiving, however, newspapers carried the startling news that the Eastman Theatre was going to be leased to Paramount:

> The Associated Press last night could not obtain confirmation of a report received yesterday afternoon in its New York office that the Paramount Pictures Corporation had announced conclusion of an agreement to operate

the Eastman, Piccadilly, and Regent theaters in Rochester
for one year from Jan. 1.[13]

The Eastman Theatre operation had fallen victim to developments
in the motion picture industry that could not have been foreseen in
1922, when the theater had opened to such high expectations. It was
not simply a matter of "talking pictures." The more essential problem was that it was increasingly difficult for independent theaters
to secure the better movies, since the control of the leading theaters
in America was now in the hands of a few large production and distribution companies. At issue was not only the Eastman Theatre,
but also the Piccadilly and Regent theaters, which were controlled
by the Regorson Corporation on behalf of the University of
Rochester. The corporation, formed in 1922 by George Eastman,
Edward Bausch, James Gleason, and Libanus Todd (the older
brother of George Todd), later acquired a controlling interest in
several other Rochester movie houses. As a result, the University
of Rochester—which was the sole owner of the Eastman Theatre—
also had a controlling interest in the Regorson Corporation and,
through Regorson, seven additional theaters throughout the
Rochester area.

On November 24, 1928, local papers reported that George
Eastman had confirmed reports of negotiations with Paramount
Pictures Corporation, and an announcement of the agreement was
reported on December 15:

> The Paramount Pictures Corporation will take over and
> operate the Eastman Theater [*sic*] as one of its chain of 700
> movie houses, beginning next Monday. The lease for the
> rental of the theater and of the Regent and Piccadilly for
> a period of ten years was signed by the University of
> Rochester last night.[14]

The lease provided that twenty days each season would be reserved
for concerts in the Eastman Theatre, not including an additional
three dates reserved each spring for the Metropolitan Opera.
Despite widespread public concern, George Eastman and Rush
Rhees probably acted wisely in striking this deal. The theater operation had consistently lost money, including $75,000 during the
1927–28 season. Revenue provided by the new lease would hopefully guarantee the survival of the concert season each year.

---

[13] *Democrat & Chronicle*, Rochester, 23 November 1928. SML.
[14] *Democrat and Chronicle*, Rochester, 15 December 1928. SML.

Even Paramount would find it difficult to operate the Eastman Theatre without incurring heavy losses. Among the many difficulties that it would face was new competition for movie audiences. Up until this time the Eastman Theatre had simply "out-classed" all the other movie houses in town, but this had suddenly changed. The beautiful Rochester Theater (later known as Loew's Rochester) opened in 1928 on South Clinton Avenue and boasted of a seating capacity of 4,000 and an "air-cooled" environment for viewing its shows. An even more serious competitor for the Eastman Theatre was the RKO Palace at 71 North Clinton Avenue, which opened in 1928 on Christmas Day. Its interior featured golden grillwork, velvet draperies, beautiful crystal chandeliers, and a magnificent Wurlitzer theater organ. Patrons purchased tickets in the outer lobby, walking on a terrazzo floor and gazing at beautiful mirrored walls and a frescoed ceiling. They then entered an even more beautifully decorated inner lobby (a feature totally absent at the Eastman Theatre), which featured plush carpeting, an ornate arched ceiling, and more crystal chandeliers. Paramount's rental of the Eastman Theatre may well have been at least partially in response to the opening of lavish new theaters by two of its main competitors.[15]

On January 16, 1929, George Eastman was interviewed by the local news media and spoke of the decision to rent the theater:

> When the Theater was built . . . it was entirely feasible, and in fact was the practice, to run individual theaters. Before long, however, the big producers began to collect groups of theaters so that it became not only possible for them to buy pictures cheaper but to put on acts more effectively and economically. Obviously if an organization could play an act successively in fifty or one hundred theaters the expense of producing the act . . . would be reduced proportionately. Another difficulty developed and that was that our public, no matter how good acts were staged got tired of seeing the same people week after week. A third development of importance is that of the advent of the so-called sound picture. When we fully realized these developments we also realized that the time would soon come when we would have to join one of the combinations. Taking time by the forelock we

---

[15] Loew's Rochester Theater closed in October 1964, and RKO ceased operating its Clinton Avenue Palace in 1965. Both were later demolished, as was the Piccadilly (later known as the Paramount), a sad example of misguided urban renewal.

selected one of the largest and best equipped of the producing companies for this alliance.[16]

The one matter of grave concern in all of this, however, was the
future of the Rochester Philharmonic Orchestra. The orchestra was
only possible because its "core" members performed in the
Eastman Theatre Orchestra. All that Paramount would guarantee
was the continuance of the theater orchestra until July 31, 1929.

Therefore, the community rallied with a bold plan to create a
full-time orchestra of forty-eight players to be known as the
Rochester Civic Orchestra, which would perform as many as sixty
concerts each year in local high schools, half being played without
charge on Wednesday afternoons to children studying music in
school. In addition, this orchestra would be augmented in numbers,
as had been done in the past, to create the full-size Rochester
Philharmonic Orchestra, which would play the same number of
Eastman Theatre concerts as in former years, namely two or three
evening performances and eight or nine afternoon concerts. The
"umbrella organization" controlling all of this would be known as
the Civic Music Association. It was estimated that the orchestra
needed an annual budget of $260,000. The Eastman School con-
tributed $75,000 towards this amount, spending the money for the
purpose of securing orchestral positions for musicians who were
also needed as teachers at the music school, particularly in woodwinds, brass, and percussion. The practice of hiring members of the
orchestra as faculty members at the school would continue for
many decades.

The Eastman Theatre Subscribers' Association committed itself
to $70,000 of support for the project, and the Rochester Board of
Education budgeted $40,000. It was estimated that admissions
would produce another $15,000, leaving the new Civic Music
Association with the task of raising the remaining $40,000 of the
$260,000 annual budget. By mid-March the campaign to raise nec-
essary funds for the "Civic Orchestra" had been reached, and the
future of the Rochester Philharmonic Orchestra was thus secure.

Another performing group, the ballet corps, was similarly
affected by the leasing of the Eastman Theatre to Paramount.
Although the Eastman Theatre Ballet officially came to an end, ballet instruction on Swan Street continued for more than thirty additional years. Olive McCue and Thelma Biracree both continued to

---

[16] *Democrat and Chronicle*, Rochester, 16 January 1929. SML.

teach in the ballet studio and to provide dancers as needed for presentations in the Eastman Theatre. Many Eastman School students
earned a little extra spending money by accompanying the classes
in Annex I. Among the many others who faced an uncertain future
because of the new lease with Paramount was the poster artist,
Batiste Madalena. He had worked at the theater since 1924, but
now in 1928 he was out of a job. One day he was riding his bicycle
down Swan Street and to his horror saw all of his posters sitting out
in the trash. He was able to salvage almost 500 posters, and the reputation that Madalena eventually enjoyed as an artist can be largely
attributed to that chance rescue of the work that had occupied him
during those four years of employment at the Eastman Theatre.

Meanwhile, the 1928–29 concert series proceeded, relatively
unaffected by the events thus described. The Eastman Theatre
season ended, as it always did, with the annual visit of the
Metropolitan Opera. On Monday, May 6, the company presented
two operas, *Hänsel und Gretel* and *Pagliacci*. The following evening
Lucrezia Bori and Beniamino Gigli had the lead roles in a production of *Manon*.

The following year the number of concerts was increased from
fourteen to fifteen, now divided once again into three series. Series
A presented the dancer L'Argentina (1888–1936), violinist Efrem
Zimbalist (1889–1985), tenor Roland Hayes, the Rochester
Philharmonic Orchestra, and soprano Dusolina Giannini (1902–86).
Series B featured performances by the Russian Symphonic Choir,
the Rochester Philharmonic Orchestra, pianist Alfred Cortot, tenor
Beniamino Gigli, and soprano Rosa Ponselle (who had starred in
Manon the previous May). Series C included concerts by the sensa-
tional young Russian pianist Vladimir Horowitz (1904–89), the
Detroit Symphony, tenor Tito Schipa, contralto Sigrid Onegin, and
violinist Jascha Heifetz. The recital by Alfred Cortot on November
29, 1929, must have been one of the outstanding events of the year,
the French pianist presenting an all-Chopin program consisting of
the four Ballades, the B-Flat-Minor Sonata, and all twenty-four
Etudes from Op. 10 and Op. 25.

The Rochester Philharmonic Orchestra, led once again by
Eugene Goossens, presented its customary schedule of matinee and
evening performances. The symphony concerts included an all-
Wagner program on November 28, 1929, and an all-Tchaikovsky
program on January 17, 1930. Among the various soloists during
the season was Raymond Wilson, who played the Grieg Piano
Concerto, the same work that his former student Roslyn Weisberg
had played with the orchestra four years earlier. Audiences at the

symphony concerts had no idea that this would be Eugene Goossens next-to-last year as conductor of the Rochester Philharmonic Orchestra. When he left at the end of the 1930–31 season to become conductor of the Cincinnati Symphony Orchestra, it was with genuine regret on his part. He had been intimately involved in one of the most exciting musical enterprises of his time, and his contributions to music in Rochester were remembered for many years with genuine fondness and respect. For the next five seasons the Philharmonic played without benefit of a principal conductor. However, Fritz Reiner served in the unofficial role of principal guest conductor, thus guaranteeing the continued artistic development of the orchestra until José Iturbi arrived in 1936 as the orchestra's new permanent conductor.

It was during Goossens' final year that the Rochester Civic Music Association was officially incorporated. It had previously been concerned only with the new Civic Orchestra, but it now absorbed the work of the older Eastman Theatre Subscribers' Association. The new corporation was now completely responsible for the management of the Rochester Civic Orchestra, the Rochester Philharmonic Orchestra, and the annual series of artist concerts in the Eastman Theatre, including the productions each May by the Metropolitan Opera. It ensured the continuation of a rich concert life in Rochester, even in the face of the economic hardships affecting the entire country at that time.

Part Two

The Beginning of the
Hanson Years

Chapter 11

1924–1925
Mr. Hanson Arrives in Town

Howard Hanson arrived in Rochester to assume his new position as director of the Eastman School of Music in September 1924. No one, not even Hanson himself, could have guessed that this would mark the beginning of a forty-year tenure in that position, forty years that would see the Eastman School of Music become an internationally acclaimed institution under his leadership. Hanson was greeted by a faculty that totaled nearly eighty members, including Rosing, Mamoulian, and others associated with opera training at the school. The largest single group was that of the piano teachers, twenty-three in number. Only five of them, however, were listed as being "faculty for degree and certificate courses." The 1924–25 annual catalogue was the first to indicate a distinction between those who taught degree students and those who did not. In later years the use of the terms "major teacher" and "secondary teacher" became customary, unfortunately suggesting two different classes of teaching ability rather than simply different teaching assignments at the school.

The five piano faculty members responsible for the degree and certificate students in 1924 were Pierre Augieras, Max Landow, Edgar Rose, Raymond Wilson, and Sandor Vas. With the exception of Wilson, they were all European-trained. Rose, like Wilson, had been hired to teach in 1921. He came to the Eastman School with an impressive résumé, having studied in Berlin with Martin Krause (with whom Rosita Renard had also studied). Rose was also a student of the Russian virtuoso Josef Lhevinne (1874–1944) and took master classes with Ferruccio Busoni (1866–1924) in Basel, Switzerland, and with Ernest Hutcheson in America. Among the other eighteen piano teachers could be found many who subsequently had long careers at Eastman, including Marie Erhart, Ernestine Klinzing, Donald Liddell, George MacNabb, and Marjorie Truelove MacKown. In addition to the regular faculty,

Figure 38. Organ faculty members Harold Gleason, Abel Decaux, and Warren Gehrken (front row fourth, fifth, and sixth from the left) with members of the Eastman School organ club. (Collection of the author.)

Figure 39. A rare photo of a class for training theater organists.

Frederic Lamond was on hand for yet another year of his course for advanced piano students as well as for another series of lecture-recitals.

The two principal organ teachers were Harold Gleason and the Frenchman Abel Decaux. The third member of the organ teaching staff, although not listed as being a teacher of degree and certificate students, was Warren Gehrken, who came to Rochester to succeed Guy Fraser Harrison at St. Paul's Episcopal Church when Harrison's interests were redirected towards conducting and coaching. Gehrken's educational background included piano study with Arthur Friedheim (1859–1932) and organ study with E. Power Biggs (1906–77), and he had served as organist at several important churches in the New York City area prior to being appointed to the organ teaching staff at Eastman.

The organ faculty also included the two organists from the Eastman Theatre, Robert Berentsen and Harold Osborn Smith. Neither of them was lacking a credible background. Berentson had studied in his native Norway and also at the Hochschule in Berlin. He held a number of important church positions in Norway and in the United States before accepting a position as first organist at the Capitol Theater in New York City. Harold Osborn Smith had studied at Ohio State University and at the Berlin Conservatory. His background included piano study with Harold Bauer and organ study with Henry Bird (1842–1915). Like Berentson, he held a number of important church positions before working as a theater organist at the Capitol Theater in New York and the Strand Theater in Brooklyn.

Berentsen and Smith provided instruction in the motion picture organist course, which had been established when the Eastman Theatre opened and which somehow survived until the end of the decade. The course was a three-year program and was said to be the only one of its kind in America to be associated with a school of music. Teaching facilities were located on the sixth floor of the Eastman Theatre and included a small theater with two motion picture projectors and a fully equipped theater organ. In addition to courses in theory, orchestration, keyboard harmony, and music history, students in the motion picture course took weekly "motion picture organ" lessons for each of their three years in the program, plus two years of scoring, extemporization, and repertoire. In addition, all students in the motion picture organist course were required to view performances in the Eastman Theatre four hours each week. Unfortunately, this well-structured and thorough program was preparing organists for a profession that would soon practically disappear with the coming of "talking pictures."[1]

There were six voice teachers on the faculty in 1924. Frederick Benson, Lucy Lee Call, Adelin Fermin, and Oscar Gareissen were all charter members of the faculty, having been among the original teachers when the school opened three years earlier. Thomas Austin-Ball joined the faculty in 1922, coming from a teaching post at Skidmore College in Saratoga Springs, New York. He had studied voice, opera, and oratorio in Belfast, London, and Paris, and had enjoyed a rich professional life in opera and oratorio before deciding to pursue a teaching career. The sixth member of the department was Jeanne Woolford, who had studied with Fermin at Peabody. In addition to teaching voice, Woolford also taught English diction. The only member of the voice faculty who had sung with the Metropolitan Opera was Lucy Lee Call. She taught privately in New York before coming to Rochester in 1919 to join the faculty at the Prince Street school.

The string department consisted of eight teachers. Vladimir Resnikoff, Gerald Kunz, Samuel Belov, and Joseph Press were designated as the teachers of the degree and certificate students, as well as being the members of the Kilbourn Quartet and occupying the principal string positions in the orchestra. The other members of the string department included cellist Samuel Maslinkowsky and violinists Hazel Dossenbach, Effie Knauss, and Ludwig Schenck. Among the eight string teachers, only two remained on the Eastman faculty for any real length of time, Belov retiring in 1949 and Knauss in 1954. Rochester Philharmonic Orchestra harpist Lucile Johnson Bigelow was the harp teacher. Her study had been with Alfred Holy (1866–1948), the principal harpist of the Boston Symphony Orchestra, and then with Carlos Salzedo (1885–1961) in New York and Marcel Tournier (1879–1951) at the Paris Conservatory. After touring for several seasons with the Salzedo Harp Ensemble, she served as Salzedo's assistant at the University of Michigan School of Music in Ann Arbor, and then came to Rochester to play in the orchestra and teach at the school.

The 1924–25 catalogue was the first to list teachers of orchestral instruments. Nine such teachers were identified in the catalogue, all members of both the Eastman Theatre Orchestra and Rochester

---

[1] The last mention of the Eastman School's theater organ program was in the 1929–30 catalogue. Robert Berentsen remained in Rochester after his work at the school and theater came to an end, serving with distinction as organist and music director at Central (Presbyterian) Church on North Plymouth Avenue.

Philharmonic Orchestra. The practice of securing faculty from among the personnel of the orchestra, therefore, had its origins during the earliest years of the Eastman School of Music, and it would continue for the next four decades. At first this policy was very advantageous to both organizations. Opportunities for teaching orchestral instruments at the school were initially very limited because so few students applied to study these instruments. Therefore, the most practical way of providing a faculty in these areas was to employ people who were already drawing a salary for playing in the orchestra. When the Eastman School of Music began to subsidize the Civic Music Association in 1929, it viewed its annual $75,000 subsidy as a prudent investment towards maintaining the availability of these teachers.

Within this system, however, was a potential of exploiting these musicians, especially as teaching schedules began to grow from a handful of students to more full-time responsibilities. Faculty members, thus affected, began to feel that they were suddenly doing two full-time jobs for the equivalent of one full-time salary. Although the Civic Music Association and the Eastman School of Music were technically separate organizations, both knew the salaries which each was paying. A growing unfairness in this situation led to increasing accusations in the years to come that the Eastman School of Music had a deliberate policy of underpaying musicians who were also employed by the orchestra, and there was no real attempt to address the problem with any degree of fairness until the mid-1960s.

Nine members of the Eastman Theatre Orchestra formed the original Eastman School faculty for orchestral instruments. They included Lewis Catalano, oboe; Otto Conrad, clarinet; Leonardo DeLorenzo, flute; Harry Freeman, trumpet; Wendel Hoss, French horn; Emory Remington, trombone; George Waterhouse, timpani; Nelson Watson, double bass; and Adolph Weiss, bassoon. Catalano remained for only one year and was replaced by Arthur Foreman, who played in the orchestra and taught at the school until 1936. His successor was Robert Bloom, who remained in Rochester for only one year. Robert Sprenkle arrived in the fall of 1937 to become the oboe teacher at Eastman and to play oboe in the Rochester Philharmonic Orchestra, remaining at the school until his retirement in 1982.

The clarinettist Otto Conrad was in Rochester for only a few years, but the story of how he came to become the school's first clarinet teacher is interesting and deserves to the related. Conrad had played principal clarinet in Berlin under Arthur Nikisch but came to the United States because Frederick Stock (1872–1942) wanted a German clarinettist for his orchestra in Chicago. Upon arriving in New York, however, he learned that the Chicago position had been filled by another German, but he was told to proceed to upstate New York for a position which had become available in Rochester. He arrived in time to become the first clarinet teacher at the Eastman School of Music, remaining for only three years before leaving for a position with the New York Philharmonic. Rufus Arey succeeded Conrad in the Rochester Philharmonic Orchestra and at the Eastman School in 1927.

Harry Freeman, the first trumpet teacher at Eastman, was born in England in 1875 and raised in Australia. There is evidence that he was largely self-taught. After returning to England, Freeman joined the Band of the Grenadier Guards as solo cornetist. Several years later he left the Grenadier Guards and came to the United States, where he toured with the Sousa Band. Eventually he started to perform in various theater orchestras in New York, including the Criterion on Broadway, where Victor Wagner was the conductor. When Wagner came to Rochester to lead the Eastman Theatre Orchestra, he asked Freeman to come with him to become principal trumpet in the orchestra. Freeman's tenure as the trumpet teacher at Eastman was relatively brief, but he continued to perform professionally in Rochester until his retirement in 1933. His son, Henry S. Freeman, a 1930 graduate of the Eastman School of Music, was a member of the double bass section of the Rochester Philharmonic Orchestra until 1945, when he left Rochester to join the Boston Symphony Orchestra under Serge Koussevitzky. Henry Freeman's son, Robert, became director of the Eastman School of Music in 1972, serving in the position for twenty-four years.

The Eastman teaching careers of George Waterhouse and Adolph Weiss, like that of Harry Freeman, were relatively brief, but Wendell Hoss remained in Rochester until the early 1930s. It was Hoss who organized and conducted the Eastman School's first wind ensemble. Leonard DeLorenzo, Eastman's first flute teacher, taught until the mid-1930s when he was succeeded by Joseph Mariano. DeLorenzo was one of the more successful teachers among the early woodwind faculty, and he was also a very solid and dependable player. He was trained in Italy at the conservatory in Naples and came to America in 1910 to serve as first flutist of the New York Philharmonic. Before coming to Rochester he also played for five years with the Minneapolis Symphony and two years with the Los Angeles Symphony. The bass teacher, Nelson Watson, enjoyed an even longer association with the school and orchestra. His training had been in London at Trinity

College and at the Royal College of Music, and he came to Rochester from the Philadelphia Orchestra. Watson died in 1945, and the position of bass teacher at the school was then filled by Oscar Zimmerman.

The practice of hiring teachers from the orchestra was not without its dangers, since most of the orchestral players in the 1920s were theater orchestra men, often with somewhat limited experience as symphony players and even more limited experience as teachers. Many of these early Eastman faculty members are remembered as being perhaps solid and dependable players, but without the kind of musical and pedagogical skills found in the teachers who gradually came to replace them at the school in later years. However, that could not be said of Emory Remington, the theater orchestra man chosen to be the Eastman School's first trombone teacher.

Although Remington came to the faculty without an impressive résumé, he became one of the most beloved and successful teachers in America, affectionately known to practically everyone as "The Chief." Remington was born in Rochester on December 22, 1891, and received his earliest exposure to music as a member of the choir at St. Andrew's Episcopal Church. In later life he said that if he had a special distinction, it was that he tried to make the trombone sing, and he attributed that approach at least in part to his experience at St. Andrew's. At the age of fourteen Remington was given his first trombone and received lessons from his father, who was a cornetist and trumpeter. At age seventeen he became a member of the Rochester Park Band, an accomplished group of players lead by Herman Dossenbach's brother, Theodore. In 1917 Remington enlisted in the Navy and was sent off to play trombone in an orchestra. After the armistice he was selected as one of twenty-five Navy musicians who sailed to France with Woodrow Wilson when he attended the Versailles Peace Conference. In 1922 Remington became principal trombonist at the Eastman Theatre, a position he held for about a quarter century. Around the same time he began teaching at the Eastman School and was still teaching full-time at the time of his death almost fifty years later.

Remington's influence as a teacher of trombone and the influence of the countless numbers of his students who began to take positions in colleges and conservatories and in orchestras throughout the country is immeasurable. The affection that everyone had for him throughout his long career was as much an indication of his warmth and humanity as it was the success of his teaching. Donald Hunsberger, a Remington student who later

Figure 40. Emory Remington, trombonist, Eastman School faculty 1922–71. (Photograph by Alexander Leventon. Used by permission.)

became conductor of the Eastman Wind Ensemble, commented that "this was a man who believed in people, who took pleasure in their accomplishments, who understood their frustrations, who sympathized in their moments of sorrow, and who reveled in their love and devotion to music and to music performance in particular."[2]

The presence of teachers for the orchestral instruments in September 1924 did not signify large numbers of collegiate students for these members of the faculty. As a matter of fact, at that time there were no students in the degree or certificate programs who were majoring in any woodwind or brass instrument or in percussion. The collegiate enrollment for 1924–25 included ninety-two students majoring in piano, twenty-one in organ, an additional eight in motion-picture organ, fifty-four in voice, five in opera, thirteen in violin, six in cello, two in harp, one in composition, and twenty-nine in public school music. To stimulate enrollment for the study of orchestral instruments, the school offered twenty-one scholarships the following year: four in French

[2]   Donald Hunsberger, interviewed by the author, Rochester, 23 September 2002.

Figure 41. Theory faculty members. Back row from left: Donald Tweedy, George MacNabb, Melville Smith. Front row from left: Selim Palmgren, George Barlow Penny, Marjorie MacKown, Edward Royce. (Collection of the author.)

horn, three in trombone, one in timpani, one in tuba, plus two each in flute, oboe, clarinet, bassoon, trumpet, and double bass. One can see in these numbers the necessary personnel for the school orchestra.

In addition to those who were providing instrumental and vocal instruction, the 1924–25 faculty included ten people who taught the more academic aspects of music. The catalogue listed five individuals under the general heading of "Musicianship," which included harmony, counterpoint, composition, and instrumentation: these included George Barlow Penny and Selim Palmgren, as well as the new director, Howard Hanson. Penny also had the responsibility of teaching music history, music literature, and music appreciation, retaining his now customary role of being somewhat a "jack of all trades."

Two newcomers to the theory teaching staff the previous September had been Edward Royce and Donald Tweedy, both of them graduates of Harvard University. Tweedy remained at

Eastman for only a half-dozen years, but Royce was a faculty member from 1923 until 1947. In addition to his studies at Harvard, Royce had spent two years at the Stern Conservatory in Berlin. Prior to coming to Eastman, he had taught at the University of Illinois, Middlebury College, the Ithaca Conservatory of Music, and the New York School of Music and Arts in New York City. In addition to the regular faculty, Ernest Bloch (the man who had not wanted to be "bothered" by an important position and a high salary) was engaged to teach a special "Master Course in Theory and Practice" during the year. Contrary to what might have been expected from a composer of Bloch's stature, his course dealt with pedagogy, harmony, counterpoint, form, and fugue. Bloch was at Eastman for a total of five weeks. He lectured for two hours each day, devoting one week to each of the five topics chosen for his Eastman School "master course."

The faculty for what was then called Public School Music was represented by Sherman Clute, Catherine Eaton, David Mattern, and Charles Miller. Miller and Clute, who were also employed by the city public schools, each had a long association with the Eastman School of Music, Miller until 1938 and Clute until 1949. Charles Miller was a graduate of Nebraska Wesleyan University in Lincoln, and had worked in Lincoln for fifteen years prior to coming to Rochester. In Rochester he worked with Joseph E. Maddy[3] in developing the music curriculum for the city's public schools. In 1917 he was appointed director of music for the public schools and then joined the Eastman School faculty in 1924.

Sherman Clute was hired by the Rochester public school system in 1920 and became supervisor of instrumental music. His training had been in Potsdam, New York, at what was then called Potsdam Normal and the Crane Normal Institute of Music, but he had also done additional study at Eastman under Thomas Henry Yorke Trotter, Albert Coates, and Eugene Goossens. Clute was a very versatile man and an accomplished trumpet player and conductor. He spent twenty-five years on the Eastman faculty before retiring in 1949. The employment of Miller and Clute by both the Eastman School of Music and the Rochester public schools was a clear indication of the close connection between the school and the city school district, a connection which would endure for a long time.

---

[3] Joseph E. Maddy is best remembered for establishing the National High School Orchestra Camp at Interlochen in 1928, which became the National Music Camp in 1931 and is now known as the Interlochen Arts Camp.

Between 1921 and 1946, nine members of the Rochester city school district music department were appointed to Eastman School faculty positions.

In addition to the regular Public School Music curriculum, which was a degree course, the school offered "normal training" during its earliest years. The Normal Training Courses were open to persons who were not enrolled in the regular courses of the school. It provided an opportunity for such students to complete their teacher training by attending various lectures and demonstrations and by taking specialized classes. Instruction in this program was provided by Oscar Gareissen in voice, Majorie MacKown in piano, George Barlow Penny in pedagogy, and Vladimir Resnikoff in violin. The school also offered a "Vocal Normal Course for Public School Teachers," which taught methods and principles of singing applicable to class teaching in public schools. Frederick Haywood was the faculty member in charge of this particular course. The separate "normal training" programs at the school were all soon discontinued, but Haywood remained involved in the Public School Music program at the Eastman School until his retirement in 1954.

Three more faculty members deserve mention, namely Marian Weed, Anne Theodora Cummins, and Hazel Stanton. Weed, who was a native Rochesterian, was advisor to women (i.e., dean of women) and instructor in German and English. Her professional background, however, had been in opera, including three seasons at the Bayreuth Festival and five seasons with the Metropolitan Opera. She retired from Eastman at the end of the 1937–38 school year, after having served as advisor for women since the school's opening in 1921.[4] Anne Theodora Cummins came to the school in 1924 as the teacher of French language and diction. Her long career at Eastman brought her into contact with countless numbers of students, and she was certainly one of the most unique and well-loved personalities at the school during all of those years. Cummins was born in England and had been educated in London and in Paris, including receiving a diploma from the Sorbonne. She taught for a while in India, a fact that seemed to deserve frequent mention in her Eastman classes during her long career at the school.

Hazel Stanton served as the school psychologist, with important responsibilities concerning admission and evaluation of students.

---

[4]   The new advisor for women in 1938 was Jessie Hoskam Kneisel. There was no advisor for men until the 1939–40 school year.

She had been a student of Dr. Carl Seashore at the University of Iowa and had been recruited to the Eastman School of Music in 1921. The school first attempted to entice Seashore away from Iowa, but he declined and suggested Stanton might come in his place. She accepted the position at the school partly because it provided an opportunity to make a study of the value of measuring musical capacity to determine probable achievement in music. During her tenure at the school—and for many years after she had left—the famous "Seashore Tests" were administered not only to incoming Eastman School of Music students but also throughout the city's public schools. These tests measured six aspects of musical capacity: sense of pitch, sense of intensity, sense of time, sense of rhythm, sense of consonance, and tonal memory. They were designed to measure the potential for musical growth and development rather than actual musical attainment. Although their value was called into question in later years, the Seashore Tests were an important part of the admissions process during the early decades of the school and were enthusiastically endorsed at the time by Howard Hanson.

The new director quickly established a good working relationship with his faculty and showed the kind of energy and initiative that seemed to justify the confidence George Eastman and Rush Rhees had placed in him. Hanson was apparently not the kind of person who would spend his first year merely assessing the situation. All of this pleased Rhees, who reported his favorable impressions to George Eastman in a letter dated October 1:

> You will be much interested to know that Hanson seems to be taking hold of the work at the School of Music with equal discretion and vigor.
>
> He seems to have established very friendly relations both with students and members of the faculty. I have had incidental opportunity to observe his mode of greeting, both to students and members of the faculty, and have remarked a friendliness and winsomeness which seem to have very great promise. On the other hand, no one can question the fact that a strong hand is at the wheel.
>
> Of course we must anticipate some problems with reference to any new man in the organization, but I confess that I have not yet seen them coming over the horizon and believe that we have made an excellent choice for our great undertaking.[5]

[5]   Rush Rhees, Letter to George Eastman, 1 October 1924. RRL.

One of the first areas of the curriculum which Hanson addressed was the program of theory instruction, which he found somewhat deficient. In a letter to Rush Rhees, dated October 17, he commented that the "curricula leading to the degree bachelor of music have been handed down to us from the old Institute of Musical Art and do not for that reason fit the conditions of an institution of the size and prominence of the Eastman School of Music."[6] Part of Hanson's concern arose from observing that there was little coordination of work in the various theory courses. In his letter to Rush Rhees he commented on this basic structural weakness in the program:

> I find students who have completed work in Advanced Form who apparently have had no work in Elementary Form; students who have passed to an advanced subject without having completed satisfactory work in the elementary subject; and students who have pursued work in an advanced and elementary subject at the same time to the detriment of both.

In addition, Hanson thought that the theory curriculum did not place enough emphasis on practical subjects, such as keyboard harmony, or sufficient work in dictation and sight-singing. Therefore, he mandated immediate changes in the theory program, which at the time extended through all eight semesters of the undergraduate curriculum.

At about the same time, Hanson traveled to Pittsburgh for the first meeting of the National Association of Schools of Music (NASM), which was being held at Hotel Schenley on October 20 and 21. The association was being formed because of a growing feeling among leaders of independent and university-based music schools that a basic agreement regarding curricula and performance expectations was to everyone's advantage. At issue was the basic credibility of the professional music degree and the credibility of music study as a discipline in higher education. Although Kenneth Bradley from the Bush Conservatory in Chicago was elected the first president of NASM, Hanson was chosen for what proved to be the more important position of chairman for the commission on curriculum. NASM members serving on Hanson's commission included G. R. Combs from the Combs Broad Street Conservatory in Philadelphia, John Hattstaedt from the American Conservatory

---

6   Howard Hanson, Letter to Rush Rhees, 17 October 1924. RRL.

in Chicago, Earl Moore from the University of Michigan, Harold Randolph from Peabody Conservatory, and Louise Westervelt from the Columbia School of Music in Chicago.

Hanson held this highly influential position from 1924 until 1933 and was perhaps the single most important influence in the development of standards for professional degrees in music and for the accreditation of such degrees. In reporting to Rush Rhees on October 23 following his return to Rochester, Hanson spoke of his selection to lead the curriculum committee:

> The leadership of this campaign for higher standards in music schools was thrust upon me as I felt that I had plenty to do in Rochester without championing any other cause, but since they seemed to feel that I was the logical man for the position, I felt that the opportunity was too great to turn down as it will virtually place the Eastman School of Music at the head of the institutions demanding high requirements for music school degrees.[7]

While all of this was transpiring, the Eastman faculty was holding regular meetings and making some decisions of its own concerning the bachelor's curriculum. Of particular interest was the decision approved on October 8, 1924, that students who were admitted as piano majors would henceforth be graduated either as artists (i.e., performers) or teachers. Later in the semester the faculty decided that students who were graduating as teachers would be required to take two years of pedagogy, as opposed to a one-year requirement for those graduating as performers.

Just before the Christmas holidays Hanson presented a new plan to Rush Rhees, one which would have long-term implications for the school's strong commitment towards the encouragement of American music. His plan was to present two concerts at the end of the spring semester which would consist entirely of new orchestral works by American composers. Hanson suggested that the concerts would be considered "rehearsal performances" with no admission charge, and that he would invite American composers to submit manuscript scores from which he would select the programs. If Rhees approved, the concerts would take place on March 26 and April 25 and be known as the "American Composers' Rehearsals Concerts." To give the event national exposure, Hanson suggested that critics from other cities be invited to the performances, with

---

[7]   Howard Hanson, Letter to Rush Rhees, 23 October 1924. RRL.

expenses being paid by the Eastman School of Music. He submitted a budget for these concerts which estimated the total cost for each concert at $1,800. Rush Rhees approved the proposal on December 27, 1924.

The original proposal for two concerts, however, was eventually scaled back to a single event which took place on Friday, May 1, 1925, with Hanson conducting the Rochester Philharmonic Orchestra in the first "American Composers' Concert." This concert inaugurated a project which would continue with similar programs each year and then lead to the establishment of the annual Festival of American Music. The two-fold purpose of the concerts was to give composers an opportunity to hear professionally competent performances of their works, while also giving them the opportunity to receive the reaction of the audience and comments from the attending music critics. Composers selected for the first of these concerts in 1925 were Aaron Copland, Quincy Porter, Bernard Rogers, Mark Silver, Donald Tweedy, and Adolph Weiss.

Another event of note during the second semester of the 1924–25 school year was the inaugural concert of the Rochester Little Symphony, conducted by Albert Coates. This was a small chamber orchestra consisting of only twenty-four players. The orchestra members were mainly the principal teachers at the school and the principal players of the Rochester Philharmonic Orchestra. For their first program on February 9 they performed Ravel's *Mother Goose Suite*, Mozart's Symphony in G Minor, Carl Rorich's Woodwind Quintet, Mendelssohn's Overture to *A Midsummer Night's Dream*, Eight Russian Folk Songs of Liadov, and the Suite for Flute, Harp, and Violin by Eugene Goossens. Soloists in the latter work were Lucile Johnson Bigelow, Leonardo DeLorenzo, and Vladimir Resnikoff.

It was also at this time that Sigma Alpha Iota, Mu Phi Epsilon, and Phi Mu Alpha were established at the Eastman School of Music. Sigma Alpha Iota was the oldest music sorority in America, and their new Eastman chapter, Sigma Theta, was established on January 16, 1925, with twenty-two active members. It was the first national sorority chapter at the University of Rochester. Alpha Nu chapter of Phi Mu Alpha was established on January 24, 1925, by the fraternity's national president, Peter W. Dykema, a man who later became head of the music department at Teachers College, Columbia University. Twenty-five men, including several members of the faculty, were installed as charter members at ceremonies in Kilbourn Hall, which was followed by an informal banquet at the Sagamore Hotel. Mu Phi Epsilon sorority established its Eastman chapter (Mu Epsilon) on February 28, 1925, with thirty active members. The installation ceremony was followed by a banquet at the Hotel Seneca. Both of the new sorority chapters had previously existed as local organizations before affiliating with national groups. The Mu Phi Epsilon chapter had originated as Beta Gamma Mu, the first sorority at the Eastman School of Music. The Sigma Alpha Iota chapter had been Alpha Phi Alpha, also founded in the school's first year.

Howard Hanson's first year as director was a time of new developments and initiatives, and most observers must have been pleased with the creative and energetic leadership he brought to the school in 1924. Part of that leadership, however, needed to be directed towards emerging problems in the faculty. This was the year that saw the resignation of Albert Coates and Frank Waller, as well as being the year that Vladimir Rosing left the Eastman School opera department to concentrate his energies on the new Rochester American Opera Company. Early in the second semester Vladimir Resnikoff also announced his resignation, effective at the end of the school year. He was rather embittered by what he saw as an unreasonable workload. He thought, perhaps with some justification, that the combination of teaching at the school, playing in the orchestra, and playing in the quartet made it extremely difficult for him to develop his own career as a solo violinist:

> For three tedious, heart-breaking years I have been laboring here. . . . It is too much for one man. There should be at least three doing this work. Worst of all, it is keeping me from the public and my art. I have no time to practice. . . . I want to play the violin. I do not want to be a machine.
>
> Were I satisfied that I never could become a great artist, then this job might be for me. The job prevents one from becoming great.[8]

Although Resnikoff was a gifted violinist, he never achieved the prominent career as a soloist to which he aspired. After leaving the Eastman faculty he established his own music school only a few blocks away from the Eastman School of Music, doing this in partnership with the cellist Gerald Maas. The Resnikoff-Maas School of Music opened on September 8, 1925, with a faculty of seventeen; the stated aim of the new school was to develop talent for professional

---

[8] *Rochester Journal and Post Express*, Rochester, 19 February 1925. SML.

Figure 42. Paul Kefer, cellist, Eastman School faculty 1921–41. (Photograph by Alexander Leventon. Used by permission.)

careers, a rather lofty goal. The school lasted only a short while, however, and Resnikoff went on to become a long-time member of the Boston Symphony rather than realizing his dream of becoming a great solo artist.

Resignations from the faculty were not the only personnel problems confronting Howard Hanson. Death claimed three highly valued teachers during his first year as director. On October 4, 1924, Joseph Press died as a result of complications of pneumonia. He was one of the most gifted members of the early Eastman faculty, and the loss was deeply felt throughout the Eastman community. In expressing their sympathy to the cellist's widow, the faculty described his death as an irreparable loss and spoke of him as a great artist, a superior teacher, and a dear friend. On October 23 Hanson was able to announce that Paul Kefer, a distinguished French-American cellist would immediately become the new cello teacher at Eastman. Kefer was a graduate of the Brussels Conservatory and came to America in 1900 after holding a number of orchestral positions in Europe. During his early years as a cellist in Europe he had been a member of a string quartet which included

Pierre Monteux (1875–1964) as its violist.[9] Prior to Kefer's appointment to the Eastman School faculty in Rochester, he served for five years as first cellist of the New York Symphony.

The death of Joseph Press was followed a few months later by that of Oscar Gareissen on December 9. He was deeply mourned, especially by those who had known him in the earlier days of the D.K.G. Institute of Musical Art on Prince Street. Among his many contributions to the Eastman School was his role in establishing the Eastman School Chorus. The leadership of that group was soon given to Herman Genhart. In late May, several weeks before the annual university commencement, the Eastman School community suffered yet another loss with the death of Pierre Augierras due to complications following an operation for appendicitis. Augierras was a pianist of the first rank, and he served on the Eastman faculty as an important representative of the French school. That influence was now lost, and its absence within the piano department in the immediate future was an unfortunate development.

The University of Rochester commencement ceremony was held on June 15, 1925, and included the conferral of nineteen degrees and fifteen certificates earned by Eastman School of Music students. Among the degree recipients was Jerome Diamond, who served as a member of the Eastman piano faculty from 1926 until his death in 1966. The certificate recipients included Elvira Wonderlich, who had a similarly long tenure at the school, mainly as an uncompromising but meticulously thorough teacher of undergraduate theory. Most of her students in later years had little idea that she had been a first-rate pianist in her day, even including in her repertoire the Rachmaninoff First Piano Concerto, which she performed in Kilbourn Hall as a post-graduate student the following November.

Diamond and Wonderlich joined an increasing number of Eastman School graduates who had been hired to teach at the school following their graduation. This practice continued for many years and led to accusations of a musical "inbreeding," which some felt was not in the best interests of the school. Although Hanson certainly endorsed the practice, he was still quite capable of looking beyond the school's alumni to make important faculty appointments. The necessity of making some important new faculty appointments must have been foremost in the mind of Howard Hanson

---

[9] Monteux, as is well known, went on to a highly distinguished career as a conductor. The author recalls hearing him speak of his early experiences as a chamber music player, including one occasion when he played chamber music with Johannes Brahms.

throughout the second semester and into the summer months. The loss of so many good people during his first year was perhaps the only blemish on an otherwise exemplary freshman year as leader of Mr. Eastman's School. In all other respects he could look back over his initial year with satisfaction and pride, while at the same time awaiting the many challenges which lay in the future.

Chapter 12

1925–1927
New Directions under New Leadership

Howard Hanson began his second year as director of the Eastman School of Music in September 1925, after having made several important appointments to the Eastman faculty. Gustave Tinlot, a French violinist, was the school's new principal teacher of violin, replacing Vladimir Resnikoff. Like Resnikoff, he was also to be the concertmaster of the Rochester Philharmonic Orchestra and first violinist of the Kilbourn Quartet. Tinlot had received his education at the Paris Conservatory and had played with the Paris Conservatory Orchestra. He then became concertmaster of the Paris Opéra Comique and served as a member of the jury at the conservatory. After coming to the United States he was the concertmaster of Walter Damrosch's New York Symphony from 1918 to 1924, and then spent one year in Minnesota as concertmaster of the Minneapolis Symphony.

Tinlot also had previous teaching experience, both in Paris and in New York where he had taught at the David Mannes Music School. He was also an experienced chamber music artist. When the Franco-American String Quartet was organized, Tinlot was its first violinist and Paul Kefer its cellist. Therefore, these two men, who were now members of the Kilbourn Quartet in Rochester, had already been associated as chamber music performers. Tinlot was the third person since 1921 to be the principal violin teacher at the Eastman School of Music, and the criteria for his selection were probably not too different from those used in hiring Hartmann and Resnikoff. The principal string teachers at Eastman during the 1920s had to be good solo performers with an orchestral and chamber music background, and with at least some previous teaching experience. The position required all of these things. Unlike Hartmann and Resnikoff, however, Tinlot's selection would appear

Figure 43. Gustave Tinlot, violinist, Eastman School faculty 1925–42. (Photo by Alexander Leventon. Used by permission.)

to have been based more on his orchestral experience than other factors in his background.

Also new to the faculty was a young American pianist named Ashley Pettis. He was presumably taking Pierre Augieras' position on the faculty, but he simply did not have the Frenchman's extensive background or his experience. His keen interest in American music, however, must have made him a particularly attractive to Hanson. Pettis proved to be a thorough and skillful teacher, but he stayed at Eastman only until 1932. He later joined a Roman Catholic religious order and lived in Italy, where several friends from Rochester visited him from time to time. Another newcomer to the faculty was Melville Smith, who joined the theory teaching staff in September 1925. Like Tweedy and Royce, he held an A.B. degree from Harvard. Prior to coming to Eastman, Smith had taught at the David Mannes Music School in New York City.

As previously noted, Hanson was also faced with the necessity of making some important personnel decisions for his opera department, with Rosing now pursuing his dreams of a professional opera company and Mamoulian involved with the new

Eastman School of Dance and Dramatic Action. First of all he appointed Otto Luening and Emanuel Balaban as opera coaches, but he also needed a new general director for the department. Albert Coates was now gone, but Hanson quickly recognized Eugene Goossens' abilities and appointed him to head the opera department in addition to his responsibilities as music director of the Philharmonic. Goossens may have been very young and slightly inexperienced in this new role, but he was a person of genuine talent and ability who could give the school's opera program firm and steady direction.

Steady direction was what Hanson was seeking throughout the school. The annual catalogue for 1925–26 was the first to include detailed listings of the Eastman curricula, probably reflecting the active role Hanson took in curricular matters during these early years. The catalogue listed five courses of study leading to the certificate (diploma) of graduation: piano, organ, voice, composition, and instrumental (violin, violoncello, or any orchestral instrument). The courses of study leading to the bachelor of music degree included these same five majors plus three more in public school music (piano, instrumental, and vocal). The catalogue also mentioned the bachelor of arts with a major in music, a degree offered by the College of Arts and Science, which included thirty credits taken under the direction of the Eastman School of Music. There was, however, no graduate program yet in existence. Therefore, when Hanson met with the faculty on September 23, 1925, he appointed a committee consisting of Raymond Wilson, Donald Tweedy, Melville Smith, and Edgar Royce to consider the question of formulating the course of study for master's and doctorate degrees. The three Harvard graduates were, therefore, central to the initial planning for graduate degrees, along with the steady and dependable Raymond Wilson. Their European-trained colleagues were conspicuously absent from the committee, and no one on the committee, not even the Harvard men, had ever earned a graduate degree.[1] It would be two years before the Eastman School would announce the establishment of a graduate department.

At this time Hanson and his faculty also began to deal with establishing recognizable standards for admission and for graduation. Being admitted to the Eastman School during its first few

---

[1] Hanson had earned only a bachelor's degree, but Northwestern University had recently given him an honorary doctor of music degree; Hanson was the youngest man thus honored by his alma mater.

years had been a rather simple procedure, but as the school began to gain in stature and national reputation a more rigorous application process was necessary. Up until this time, the entrance requirements were restricted to being a high school graduate, taking the "psychological test" (i.e., Seashore test), and playing an audition for the director to demonstrate musical ability and level of accomplishment. The results of the Seashore tests, however, were only advisory in nature and had no direct bearing on the question of acceptance for study at the school. In November, however, the faculty voted to establish a specific score on the Seashore tests as being necessary for admission at all levels (preparatory, special, and regular course).

The faculty also became directly involved in the Seashore tests and in Hazel Stanton's research by being required twice a year to submit a talent estimate and an achievement rating for each of their students, using the same six ratings (A, B, C+, C−, D, E) as were used in scoring the Seashore tests.

> [The] talent rating is a factor to be discriminated from the achievement rating on the same rating blank form. Students with a considerable degree of recognized talent may have an estimated achievement commensurate with their estimated talent or very much lower or higher than the estimated talent. An achievement rating which is lower than the talent rating occurs more often than an achievement rating which is higher than a talent rating.[2]

This system, which was merely an elaborate means of evaluating if a student was working to his/her full potential, was probably beneficial mainly to Hazel Stanton's research. Nonetheless, the Eastman School of Music gave considerable credibility to all these ratings for many years to come.

The situation that Hanson was attempting to avoid through the use of the Seashore tests was the admission of students who were later found to be unprepared or unable to complete the course of study. Each year, a significant number of such students needed to be placed on probation or dismissed from the school. For example, at the end of the 1925–26 school year, forty students were dismissed, of whom only four successfully applied for reinstatement. Fourteen others were informed that they could reregister for the

---

[2]   Hazel M. Stanton, *Prognosis of Musical Achievement: A Study of the Predictive Value of Tests in the Selection of Degree and Certificate Students for the Eastman School of Music* (Rochester, 1929), 15.

1926–27 school year "on their own responsibility," the faculty being unable or unwilling to make a definite recommendation concerning their status. Six additional students were allowed to return on probation. The total number of students affected by dismissal or probation represented one out of every six persons enrolled in the degree and certificate programs, a figure Hanson considered much too high.

This was not simply an issue of academic non-performance, but most often involved a basic lack of talent and skills, something that should have been properly assessed before the student was accepted for study at the school. At the time it appeared that the use of the Seashore tests might be an accurate means of assessing future performance and, therefore, a highly useful tool in the entire admissions process. Hanson was obviously struggling to establish the criteria that would lead to a better selection of students, and he even went so far as to insist that all "doubtful cases" be discontinued at the end of their freshman year. He referred to the problems of retaining and graduating students as "student mortality," and by 1929 he was able to report considerable progress to Rush Rhees:

> [G]reater stability has been attained due to two factors, first a greater stability in our own curriculum and second, and more important, a more careful selection of applicants for the entering classes. We are now using as the basis for selection the questionnaire of the applicant, confidential reports from the high school principal and the music teachers, the high school records, the two psychological tests and an examination in applied music. In admitting students, I am indebted to Dr. Hazel Stanton for her most excellent administration of the psychological tests and for help in drawing up the various questionnaires and to the various examiners in applied music for their painstaking care.[3]

A fundamental problem in the admissions process, however, was not addressed by psychological testing or by confidential reports from principals and music teachers. Central to the issue was the simple fact that the Eastman School of Music was attracting students from a wide geographical area and often finding it difficult or even impossible to insist upon an audition as part of the application process. As a result, there were students who were

---

[3] Howard Hanson, *Report to the President of the University*, May 1929. Draft contained in the Hanson papers. SML.

admitted to the school solely on the strength of their high school transcript and recommendations, but without an audition of any sort. While the practice of not insisting on an audition may now seem either rather strange or even absolutely foolhardy, it reflected the great difficulties confronting applicants who were from areas of the country at a considerable distance from Rochester. Without the convenience of modern air travel, many such students would have had an extremely difficult time in coming for an audition. Moreover, there was no cassette, video, or compact disc technology at that time by which these students could submit a recorded audition program. It is difficult to estimate how many students entered degree study at the Eastman School of Music without having played an audition, but the number was by no means insignificant. It was not until the 1950s that an audition was routinely required of all applicants.[4]

In addition to dealing with the admissions process, Hanson continued to address various aspects of the curriculum, especially the theory program. Although he had already instituted some changes in the curriculum during his first year as director, he now asked the faculty for their suggestions on how it might be further improved. This request was made at a faculty meeting on February 10, 1926, and the resulting changes in the four-year curriculum were approved by the faculty on April 28, 1926. Counterpoint and orchestration, which had previously been taught during the junior year, were now to be divided between the final two years of study. Modern harmony, which had been taught during the senior year, was now to be an elective. Even with a four-year, eight-semester theory curriculum, the prevailing opinion was that too much was being attempted. It is interesting to note that the study of orchestration was considered more important at the time than modern harmony.

If there was only a relatively small amount of streamlining to the theory curriculum, the music history requirements were being severely curtailed. The original Eastman School curriculum for history and literature of music was so comprehensive that it deserves to be fully described:

First Year: Ethnomusicology: the Music of the American
              Indians, West Indians, Polynesians, Africans,
              Australians, etc.

---

[4]   The auditioning of all applicants was a policy instituted by Edward Easley, who became the school's first director of admissions in 1953.

	Archeology: The Architecture, Sculpture, Painting and Music of Chaldea, Babylonia, Assyria, Egypt, Palestine, Greece and Rome.
Second Year:	Medieval History: The Art and Music of the Christian Church to the time of the Reformation and Palestrina.
Third Year:	Modern History: The first term is concerned with the beginnings of Opera, Oratorio, and Orchestra; Classicism, Scarlatti, Bach, Handel, Haydn, Mozart, Beethoven, Gluck. The second term is concerned with Romanticism: Beethoven, Schubert, Mendelssohn, Schumann, Von Weber, Chopin, etc.
Fourth Year:	The modern movements of Neo-Romanticism, Neo-Classicism, Ultra-Modernism and Nationalism; Berlioz, Liszt, Wagner, Brahms, Caesar [*sic*] Franck, and contemporary composers, including and closing with American composers.
	The subjects of Aesthetics, History of Music, History of the Fine Arts, Biography, Music Appreciation and Criticism are combined in this course.[5]

One cannot imagine a more comprehensive curriculum, with so many interdisciplinary characteristics. However, this may have been its very weakness, and it is easy to imagine that the curriculum had little support among most members of the Eastman faculty. The problem was that it was *too* comprehensive, *too* interdisciplinary. In a four-year curriculum students had to wait until their junior year before Bach's name was even mentioned, and until their senior year before there was any discussion of Brahms and Wagner. Perhaps it might have been an exemplary learning experience in a liberal arts program, but its place in a program of study leading to the bachelor of music degree was open to question. It simply did not coordinate with anything else that the students were learning. Therefore, this comprehensive approach to history and literature of music was replaced by two separate courses, the first (taken in the freshman year) being a basic music history lecture-course, and the second (taken in the senior year) a history of

---

[5] *First Annual Catalogue of The Eastman School of Music of The University of Rochester, 1921–22* (Rochester, 1921), 21.

fine arts in relation to music. In time the latter course was elimi-
nated, and the undergraduate music history requirement for many
years was limited to a one-year music survey course.

While all of these matters were being decided, a new
development arose concerning the WHAM radio station. A New
York State Network was being formed, of which WHAM was to be
a member. Member stations were WGY in Schenectady (the anchor
station), WJZ in New York City, WBFC in Syracuse, WHAM in
Rochester, and WMAK in Lockport (near Buffalo). Engineers from
WJZ had gone around to each station in October to check its equipment in preparation for the new network. General Electric, owner
of the anchor station in Schenectady, considered WHAM to be a
highly important part of the new network because it was counting
on its connections with the Eastman School of Music. The first
WHAM network broadcast, a concert by the Rochester Little
Symphony conducted by Eugene Goossens, was on December 23,
1925. The concert was carried over a special long-distance line of
the Postal Telegraph Company to Schenectady, where it was broadcast by WGY to an audience estimated at more than a million
persons.

A little more than a year later, Stromberg-Carlson assumed
operation of WHAM, but with expectation that the Eastman School
of Music would continue to supply the station with classical music
programming. The company upgraded WHAM's operation by providing new studios, adding to the professional staff, and increasing
the station's power. In addition, it increased programming from
three to seven and a half hours per day. The station management
worked closely with the Eastman School to develop educational
broadcasting, and by the mid-1930s it was supplying the NBC
"Blue Network" with four symphonic concerts each week. By the
end of the decade, WHAM was the supplier of more symphonic
programming than any other station outside of New York and
Chicago. All of this worked enormously to the advantage of the
Eastman School of Music, a fact that the school's young director
quickly appreciated.

These early years of administration were extremely busy and
challenging for Howard Hanson. Faculty appointments, changes in
the curriculum, matters concerning admission and graduation,
annual concerts devoted to the works of American composers,
working arrangements with WHAM, an emerging leadership position with the newly organized NASM should have been more
than enough to occupy the attention of Eastman's new Director,
who also had to keep a watchful eye on Rosing's opera venture and

Mamoulian's activities. Yet he was still able to accept invitations for guest conducting appearances throughout the country and to accept invitations to speak before important national organizations, while also reserving time to devote to composition. Perhaps he was overly committed to these outside activities. In 1929 Rush Rhees suggested that he might be spending too much time away from the school, and Hanson agreed to eliminate as much as possible his speaking engagements and the like around the country. Hanson's willingness to seek and accept out-of-town professional commitments stands in rather stark contrast with his de facto policy of not encouraging his faculty to do likewise. During his forty-years as director, very few members of the Eastman faculty had outside concert careers. As a matter of fact, Hanson seemed to be deeply mistrustful of people who attempted to balance a concert career with teaching at the school. A commitment to the education and well-being of the students was the sole reason for being a member of the faculty.

A commitment to the well-being of the student body soon included concern for the lack of adequate dormitory accommodations, a development that was not unanticipated. When the school had opened in 1921, collegiate enrollment had been limited and largely made up of local students from the Greater Rochester area. However, enrollment in the certificate and degree programs had risen from about one hundred students during the school's first year to three and a half times that number in 1925–26. More significantly, the school was now attracting students from a wide area of the country, students who needed accommodations when they came to study in Rochester. This was especially true of the school's female students, since few parents at the time would have been in favor of sending their daughters to the school unless such accommodations were available. Therefore, the decision to build dormitories was taken prior to Hanson's arrival in 1924, and these were under construction on University Avenue adjacent to the University of Rochester campus during his first year as Director. The original plan for adding an eight-story dormitory to the school's heating plant building on Swan Street had been abandoned. That site would soon be used for another important new project.

Plans for the dormitories called for initial construction of three connecting buildings facing an internal courtyard. Two of the buildings were completed in time for the opening of the 1925–26 school year and provided accommodations for 123 female students. They were four-story structures, with dining rooms, living rooms, offices, and a kitchen on the ground floor, and student rooms on each of the upper three floors. The third dormitory building was available for

Figure 44. Eastman School dormitories for women in 1925–26, shown prior to the construction of the east wing and the portico facing University Avenue.

occupancy the following September, raising the number of available accommodations to 210. Since the Eastman School did not need quite so many rooms, twenty were reserved to be used by students from the Women's College of the University of Rochester.

It was not until the following school year that a decision was made concerning naming the new dormitories. George Eastman suggested names of older, established musicians, but Hanson argued that the Eastman School of Music was an American school with a American faculty, dedicated to stimulating American composition and musical advancement. Therefore, he suggested Francis Hopkinson, Edward MacDowell, and Horatio Parker as names for three dormitory buildings. Although these became the official names, students for many years simply called the buildings "A House," "B House," and "C House." (While students surely had some familiarity with MacDowell and his music, Francis Hopkinson and Horatio Parker were names that may have meant very little to them.) Plans existed for the construction of two more dormitory units along University Avenue, the whole group to form a letter "E," but these additional units were never built.[6] Appropriate housing for male students was not provided until 1955. For a while, a men's dormitory with limited accommodations was operated in the old Institute building at 47 Prince Street, which had also been used as a women's dormitory prior to the opening of the University Avenue buildings.

Another concern facing the Eastman School at the same time was the lack of adequate practice facilities. The handful of practice rooms in the basement of the school building could hardly provide for the needs of a collegiate student body that now numbered about 350. The use of several studios for student practicing did little to alleviate the woeful lack of practice facilities for the students, and the situation was little improved when the school provided access to several old houses along the east side of Swan Street in which they had placed practice pianos. This was obviously only a temporary solution to a growing space problem that could only be properly addressed by new construction.

Therefore, the school announced plans in June 1926 for the erection of a twelve-story building on Swan Street, for which the existing power plant of the school would serve as a foundation. The announcement stated that the new building would contain practice

---

[6] When additional dormitory facilities were finally constructed about a decade later, a new building (connecting with the earlier buildings) was constructed on Prince Street.

Figure 45. The eleven-story Annex II under construction on Swan Street.

rooms, class rooms, assembly rooms, and a fully equipped gymnasium, all to be constructed at an estimated cost of a half million dollars. When completed the following year, the new 800,000 cubic foot, twelve-story structure provided space for 109 practice rooms (including 90 with pianos), nine classrooms, eight offices, and a gymnasium with dressing rooms and showers. The building was known simply as Annex II (or Annex B) and was connected to the main Eastman School building by means of a two-level bridge crossing Swan Street.

Hanson began his third year as director in September 1926, with construction of the new annex well underway. There were several new faculty members, including Jerome Diamond and Cecile Staub Genhart in the piano department. Diamond, as previously noted, was a 1925 graduate of the Eastman School and had studied with Edgar Rose. Cecile Genhart was the wife of Herman Genhart, who had just been "promoted" from opera coach to conductor of the Eastman School Chorus. His young wife, a pianist of exceptional skills, had studied at the conservatory in Zurich, Switzerland. Cecile Genhart's teachers had included the Swiss pianist and composer Emil Frey (1889–1946) and Edwin Fischer, with additional coaching from

Busoni. Joining the Eastman piano faculty in 1926 was the first step in what proved to be a long and highly successful career at the school.

Another newcomer to the school was Karl Van Hoesen, who joined the Public School Music faculty. Like all of his colleagues in that department, Van Hoesen was also employed by the Rochester school district. He was a native of Ithaca, New York, where he earned a bachelor of arts degree at Cornell University, while also studying with Otakar Ševčik at the Ithaca Conservatory.[7] He may have been the only man ever to teach music education at Eastman who did not have a degree in education, his degree being in English literature. Van Hoesen originally came to Rochester to play violin in one of the many theater orchestras in town. He remained on the faculty at Eastman until his retirement in 1966.[8]

Two other faculty appointments in 1926 were Arthur Foreman as the oboe teacher and Arkaty Yegudkin as the French horn teacher.[9] Foreman was English by birth and training, having been educated at the Royal College of Music. He taught at the Guildhall School in London from 1908 until 1923, while also serving as the first oboe in the Royal Philharmonic Orchestra. Among Foreman's students at Eastman during his ten years as a member of the faculty was Mitch Miller. Yegudkin was one of the most memorable and colorful characters in the history of the school. Born in Russia, he had received his training in Tiflis (Tbilisi) and Kiev, and had been the solo horn player with both the Warsaw Imperial Opera and the Symphony Orchestra of Petrograd (St. Petersburg). Yegudkin had taught at both the Tiflis Conservatory and the Kiev Conservatory before fleeing Russia, like many others, in the aftermath of the Bolshevik Revolution. Known to students and friends alike as "The General," he spoke with a heavy Russian accent that faded little during his many years in America, an accent which was known to have caused considerable embarrassment and misunderstanding on at least several occasions.

The new school year also led to an important administrative change at the Eastman School. At a faculty meeting on March 2,

---

[7] Ševčik taught in Vienna from 1909 until 1919 (which is where Hochstein and Resnikoff studied with him), but he spent the years 1921–31 teaching in the United States.

[8] Karl Van Hoesen was the father of K. David Van Hoesen, the teacher of bassoon at the Eastman School of Music from 1954 until 1991.

[9] Academic rank was not introduced at the Eastman School of Music until the 1960s. Therefore, Foreman and Yegudkin, like all of their Eastman faculty colleagues, had no academic title.

Figure 46. Various members of the faculty ca. 1930. Back row from left: Gerald Kunz, Harold Gleason, Paul White, Alexander Leventon, Arkaty Yegudkin, George MacNabb. Front row from left: Gustave Tinlot, Arthur See, Eugene Goossens, Edward Royce, Samuel Belov. (Collection of the author.)

1927, Hanson announced that Raymond Wilson was being appointed director of the Preparatory and Special Departments. With collegiate enrollment now numbering around 350 students, including 281 students in the bachelor of music program, Hanson had enough responsibilities without also being concerned with the 1200 non-collegiate students in the Preparatory and Special Departments. A separate administrative director relieved him of unnecessary responsibilities in this area of the school's work and placed these responsibilities into the hands of someone with proven leadership skills. Wilson remained in this position until his retirement twenty-six years later.

It is interesting to note that there was considerable discussion at the same faculty meeting that the school was expecting too much work in the degree program, the principal problem being the time required in preparing the classwork in the academic courses. Some faculty even suggested that the degree program should be extended to six years. Obviously, this suggestion was not implemented, but concern for the heavy academic requirements taking valuable time away from practicing has been a constant topic of discussion throughout the school's history. On March 16 the faculty met once again, deciding that all incoming freshman must have achieved a minimum average of 80 percent in their senior year of high school. At the same time, the faculty decided that Eastman collegiate students would remain in good standing only if they had maintained grades of A or B in their major subjects, and an average of C in all other subjects.

Life at the Eastman School of Music for the students, however, was not confined to studying and practicing. As previously noted, this period of time was particularly rich in opportunities to hear exceptional concerts and recitals. Although concert life centered around events in the Eastman Theatre, already described, there were also outstanding events in Kilbourn Hall. The school sponsored eight recitals each year, divided into two series. The programming was a mixture of internationally known artists and local musicians. Two of the programs each year were supplied by Eugene Goossens and the Rochester Little Symphony. Raymond Wilson and Sandor Vas shared a recital during the 1925–26 season, as did Gustav Tinlot and Paul Kefer. Vladimir Rosing and Lucile Johnson Bigelow appeared together during the following season.

The guest recitalists during this two-year period were all pianists, but they certainly represented a stellar group. Josef Lhevinne and Myra Hess each gave Kilbourn recitals during the 1925–26 season, while Wanda Landowska (1879–1959) and Walter Gieseking (1895–1956) were guest artists during the following year. Landowska performed on both the piano and the harpsichord, and her recital included music of Handel, Mozart, Bach, Haydn, Weber, Couperin, and Daquin. Eighteenth-century music was rather infrequently included on piano recitals at the time, and Couperin and Daquin were probably heard for the first time by many members of her Rochester audience. The remaining programs during these two seasons were all string quartets, with appearances by the Flonzaley Quartet, the Hart House Quartet, and the London Quartet (the latter appearing both seasons).

In addition to these public concerts, the school began to also offer an Educational Concert Series that consisted of events where admission was restricted to students and faculty. In some instances the performers were the same as those engaged for public recitals in Kilbourn Hall, playing for the students in the morning or afternoon and then repeating the recital for the general public in the evening. On other occasions however, the Educational Concert Series presented recitalists and ensembles who were appearing solely for the benefit of the Eastman School community. During 1926–27 there were ten educational concerts, including four recitals by the Kilbourn Quartet, a concert by the Rochester Little Symphony, and a recital featuring Lucile Johnson Bigelow and Vladimir Rosing. Guest artists appearing on the series included the Hart House Quartet from Canada; pianist E. Robert Schmitz (1889–1949), who was an important early authority on the music of Debussy; pianist Walter Gieseking; and the noted French organist Louis Vierne (1870–1937). At the time Vierne was organist at Notre Dame in Paris, and his Rochester program included some of his own music plus the Bach Toccata and Fugue in D Minor, the Franck Chorale in A Minor, and selections by Lazare Levy and Alphonse Marty.

The year 1927 marked the hundredth anniversary of the death of Beethoven, and there were a number of special Beethoven recitals throughout the year. The centenary was officially celebrated at Eastman, however, with a special concert in Kilbourn Hall on April 12. The program included the *Coriolan* Overture performed by the Rochester Little Symphony under the direction of Eugene Goossens, the "Appassionata" Sonata played by Max Landow, two songs sung by Jeanne Woolford and accompanied by the Rochester Little Symphony, and the Mass in C Major. The Mass featured the Rochester Festival Chorus and the Rochester Little Symphony conducted by Howard Hanson. It is interesting to note that the Eastman student orchestra was not utilized for the performance. At this time the Rochester Little Symphony, essentially a professional organization, was the school's performing ensemble. The Eastman School Orchestra, now being led by Samuel Belov, would need several more years before developing into a genuinely creditable ensemble.

Meanwhile, the American Composers' Concerts were continuing to attract attention and praise under Hanson's careful direction. There had been two such programs during the 1925–26 school year, and two more during the 1926–27 school year. The latter pair of concerts, however, took place in Kilbourn Hall with the Rochester Little Symphony rather than in the Eastman Theatre with the Rochester Philharmonic, as had been the done in the previous two seasons. Hanson was quickly establishing himself and his school in the forefront of championing the cause of American music. He was passionately committed to this cause and preached it whenever and wherever he could. For example, in December 1925 he was given the opportunity to speak at the Music Teachers National Association (MTNA) national convention, which was being held in Dayton, Ohio. He included this stirring challenge:

> Let us fight for a lofty American art, for a spirit of idealism and a love of beauty in a mechanistic age, for a spirit of reverence for the best of the past and a spirit of toleration and sympathy for every honest creative effort of the present—whether or not we understand it. Above all, for the development of our own American music in America.[10]

The following December, MTNA held its annual national convention in Rochester, and Hanson was once again invited to address the group. In his comments he made some interesting observations concerning American music:

> An American school in the technical sense of the word, is not likely to develop, however, because in this country we have no single set of traditions, racial characteristics, environment and consensus about creative art, but rather many separate conditions. If you want to develop music of so marked a character that you will say immediately upon hearing it, "Ah, that is American music," I do not think that you will succeed. At least I hope you won't. If, on the other hand, you mean by American music, music of many different styles, tracing origins back to many different countries and to different races, but at the same time music which could only be written by an American, you are already succeeding.[11]

---

[10] *Democrat & Chronicle*, Rochester, 10 January 1926. SML.
[11] *Democrat & Chronicle*, Rochester, 27 December 1926. SML.

In later years Hanson was certainly less receptive to different styles and different ideas. In these early years of the American Composers' Concerts, however, he seemed much more willing to embrace a broader spectrum of compositional style. Hanson's advocacy of American music may have been his single most important accomplishment as an educator. Among the many composers whose works were heard during these early years were Randall Thompson, Roy Harris, Aaron Copland, Quincy Porter, Leo Sowerby, and Bernard Rogers, to name but a few.

The end of the 1926–27 school year brought a close to Hanson's first three years as director of the Eastman School of Music. The school had grown immeasurably under his leadership during that period of time, with increased collegiate enrollment (especially for the degree program), improvement to the curriculum and the school's facilities, and many significant additions to the faculty. There is every indication to assume that he had the cooperation of his faculty, and he certainly had the confidence and support of Rush Rhees and George Eastman. Many years later Hanson remarked that "President Rhees was much more like a father to me than an employer."[12] His relations with Eastman were understandably different:

> For Mr. Eastman I had also great affection and admiration certainly not un-mixed with awe and hero-worship. We were all probably a little afraid of him. It was not merely a matter of power and money, the fact that he could with the initialing of two magic letters, G. E., wipe out the entire deficit of a school or a university; or, perhaps, in another context, change the direction of an entire community. It was more than this. It was the keenness of his mind, the quickness of his decisions. I have read frequently of men with "minds like steel traps," but I have not observed many like that of George Eastman. Perhaps he could also be ruthless in his decisions although I never saw or experienced such a trait personally.[13]

In 1927 it was still Mr. Eastman's school, and Howard Hanson was wise in understanding that fact.

---

[12] Howard Hanson. "Music Was a Spiritual Necessity," in *The University of Rochester Library Bulletin*, 26, no. 3 (Spring 1971): 83.
[13] Ibid.

Chapter 13

1927–1932
The Eastman School during
George Eastman's Final Years

Howard Hanson had accomplished a great deal in his first three years as director of the Eastman School of Music. He did so with the full cooperation of Rush Rhees and the quiet support of George Eastman. Eastman would now begin quietly to withdraw from much of the everyday operation of the school, limiting his active involvement to the challenges now confronting the theater and its orchestra. For the school's director, the first important order of business at the start of the 1927–28 school year was the establishment of a graduate department that would offer curricula leading to the master of music and master of arts degrees. The admission of doctoral students did not occur until the fall of 1931, when the Eastman School was authorized by the Committee of Graduate Studies of the University to accept candidates for the degree doctor of philosophy in music.[1] The new department opened with six students who were candidates for master's degrees, as well as postgraduate students who were not pursuing degree study. All graduate students at the time worked under Hanson's direct supervision. The department grew rapidly during the next several years. Enrollment for the master's degree rose to nine students in 1928–29, sixteen in 1929–30, and twenty-seven in 1930–31. The number of non-degree postgraduate students similarly increased each year.

It was also determined at this time that total enrollment should be limited to 2,000, of whom 400 would be degree students. In retrospect it was overly optimistic to assume that the school could sustain an enrollment of 1,600 preparatory and special students. As a matter of fact, enrollment of these students had been steadily

---

[1]   The doctor of musical arts degree was not introduced until the early 1950s.

declining since the 1923–24 school year, when it had reached 1,667. The 1927–28 school year saw a somewhat more realistic total of 1,347. But troubles lay over the horizon with the deepening economic crisis that was leading the country into the Great Depression. The number of preparatory and special students fell from 1,310 in 1927–28 to 1,095 the following year. The downward spiral worsened as enrollment dropped to 897 in 1929–30 and then to 816 in 1930–31. The worst was yet to come, however, with numbers of preparatory and special students finally reaching an all-time low of 417 in 1934–35, a far cry from the planned level of 1,600 students. With many wage-earners out of work and with families unable to pay for basic necessities such as their mortgage, Eastman lessons for their children became an unaffordable luxury.

The downward trend in enrollment must have been a great concern to Raymond Wilson, but he did not waver at all in his commitment to this area of the Eastman School's mission. Throughout his twenty-six years as director, Wilson provided exceptionally strong leadership for the Preparatory Department. Prior to assuming overall responsibility for preparatory and special students in September 1927, he had been "supervisor" of piano. Since piano students represented a very large percentage of the enrollment, Wilson had really served as the *de facto* director since his arrival at Eastman in 1921. As early as 1922 he introduced for the preparatory students what were known as "practice recitals" as a means of encouraging his faculty to achieve the very best in the area of student performances. These generally took place each Wednesday afternoon in the large classroom on the school's second floor. Students who had been recommended by their teacher had to perform for the faculty, who voted on the quality of the performance. The object of these practice recitals was to earn the right to participate in a Kilbourn Hall recital. The system allowed students to participate in what was known as a Public Recital if they obtained 50 percent of the faculty vote in the practice recital, and to participate in what was known as an Honor Recital if they obtained 80 percent of the faculty vote.

Wilson controlled these practice recitals very carefully, even to the extent of eventually using assigned seating for his faculty. He personally tabulated the voting, often working late into the night to accomplish this task. Faculty members who were found to be in disagreement with a vast majority of their colleagues were often asked to justify or explain their vote. This system of practice recitals and faculty voting eventually led to the development of Wilson's annual reports in which he tabulated statistics in twenty-one different categories, and then ranked the faculty according to an elaborate point system. Anonymity was guaranteed by identifying the faculty members by number only, but the system permitted each teacher to see his or her own performance in relation to that of colleagues in the department. All of this allowed Wilson to retain a very tight control over the department's faculty, and it is hardly surprising that the faculty almost always called him "Mr. Wilson" rather than Raymond.

The precipitous decline in Preparatory Department enrollment as the depression deepened in the United States was not his only concern. He was also director of the Eastman School's summer session, where enrollment was similarly affected by economic hardship. Enrollment in the summer of 1926 was 535 but had dropped to only 382 five years later. Regular collegiate enrollment, however, did not suffer any similar decline. As a matter of fact, the number of collegiate students actually rose into the early 1930s, reaching a level of 455 by the 1930–31 school year and climbing to 481 the following year. Not only were the numbers gratifying, but equally encouraging was the geographic area from which the school was drawing its student body. In its earliest years, the Eastman School of Music was primarily a regional institution with significant numbers of students coming from New York State, including many from the Rochester area itself. By 1930 members of the student body came from thirty-six states, including 79 percent from outside Rochester and 59 percent from beyond New York State, plus a handful from several foreign countries. This was a welcome development, especially welcome in the face of economic hard times. The Eastman School could hardly claim to be an institution of international or even national stature if its student body continued to reflect a heavy concentration of upstate New Yorkers.

The fact that collegiate enrollment did not decline in the face of the economic hardships being experienced by Americans at that particular time may seem rather surprising. However, the financial situation at the school was excellent and less seriously affected by the stock market crash and subsequent economic problems. The market value of the Eastman endowment actually rose steadily through June 1931:

June 30, 1927	$2,715,913.06
June 30, 1928	$2,820,761.25
June 30, 1929	$2,974,990.09
June 30, 1930	$3,157,811.15
June 30, 1931	$3,259,700.65

During 1931–32 the endowment declined by about a quarter million dollars, but its market value still remained in excess of $3,000,000. During this period of time from 1927 through 1932, the endowment provided an average of $178,500 in usable income each year that could be applied towards annual expenses averaging about $600,000. In other words, the endowment was providing about 30 percent of needed annual revenue. There were deficits, however, but only twice during the six-year period. The first occurred during 1927–28 and was entirely due to an expenditure of $102,000 for construction, which left the school with a $49,070.10 deficit for the fiscal year. The second deficit year was 1931–32, when expenditures exceeded income by $46,583.65. However, total income for the other four years during this six-year period of time exceeded expenses by $235,463.70. It is obvious that the Eastman School had the necessary resources to meet its obligations and to ensure that there would be no decrease in collegiate enrollment.

The difficult economic times also contributed to the return of the Eastman Theatre for full use by the Eastman School of Music. Although Paramount Pictures Corporation had signed a ten-year lease in 1928, the theater's "career" as a movie house was now at an end. Regular shows were discontinued on April 2, 1931, and the following January negotiation began with the University of Rochester to relieve Paramount of its obligations under the lease it had signed less than four years earlier. An agreement was finally signed on March 1, 1932, and control over the use of the theater now reverted back to the school. At the end of the 1931–32 school year, Hanson commented that having the full use of the theater was of great benefit to the operation of the Eastman School of Music, adding that it had previously "been difficult to provide opportunities for the adequate presentation of such large school ensembles as the Eastman School chorus . . . and the Eastman School orchestra."[2]

The school was not entirely free from the movie business, however. It remained involved with the Piccadilly Theater on Clinton Avenue, for which the school was receiving a substantial annual rent. Regorson Corporation had transferred its Clinton Avenue property to the Eastman School of Music in 1931, but it was not dissolved as a corporation until the spring of 1935, at which time it still owed the school over $50,000. The school also retained its connection with the Regent Theater on East Avenue, which it

[2]   Howard Hanson, *Report of the Director of the Eastman School of Music* (Rochester, May 1932). SML.

owned through the East Avenue Amusement Corporation. In addi-tion, the school held the mortgage on the sale of the Gordon Theater in 1932. The complex series of agreements and purchases made in the 1920s, which heavily involved the Eastman School of Music in many of Rochester's movie houses, is a fascinating chapter in the school's history. It is highly likely, however, that Howard Hanson was relieved to see the school gradually becoming disengaged from the distraction of these business enterprises.

With consistent numbers of collegiate students entering the school throughout these years of economic hardship, Hanson's principal challenge during this period of time was maintaining a strong faculty. New to the faculty in September 1927 were Rufus Arey and William Street. Arey came to Rochester to replace Otto Conrad as principal clarinet in the Rochester Philharmonic Orchestra and as teacher of clarinet at the Eastman School. Unlike Conrad, who was European-born and European-trained, Arey was thoroughly American, born in Maine and educated in Boston. Prior to coming to Rochester, he had played with the Philadelphia Orchestra and with the Detroit Symphony. William Street and his brother Stanley were the percussionists in the Eastman Theatre Orchestra and the Rochester Philharmonic Orchestra, and they were favorites of Eastman Theatre concertgoers for many years. "Bill" Street spent forty years on the Eastman faculty.

The 1928–29 school year saw the appointment of Gustav Soderlund to the theory faculty. Born and educated in Sweden, he had traveled far from his homeland to become director of the Conservatory of Music in Valparaiso, Chile. He spent three years studying at the University of Kansas, where he also taught for a while, and then came to the Eastman School, where he earned his master of music degree, subsequently teaching at the school for twenty-six years. Also joining the faculty in September 1928 was Paul White, a graduate of the New England Conservatory. He had studied composition with G. W. Chadwick and violin with Felix Winternitz, the concertmaster of the Boston Symphony Orchestra, before spending three years with the great Belgian violin virtuoso Eugène Ysaÿe (1858–1931). White was a member of the Cincinnati Symphony and then the Rochester Philharmonic before being named assistant conductor of the Rochester Civic Orchestra. He joined the Eastman faculty as a teacher of violin and later became one of the school's principal orchestral conductors.

Paul White was a familiar figure to the Rochester public because of a degree of notoriety he gained through his marriage to Josephine Kryl. She was the daughter of Bohumir Kryl, the famous cornet virtuoso and noted bandmaster. Josephine was an incredibly gifted violinist and was sent by her father to study with Ysaÿe, living with the Ysaÿe family in Belgium prior to the First World War. Kryl was determined that his daughter should have every opportunity to develop her own musical career and offered her $100,000 if she remained unmarried until her thirtieth birthday.[3] But Josephine had other ideas and eloped with Paul White, whom she had met in 1918 when they were both studying with Ysaÿe in Cincinnati. Their marriage took place in September 1922, and the reconciliation with Bohumir Kryl did not take place for several years. Rochester papers gleefully seized on this human interest story in January 1924 with headlines such as "$100,000 Eloper Unforgiven,"[4] reporting that Kryl's anger with his daughter had not softened.

The 1929–30 school year witnessed two particularly significant faculty appointments, Allen Irvine McHose and Bernard Rogers. As the long-time chair of the theory department, McHose was well known to many generations of Eastman students, and his theory text (affectionately known among students as the "Green Bible") was very much a part of Eastman student life. Before turning his energies toward music, McHose had earned a bachelor of science degree from Franklin and Marshall College in 1923, and had taught chemistry and mathematics at the Moravian Parochial School in Bethlehem, Pennsylvania. He then came to Eastman, earning his bachelor's degree in 1927 and his master's degree two years later. Hanson appointed him chair of the department in 1931, a post he held until his retirement in 1967. Bernard Rogers joined the faculty as a teacher of theory and composition. In later years he also taught orchestration and wrote a fine textbook on that subject. Like McHose, his initial professional training was not in music, but he was drawn towards the life of a composer and studied with Ernest Bloch, Percy Goetschius, Frank Bridge (1879–1941), and Nadia Boulanger (1887–1979). In 1916 Rogers was awarded a Pulitzer Traveling Scholarship at Columbia University, and he was also the recipient of a Guggenheim Fellowship in 1927–29, just prior to his appointment to the Eastman faculty.

---

[3] Josephine White's son-in-law, Milan Yancich (who taught French horn at Eastman from 1957 to 1992), claimed that the amount was $50,000 rather than the $100,000 amount reported in local newspapers; cf. Milan Yancich, *An Orchestral Musician's Odyssey* (Rochester: Wind Music Inc.), 140.
[4] *Journal*, Rochester, 20 January 1924. SML.

Two other new faculty appointments in 1929 were William Larson and Nicholas Konraty. Larson came to Eastman to serve as the psychologist and was responsible for maintaining, administering, and preserving the Seashore Tests long after anyone else at the school seemed to attached any relevance to them. Larson became a member of the public school music faculty, being the only full-time appointee in that department until the 1960s. He came to Eastman with impressive academic credentials, having earned a bachelor of fine arts degree from the University of Nebraska, a master of arts degree in music education from Columbia University, and a doctor of philosophy degree in the psychology of music from the University of Iowa. Nicholas Konraty, who joined the voice department, had been trained at the Moscow Conservatory and had sung at the Moscow Opera. After leaving Russia he pursued further study in Italy and sang various operatic roles in many European opera houses. Also appointed to the voice faculty in 1929 was Leroy Morlock, a Canadian who had graduated from the Kitchener Conservatory and who was working towards completion of his master's degree at Eastman. Both Konraty and Morlock enjoyed long careers at Eastman, the former retiring in 1957 after twenty-eight years on the faculty, and the latter retiring in 1967 after thirty-eight years of teaching.

Several other faculty appointees from this period of time deserve mention, the first being Charles Riker, who was hired to teach English in September 1930. Riker had earned his bachelor's degree from Kenyon College and his master's from Princeton University, and he later became secretary of the Eastman School, head of the humanities department, and director of the Preparatory Department (succeeding Raymond Wilson in that position when Wilson retired in 1953). He was a man of immense knowledge and cultural curiosity, with a deep appreciation for music. Another appointee to the Eastman faculty who also had a great love for music was Jessie Hoskam Kneisel, who was hired to teach German. A native of Rochester, she received her undergraduate and graduate degrees in German and History from the University of Rochester, and later earned a doctorate from Columbia University. Her influence on countless numbers of students during her forty-four years on the faculty was enormous, and she brought to her teaching an ability to make the study of German an absolute joy to all of her students, even those with little real affinity or aptitude for the language. The affection that her students felt for her was immeasurable.

Also hired in 1931 was harpist Eileen Malone, whose fifty-eight-year tenure on the faculty may be a record never to be equaled or broken.[5] Born in nearby Victor, New York, Malone attended the Eastman School of Music and studied with Lucile Johnson Bigelow, graduating with her bachelor's degree in 1928. She then continued her studies in Paris with Marcel Tournier and in New York with Marcel Grandjany (1891–1975). In 1936 she became the principal harpist of the Rochester Philharmonic Orchestra and remained in that position for forty-three years. When she died in 1999, a link with Rochester's musical past was gone, since she was the last of the Eastman faculty members who had personal recollections of George Eastman himself and of the planning and construction of the school and theater.

One further faculty appointee perhaps needs a brief mention, and that would be Ralph Davis, who was hired in 1932 to teach physical education for the undergraduate men. For twenty-seven years he was a presence in the gymnasium on the ninth floor of Annex II, presiding over innumerable volleyball games except when he was otherwise occupied with a tough game of bridge in the old student lounge off the main corridor. His retirement in 1958 was mourned by many students who appreciated his relatively low-key approach to physical fitness for musicians.

Faculty appointments and dealing with economic hard times were not the only issues occupying Howard Hanson's time and energy. An important agenda item was the continuation of the annual American Composers' Concerts. The series celebrated its fifth anniversary during the 1929–30 school year with concerts on December 19 and May 1. During that five-year period a total of 183 works had been performed, including important compositions by Ernst Bacon, George Chadwick, Aaron Copland, Henry Cowell, Howard Hanson, Roy Harris, Douglas Moore, Quincy Porter, Bernard Rogers, Leo Sowerby, William Grant Still, and Randall Thompson. In honor of the fifth anniversary, messages of congratulations were received from many people including George Chadwick, the director of the New England Conservatory; Ossip Gabrilowitsch, conductor of the Detroit Symphony; Walter Damrosch, former conductor of the New York Symphony; Serge Koussevitzky, conductor of the Boston Symphony Orchestra; and John Erskine, president of the Juilliard Foundation. From Columbia University, Daniel Gregory Mason commented, "All who love

---

[5]   Some sources suggest that Eileen Malone began teaching harp in the Eastman School's Preparatory Department in 1930, in which case her tenure at the school would be fifty-nine years.

EASTMAN SCHOOL OF MUSIC
Of The University of Rochester

ℜ

FESTIVAL OF
AMERICAN MUSIC

*In commemoration of the tenth
anniversary of the founding of
the Eastman School of Music*

DR. HOWARD HANSON
Director

MAY 19 TO MAY 22
1931

Figure 47. Program (cover) for the first Festival of American Music,
19–22 May 1931.

music and all who love the finer side of the American spirit owe to this work a debt of gratitude."[6]

The American Composers' Concerts continued the following year, but with the important addition of a Festival of American Music, which was held on four days in May in commemoration of the tenth anniversary of the founding of the Eastman School of Music. The festival opened with an Eastman Theatre concert featuring music of Daniel Gregory Mason, David Stanley Smith, Herbert Elwell, and Howard Hanson, performed by the Eastman School Orchestra and Eastman School Chorus. The following evening various Eastman School ensembles—such as the Eastman School Little Symphony[7] and the Eastman School Woodwind Quintet—presented a recital of chamber works in Kilbourn Hall. On May 21 Hanson conducted members of the Rochester Philharmonic Orchestra in music of Chadwick, Sowerby, Royce, Thompson, and Wagenaar, and the Festival concluded on May 22 with presentations of William Grant Still's ballet *Sahdji* and Bernard Rogers' lyric drama *The Marriage of Aude.* The Festival of American Music of May 1931 inaugurated a series that would continue as an annual event until 1970.

Connected with the American Composers' Concerts and the new American Music Festival was a project of publishing some of the works that had been performed. By the end of 1932, a total of thirteen such works had been published by the Eastman School of Music:

Solilioquy for Flute and Strings	Bernard Rogers
Ukrainian Suite	Quincy Porter
Medieval Poem for Organ and Orchestra	Leo Sowerby
Suite of *Four Ironics*	Leo Sowerby
Darker America	William Grant Still
The Pageant of P.T. Barnum	Douglas Moore
The 144th Psalm for Voice and Orchestra	Eric DeLamarter
Ballet Suite—*The Happy Hypocrite*	Herbert Elwell
Rip Van Winkle Overture	George Chadwick
Symphonic Poem—*Far Ocean*	Edward Royce
Symphony No. 1	Randall Thompson
Divertimento	Bernard Wagenaar
Symphony No. 2, "Romantic"	Howard Hanson

[6]   American Composers' Concerts / Anniversary Concert / Eighteenth Program, 1 May 1930, unpaginated. SML.
[7]   Eastman School Little Symphony was the name given on the program for the Phi Mu Alpha Little Symphony. This was a student chamber orchestra, founded by the fraternity in 1926 and conducted by Karl Van Hoesen.

In later years the commitment towards supporting the work of American composers came to include also a series of recordings, a project first realized in 1939 in collaboration with RCA Victor.

Meanwhile, the Eastman School continued to profit from its agreements with WHAM. In September 1929, WHAM became the first independent station in the United States to produce regularly a commercial program for distribution by the National Broadcasting Corporation when they inaugurated a series of weekly concerts by the Rochester Civic Orchestra. In January 1931, the Eastman School Orchestra began a series of twenty half-hour concerts that were broadcast by WHAM over the NBC network on Wednesday afternoons at 4:00. Hanson conducted the first of these broadcasts, which featured the *Marriage of Figaro* Overture of Mozart and the final three movements of Beethoven's Symphony No. 7. This series of broadcasts continued during the 1931–32 school year, commencing with five programs featuring student chamber music ensembles. The series of student chamber music programs was followed by twenty weekly broadcasts featuring the Eastman School Orchestra conducted by Samuel Belov, the Eastman School Chorus conducted by Herman Genhart, and various smaller ensembles conducted by Paul White. The major offering among these concerts were two programs on March 9 and March 16 devoted to a performance of the *Missa Solemnis* of Beethoven. Also worthy of mention was a concert on October 23, 1931, which was the first international broadcast of American music to Germany and Austria. The program, consisting of music by Bernard Wagenaar, Leo Sowerby, Herbert Elwell, and Howard Hanson, was relayed to Berlin for distribution to stations in central Europe.

One can imagine that George Eastman viewed all of these wonderful accomplishments with quiet satisfaction. He had celebrated his seventy-seventh birthday during the summer of 1931 amid growing concerns for his health. His physical deterioration had been diagnosed at the Mayo Clinic as involving a hardening of the cells in his lower spinal cord, a condition that made walking an extremely painful experience. His physician and friend, Dr. Audley Stewart, advised him that his condition was irreversible and likely to worsen as time went on. As his decline continued Eastman made fewer and fewer visits to his office on State Street, and the once flourishing social life in his home was reduced to only a handful of close friends and acquaintances. One day he asked the Rev. George Norton, Rector of St. Paul's Episcopal Church on East Avenue, what he thought of suicide. On another occasion he told Norton that he felt there was not much to live for anymore. He quizzed Dr. Stewart about various poisons and at one point asked him to precisely tell him where his heart was located. On March 4, 1932, Eastman returned his key to the Eastman School garage on Swan Street, attaching a note saying that he would not need it any longer. The following day he signed a supplemental agreement with the University of Rochester, modifying a few details of his original agreement dated July 10, 1919. The most important of these changes involved a clarification of the method by which members would be selected for the school's Board of Managers. Eastman had originally reserved for himself the right to select people for the Board of Managers, subject to the approval of the University's Trustees. The new agreement simply made provision for this selection after Eastman's death:

> All members of said Board of Managers shall be selected by the party of the first part [i.e., George Eastman] during his lifetime with the approval of said Board of Trustees; thereafter all members of said Board of Managers shall be selected by said Board of Trustees, except that any vacancies in said Board of Managers may be filled by the remaining members of said Board of Managers with the approval of said Board of Trustees.[8]

The day after signing this supplemental agreement, Eastman asked Kodak attorney Milton K. Robinson for assistance in drawing up new codicils to his will. Except for a number of personal bequests, most notably to his niece, Ellen Dryden, and her children, the bulk of his estate (including his house) was to go to the University of Rochester. With this decision he excluded Cornell and M.I.T., which had been named as beneficiaries in the earlier version of his will. Harold Gleason visited with Eastman on Sunday, March 13. As he was leaving Eastman said, "Goodbye Harold," and then added, "Don't let anything happen to the School."[9] The following day, after conducting some Kodak-related business, George Eastman lay down on his bed and pointed the muzzle of a gun precisely to the spot on his chest that Audley Stewart had previously indicated to him as being the exact location of his heart. He died of a self-inflicted gunshot wound at 12:50 p.m. on March 14, 1932, leaving behind a note that simply stated:

[8]   Supplemental Agreement, 5 March 1932. SML.
[9]   Harold Gleason, "Please Play My Funeral March," *University of Rochester Library Bulletin* 26, no. 3 (Spring 1971): 122.

To my friends
My work is done—
Why wait?
GE

Eastman's funeral took place at St. Paul's Episcopal Church on Thursday, March 17, at 3:30 in the afternoon. Classes were canceled at the University of Rochester, and various local businesses showed their respect by closing for the day. At precisely 3:30 p.m. the lights in all of Rochester's movie theaters were dimmed for one minute, and the bell at City Hall was struck seventy-seven times, once for each year of Eastman's life. The funeral service was broadcast throughout the country by WHAM. Harold Gleason and the Kilbourn Quartet performed at the funeral, and among Gleason's selections was the *Marche romaine* by Gounod, a work that Eastman especially liked. The last time Eastman had heard Gleason play it was during the summer months of 1930. Forty years later, Harold Gleason recalled that moment:

> He was sitting at his breakfast table as if in deep thought. Suddenly he called our in a firm voice, "Harold, please play my funeral march." When I finished he fairly shouted, "We'll give 'em hell when they carry me out the front door."[10]

On March 18, the day following the funeral, the Eastman School presented a concert in the Eastman Theatre "in memoriam George Eastman," which featured a performance of the Beethoven *Missa Solemnis* with Herman Genhart conducting the Eastman School Chorus and Eastman School Orchestra. A civic memorial service was held on Wednesday of the following week. It opened with a performance of the "Good Friday Music" from Wagner's *Parsifal* performed by the Rochester Civic Orchestra. Speeches were offered by Mayor Charles S. Owens, President Rush Rhees, and Roland B. Woodward, who represented Rochester's community interests. In addition to the performance of Wagner by the Rochester Civic Orchestra, music was provided by the Kilbourn Quartet, by Harold Gleason, and by Howard Hanson conducting the school's orchestra and chorus.

In the years to come the word "suicide" was rarely mentioned in connection with Eastman's death. Rochester was a conservative place and it remained "George Eastman's town" long after his death. When Henry Clune, a local newspaper columnist and

---

[10] Ibid., 122–24.

author, wrote a novel based upon Eastman's life and death,[11] it was not well received by many Rochesterians, who found the author's use of the Eastman story to be quite distasteful. It is said that several local bookstores refused to carry the book.

For Howard Hanson and his colleagues at the Eastman School of Music, the death of George Eastman was deeply felt. Of all of his charitable interests, the music school was the one in which Eastman was most actively involved and the one which obviously provided him with the greatest satisfaction and pleasure. Perhaps in 1918 his interest had been solely to prevent Alf Klingenberg's school from sliding into bankruptcy. Within a relatively short period of time, however, Eastman was deeply involved in all aspects of planning for the new music school and theater. No part of the design for the buildings was too inconsequential to avoid his careful scrutiny. No decision could be made without at least his tacit approval. He was interested in every aspect of the school and theater from the initial designs up to and including all of the finishing details, and it was his vision and his philosophy that provided the sense of purpose and direction for the entire enterprise.

Eastman's interest and involvement showed no signs of lessening after the school and theater opened in 1921 and 1922 respectively. He was not only a member of the school's Board of Managers but also had sole authority for nominating others to serve on the board. While such nominations required the approval of the university trustees, it would have been foolhardy to assume that the trustees would have opposed any Eastman nominee. He sought and obtained authorization from the University of Rochester to make decisions concerning the management of the theater. The corporation that controlled the various local movie houses was in turn controlled by Eastman himself. It was Eastman who dismissed the school's first director. It was Eastman who dismissed the first conductor of the Rochester Philharmonic Orchestra. None of this is intended to suggest that he was ruthless or unfair. Compared with many of his contemporaries, Eastman was probably fairer than most. But he had a passionate interest in the music school and wished to remain actively involved in its management and direction. Advancing years and ill health eventually lessened his presence and influence at the school, but everyone still understood who was really in charge. It was "Mr. Eastman's School" and remained so until his death in 1932.

---

[11] Henry W. Clune, *By His Own Hand* (New York: MacMillan, 1952).

Howard Hanson was only thirty-five years old at the time of George Eastman's death, and in the eighth year of his directorship of the Eastman School. During those first eight years Hanson had provided strong leadership and vision for the school, but he had done so under the watchful eye of both George Eastman and Rush Rhees. Eastman was now gone, and Rhees was to retire in just a few years. However, Hanson had thirty-two more years of leadership as director of the Eastman School of Music. If it had been "Mr. Eastman's School" up until 1932, it would be "Mr. Hanson's School" for the next thirty-two years. Howard Hanson was now essentially in full command of the school's destiny. The story of his accomplishments from 1932 until his retirement in 1964 is no less remarkable than the story of George Eastman and the events that led to the founding of the Eastman School of Music in 1921 and its rapid advance to a position of preeminent leadership in American music education.

A Parallel Development

Chapter 14

Hiram W. Sibley and His Music Library

The Sibley Music Library has a history that predates the opening of the Eastman School of Music by seventeen years. Established in 1904 through the generosity of Hiram W. Sibley, it was initially a part of the University of Rochester's library collection on the old Prince Street campus. The founding of the library was a very noteworthy event, for there were only a few music collections of real significance anywhere in the United States at that time. Among the few were those in the Library of Congress, the Newberry Library in Chicago, the New York and Boston Public Libraries, the Harvard and Yale University libraries, plus several much smaller conservatory libraries such as those at Oberlin, New England, Peabody, and Cincinnati. It was, therefore, quite an accomplishment for the University of Rochester to acquire a significant music collection, especially since at that time in its history it did not have a music school or even a music department.

The family that gave its name to the Sibley Music Library was one of Rochester's most affluent and influential. The patriarch of the clan was Hiram Sibley, who was born in North Adams, Massachusetts, in 1807. At the age of sixteen he moved to the Genesee River valley in upstate New York. Although he had little formal education, Sibley proved to be a shrewd businessman and successfully pursued various real estate and banking interests in Rochester and the surrounding area. At one point he was even elected sheriff of Monroe County. Sibley's most important business venture, however, was to lead a group of investors in the merger of their small telegraph companies with those of Ezra Cornell. This merger led to the formation of Western Union, a corporation for which Sibley served as president. Not content with his success in the telegraph business, he also pursued other business ventures, investing in timber and lumber as well as the mining of salt and coal. All of these initiatives made the Sibley family one of the wealthiest in upstate New York.[1]

Hiram Sibley used his money to help Ezra Cornell found Cornell University, where he served as one of the original trustees. It was through Sibley's generosity that the Sibley College of Mechanical Engineering opened at Cornell in 1871.[2] Then he provided the largest share of funds for the construction of the University of Rochester's library building on Prince Street.[3] Ground was broken for the building in 1872, but it was not dedicated until 1876. The library building, which cost nearly $100,000, was appropriately named Sibley Hall and was constructed to provide space for as many as 90,000 volumes. In the summer of 1877 the university's library collection, which had previously been housed in Anderson Hall, was moved into its new facilities.

Hiram Sibley's children (and grandchildren) were also very prominent and influential in the Rochester area. His daughter Emily married the son of his business partner, Don Alonzo Watson. Emily Sibley Watson is best remembered for establishing the Memorial Art Gallery in memory of James Averill, her son by a previous marriage. She also had a major role in the establishment of the Hochstein Music School,[4] which opened its doors to eager music students in October 1920. Emily's brother, Hiram Watson Sibley, was quite unlike his self-made father; he had received a thorough education, earning a doctorate in Heidelberg in 1869 and his jurisprudence degree from Columbia in 1871. He practiced law for seventeen years in New York City, but returned to Rochester to manage the family estate and business ventures after his father died in 1888. He soon became one of the most important supporters and donors to the University of Rochester, providing funds for the university's electrical system, for central heating, and for various improvements in the library building that bore his father's name.

---

[1]   The Hiram Sibley family should not be confused with the Rufus Sibley family, which owned and operated Sibley's Department Store, for many years the largest and most prominent store of its kind in Rochester.
[2]   The Sibley College merged with the College of Civil Engineering in 1919 and is now known as the Sibley School of Mechanical and Aerospace Engineering.
[3]   The library building was perhaps the most architecturally significant building on the Prince street campus, being modeled after a section of the Louvre in Paris, France. Unfortunately, the building was sold and later demolished, and the site is now occupied by the Rochester headquarters of the American Red Cross.
[4]   The David Hochstein Music School Settlement was granted a provisional charter by the State of New York on September 3, 1920. It continues to fulfill an important role in the musical education of the Rochester community.

At some point in time, Sibley made the acquaintance of Elbert Newton, who was the organist at Central Presbyterian Church in Rochester. In addition to his work at the church, Newton functioned as a local impresario to the wealthy by arranging musicales for social events taking place in the homes of some of Rochester's most affluent families. Sensing Sibley's keen interest in music, he approached him with a suggestion that there was a need in Rochester for a music library. Sibley thought that the suggestion was an excellent one and agreed to finance the project if Newton would serve as his agent in procuring suitable material. As there was no public library or music school in Rochester at the time, he decided that the proposed music collection should be given to the University of Rochester and housed in Sibley Hall as a circulating library for the use of the people of Rochester.

In preparing to assemble such a music collection, Newton received valuable assistance and advice from Philip Hale of the *Boston Herald* and Henry Krehbiel[5] of the *New York Tribune*, both of whom were European-trained music critics. With their assistance Newton assembled a collection of about 2,000 volumes, in the process spending roughly $3,000 of Sibley's money. After it was purchased by Newton and given to the University of Rochester, it was housed in several alcoves in the southwest corner of Sibley Hall. When established in 1904, the new music collection was named the "Sibley Musical Library," a name that persisted until the late 1930s, when it was officially changed to "Sibley Music Library."

The first printed catalogue for the music collection was issued by the University of Rochester in 1906, and it offers an interesting glimpse at the kind of books and music that were considered to be a basic part of a music library at the beginning of twentieth century. In a category entitled "General Music," the acquisitions included such diverse items as George Ashdown Audsley's *The Art of Organ Building*, P. Suitbertus Birkle's *A Complete and Practical Method of the Solesmes Plain Chant*, Tobias Matthay's *The Act of Touch in All Its Diversity*, Ernest Newman's *Musical Studies*, Robert Schumann's *Music and Musicians*, Richard Wagner's *On Conducting*, and C. M. Widor's *Technique of the Modern Orchestra*. General reference works included the expected *Baker's Biographical Dictionary of Music* and *Grove's Dictionary of Music and Musicians*, along with such works as F. J. Fétis's *Biographie universelle des musiciens et bibliographie générale*

---

[5] Krehbiel was the translator of Thayer's *The Life of Ludwig van Beethoven*, a later (1921) project for which he received generous financial backing from Hiram W. Sibley.

de la musique and Hugo Riemann's *Encyclopædic Dictionary of Music*. Acquisitions in music history included the six-volume *Oxford History of Music* and Charles Burney's *A General History of Music*, along with several specialized volumes including Oscar Bie's *History of the Pianoforte*. Musical biography included standard works about Bach (by Schweitzer and by Spitta), Beethoven (by Thayer), Brahms (by Riemann), Chopin (by Liszt), Haydn (by Leopold Schmidt), etc. The area of music theory was represented by several books of both Ebenezer Prout and Percy Goetschius, and by other standard works such as the *Treatise on Modern Instrumentation and Orchestration* of Hector Berlioz.

Music acquired by Newton for the library included miniature scores, arrangements of orchestral works, opera and vocal scores, oratorios and masses, songs and song collections, a generous amount of piano music and violin music, works for cello, some chamber music, and organ music. The acquired miniature scores represented a basic collection of late-eighteenth- and nineteenth-century orchestral works, including scores to all nine Beethoven symphonies, some of the orchestral compositions of Berlioz, the symphonies of Brahms and Schumann, and selected works of Mozart, Schubert, and Mendelssohn. There was a somewhat larger collection of arrangements of orchestral works, principally for piano four-hands, which included Beethoven, Berlioz, Bizet, Brahms, Dvořák, Elgar, Franck, Gade, Goldmark, Grieg, Handel, Liszt, Mahler, Mendelssohn, Mozart, Schubert, Schumann, Sinding, Smetana, Richard Strauss, and Tchaikovsky. Playing such arrangements was not only a useful tool for music study but also an extremely popular pastime among music lovers and amateur pianists.

The collection of opera and vocal scores included works of Beethoven, Bizet, Boito, Debussy, Donizetti, Gluck, Gounod, Lalo, Massenet, Mendelssohn, Meyerbeer, Mozart, Offenbach, Puccini, Rossini, Saint-Saëns, Verdi, and Wagner, plus a number of other less stellar composers. As might be expected, because of the popularity of the piano, the collection of piano music was especially large and comprehensive, covering much of the repertoire from Bach to Fauré and Debussy. The collection of violin works was also broadly representative of the repertoire. However, Newton's acquisition of organ music was curiously limited to the works of Johann Sebastian Bach.

About a decade later, Newton was once again asked by Hiram W. Sibley to act as his agent in procuring additional material for the Sibley Musical Library. Sibley's interest in the collection around

1918 may have been motivated at least in part by the rapid development of Alf Klingenberg's school and its acquisition by George Eastman. At this time Newton was no longer living in Rochester, being employed by the New York Public Library. Nonetheless, he operated as Sibley's agent and purchased large quantities of music by contemporary French, Spanish, and Russian composers. These acquisitions were highly important in enhancing the growing reputation of the Sibley Musical Library collection.

Perhaps even more significant was Newton's purchase between 1918 and 1921 of several important antiquarian collections. Prominent among these acquisitions was the Harry P. Kreiner collection of Russian folk songs and liturgical music, which also included a rich selection of contemporary Russian editions of composers such as Rimsky-Korsakov, Mussorgsky, Glinka, Tchaikovsky, Borodin, Stravinsky, etc. Newton also procured a significant portion of Martin Fleming's library of rare literature on the violin. The third collection acquired by the Sibley Musical Library was a large part of Oscar Sonneck's library of the collected works of Palestrina, Schütz, Lassus, Sweelinck, etc., which also included many books of music history and criticism.

The construction of the new Eastman School of Music was happening at about the same time that Newton was making these important new acquisitions. In retrospect his most recent purchases almost seemed to have been made with the new school in mind. Hiram W. Sibley had established his music library for the use of the people of Rochester, but early editions of Vivaldi and the collected works of Orlando de Lassus would certainly be more appropriate for the scholar or the serious student of music than for the local amateur musician. Whether Sibley or Newton had this in mind is uncertain. However, what was obvious to everyone at the time was the Mr. Sibley's library really belonged in Mr. Eastman's school, which was soon to open on Gibbs Street. But how would these two millionaires feel about such a proposal? A carefully arranged meeting between the two philanthropists happily resulted in agreement that the Sibley Musical Library should be moved from its present location on Prince Street to an appropriate location in the new school building on Gibbs Street. Therefore, arrangements were hastily made to provide an adequate home for the library on the school's ground floor just off the main corridor, space initially deemed sufficient for a future collection of up to 40,000 volumes.

The transfer of the music collection to the Eastman School of Music necessitated hiring a professional librarian at the school, and in June 1922 Barbara Duncan arrived in Rochester to assume that position. She was born in Boston in 1882; her mother had been a librarian at the Boston Athenaeum. In 1907 Duncan became an assistant in the fine arts department of the Boston Public Library, and two years later she became curator of the Allen A. Brown music collection there. It was from this latter position that she was recruited to Rochester following a national search requested by George Eastman and led by Donald Gilchrist, librarian at the University of Rochester. Duncan, who signed a two-year contract in early April 1922, was to remain as librarian at Eastman until 1947; during her twenty-five years at the school she was responsible for many of the library's most important acquisitions.

Almost immediately after arriving in Rochester, Duncan decided to replace the classification system then in use by the University of Rochester library by introducing the Library of Congress system. The Sibley Musical Library was among the first in the country to adopt this change for classifying music and music literature. During her second year as librarian, University Librarian Donald Gilchrest made an important purchase that would greatly enrich the collections: the library of Arthur Pougin, the music and drama critic of *Le Ménestrel* from 1885 to 1921. His collection included a significant amount of French writing on seventeenth- and eighteenth-century theater and music. The works on music, including a large and important collection of French almanacs, were added to the Sibley Musical Library. Also acquired around the same time were several early theoretical texts that were received from Europe. These included Zarlino's *Istitutioni Harmoniche* printed in Venice in 1558; Fogliani's *Musica theorica docte simul ac dilucide pertractata* printed in Venice in 1529; and Pietro Aaron's *Toscanello in Musica*. In 1923 the library acquired the manuscript of Henry Rowley Bishop's opera *Clari, or the Maid of Milan*. Included in this opera is the song "Home, Sweet Home," then considered one of the most famous songs ever written. And also at about this time the library was able to purchase a collection of annotated vocal scores that had belonged to the stage director of the Berlin Opera, Joseph Kroll; beside the important records of stage settings, markings in the scores show the versions sung by such famous singers as Ernestine Schumann-Heink.

Duncan's ability to add to the library's holdings was significantly enhanced in 1925, when Hiram W. Sibley signed an agreement with Rush Rhees to give the library $100,000, half of the amount in five equal installments for five years. The agreement stipulated that income plus portions of the principal could be used as deemed necessary for the purchase of manuscripts, books, and papers relating to music. It also stated that these funds could be used for library equipment and maintenance. Sibley encouraged Duncan to spend freely and to use the principal as quickly as possible, because he understood that the depressed economic conditions in Europe presented an unparalleled opportunity to make important purchases at bargain basement prices.

> My idea was to keep the amount as a fund and spend only the income, which in those affluent days could be counted upon to amount to about twenty-five hundred dollars a year. Mr. Sibley, however, kept urging me to spend the whole sum, saying, "There is more where that came from."[6]

By 1929 Duncan had increased the library holdings to over 29,000 volumes, which were already beginning to crowd severely the available shelving, in spite of optimistic expectations that the facilities could hold up to 40,000 volumes.

Duncan made her first important trip to Europe to purchase books for the library in 1929. She was able to acquire several important items in Berlin, including a collection of about sixty manuscript leaves dating from the tenth to the sixteenth century. These had been collected by Oskar Fleischer, an author of several important works on the subject of musical notation. In addition to the manuscript leaves, Duncan purchased thirty-five volumes of manuscript transcriptions that Fleischer had made from material in various European libraries in connection with his studies. Also procured during this trip to Europe were the eleventh-century codex now known as the Rochester Codex, which contained important musical treatises by Hermannus Contractus, William of Hirsau, Bernon, and Frutolf of Michelsberg, as well as treatises on other arts of the Middle Ages. She also purchased early sixteenth-century printings of the Masses of Josquin by Ottaviano dei Petrucci.

Duncan added several other important items to the library's collection. These included a manuscript leaf from Beethoven's sketchbook for his *Missa Solemnis* and a leaf from Mozart's holograph of his Concert-Rondo in A Major for piano and orchestra, K. 386. Another purchase was the holograph of Brahms's song "Regenlied."

---

6 Barbara Duncan. "The Sibley Music Library" in *The University of Rochester Library Bulletin* 1, no. 1 (November 1945): 27.

Figure 48. Reading room in the Sibley Music Library, later used as the student lounge and currently the location of a rehearsal hall (Room 120).

In 1931 Duncan made a second trip to Europe to take advantage once again of the depressed economic conditions that made many important items available for purchase at highly favorable prices. During this trip she established many important contacts with dealers and librarians from whom she acquired many significant items for the Sibley Musical Library, most notably a copy of the *Antiphonarium Augustense*, printed in Augsburg in 1495, and a small collection of letters from Cosima and Richard Wagner to Edward Dannreuther when he was Secretary of the London Wagner Society. By the end of 1931 Duncan was able to report that she had personally added 18,162 volumes to the library's collection, no small achievement for ten years of work.

During the years from 1926 to 1932, the library also acquired a number of holographs from former Eastman faculty member Arthur Hartmann; they included works by Benjamin Godard (*Chant et baiser*), Edward MacDowell (*To a Wild Rose* and *Will O' the Wisp*), Tivador Nachez (*Violin Concerto No. 2*), and Émile Sauret (*Farfalla*). Most important was a holograph of Claude Debussy, a transcription for violin and piano of the piano prelude *Minstrels*, which Hartmann and Debussy had performed together in Paris in 1914. On the title page Debussy had written "pour piano et Hartmann."

Barbara Duncan began her eleventh year as librarian in 1932, the year of George Eastman's death. By a strange coincidence, it proved to be Hiram W. Sibley's final year as well. He passed away in June at the age of eight-seven and was praised by Howard Hanson as being "a great and distinguished benefactor of American culture."[7] Rush Rhees also spoke eloquently in memory of this generous man who had been such a firm supporter of the University of Rochester:

> In the death of Hiram W. Sibley Rochester has lost an influence which it will take many years adequately to measure. Quiet, unobtrusive in his relation to public affairs, he has nevertheless been a powerful influence in the community for the highest standard of social and political life. His gifts in money were many and generous. Large as these are, they are exceeded by those gifts of fine influence exercised principally by example. The loss to our community is felt deeply now in the show of its debt. It can be measured only as our intelligent citizens consider year by year what he has meant to the community.[8]

[7] *Alumni Bulletin of the Eastman School of Music* 3, no. 4 (August 1932): 13.
[8] Ibid., 10.

Quite incredibly this well-educated man, who had earned his law degree and who had practiced law in New York City, had died intestate. As a result, additional funds that he had promised to the University of Rochester for the Sibley Musical Library never materialized. But the future of the library was quite secure. Its many important acquisitions had established it as a collection of major importance in the United States. The principal difficulty facing the library was that it was rapidly outgrowing the space that had been provided on the ground floor of the Eastman School. With no room to expand in its present location, the only long-term solution was the construction of a new building to house the library collection. That solution, however, lay several years in the future, a future that was now without the presence of either George Eastman or Hiram W. Sibley.

Chronology

1900   Rush Rhees becomes president of the University of Rochester.

1904–5   The Sibley Musical Library opens at the University of Rochester.

1906–7   John D. Beall opens the Rochester School of Music.

1907–8   The Rochester Conservatory of Music is incorporated in December and purchases the assets of the Rochester School of Music in March.

1908–9   The Rochester Conservatory of Music moves to new facilities on South Fitzhugh Street in the center of the city.

1912–13   Alf Klingenberg is engaged as a piano teacher at the Rochester Conservatory of Music.

1913–14   Alf Klingenberg leaves the Rochester Conservatory of Music and opens the Dossenbach-Klingenberg School of Music on Prince Street in partnership with Hermann Dossenbach.

1914–15   Oscar Gareissen becomes a partner with Klingenberg and Dossenbach, and Klingenberg's school is re-named the D.K.G. Institute of Musical Art.

1916–17   The Rochester Conservatory of Music is consolidated with the D.K.G. Institute of Musical Art.

1917–18   Alf Klingenberg becomes the sole owner of the D.K.G. Institute of Musical Art.

1918–19   George Eastman purchases the property and corporate rights of the D.K.G. Institute of Musical Art, which will now be known simply as the Institute of Musical Art.

         The University of Rochester charter is amended to allow its acquisition of the Institute of Musical Art.

         George Eastman agrees to provide the University of Rochester with a new building for its Institute of Musical Art.

1919–20   The Institute of Musical Art comes under the ownership and operation of the University of Rochester.

George Eastman signs a Memorandum of Agreement with the University of Rochester to provide buildings for a school of music and a concert and motion picture auditorium.

Land is acquired and construction begins on the new school and theater.

1920–21 Construction continues on the school and theater, both of which will bear George Eastman's name when completed.

1921–22 The Eastman School of Music, partially completed, opens in September with Alf Klingenberg as its first director.

The school officially opens to the public in March, including ceremonies observing the dedication of Kilbourn Hall.

The Sibley Musical Library moves from its former location on the Prince Street campus to its new location in the Eastman School of Music.

The first bachelor of music degrees earned by Eastman School of Music students are conferred at the June commencement exercises.

WHAM radio station begins broadcasting from the Eastman School of Music in July.

1922–23 The Eastman Theatre opens on Labor Day.

An entire week of opera is scheduled in the theater in October.

Giovanni Martinelli is featured in the first Eastman Theatre artist event.

The school's bachelor of music degree is formally registered by the Board of Regents in Albany.

The Eastman Theatre Ballet is established by Enid Knapp Botsford in February.

The inaugural concert of the Rochester Philharmonic Orchestra under the direction of Arthur Alexander takes place in the spring.

George Eastman requests and receives Arthur Alexander's resignation as conductor of the Rochester Philharmonic Orchestra.

George Eastman requests and receives Alf Klingenberg's resignation as director of the Eastman School of Music.

1923–24 Raymond Wilson becomes acting director.

A five-story theater annex opens on the east side of Swan Street.

Albert Coates and Eugene Goossens begin conducting the Rochester Philharmonic Orchestra.

The Metropolitan Opera arrives in May for the first of what will become an annual series of opera presentations in the Eastman Theatre.

1924–25   Howard Hanson arrives in Rochester to become the second director of the Eastman School of Music.

Vladimir Rosing's Rochester American Opera Company is founded with George Eastman's financial support.

Sigma Alpha Iota, My Phi Epsilon, and Phi Mu Alpha all establish chapters at the Eastman School of Music.

The first American Composers' Concert takes place in May.

1925–26   Two new dormitory buildings for women open on University Avenue.

The Eastman School of Dance and Dramatic Action opens in September under the director of Rouben Mamoulian.

Martha Graham arrives in Rochester to teach at the Eastman School of Dance and Dramatic Action.

The Eastman School of Dance and Dramatic Action closes at the end of the school year.

1926–27   A third dormitory building for women opens on University Avenue.

The Rochester-American Opera Company loses George Eastman's financial support and becomes an independent professional opera company, the American Opera Company.

1927–28   A twelve-story school annex opens on the east side of Swan Street.

The Eastman School of Music announces the establishment of a graduate department.

1928–29   Paramount Pictures Corporation takes over the operation of the Eastman Theatre.

1929–30   The American Composers' Concerts celebrate their fifth anniversary.

1930–31   The first Festival of American Music takes place in May.

1931–32   Control of the Eastman Theatre reverts back to the Eastman School of Music.

George Eastman dies of a self-inflicted gunshot wound on March 14.

Hiram W. Sibley dies in June.

Appendix 1

Members of the Institute of Musical Art Faculty, 1913–1921

The following is a listing of individuals who taught at the Institute of Musical Art during the period dating from September 1913 through June 1921. The dates of their faculty service are indicated. The listing includes teachers at the original Dossenbach-Klingenberg School of Music, the D.K.G. Institute of Musical Art, and the Institute of Musical Art, all of which were essentially the same institution functioning under evolving ownership during its eight years of existence prior to the opening of the Eastman School of Music. Annual year books (i.e., bulletins) issued by the institute provide the only reasonably accurate source of information concerning the faculty, and this listing is derived from these year books. Unfortunately, these sources provide very little information concerning teachers of percussion or woodwind and brass instruments, only indicating as a rule that such instruction is "available." Therefore, it is safe to assume that there were additional faculty members at the Institute of Musical Art who are not identified in any of the year books. The listing includes Rosita Renard, who was appointed to the faculty in 1916 but never actually taught at the institute. Members of the institute faculty who subsequently taught at the Eastman School of Music are indicated in italics.

Alexander, Arthur	*Voice*	*1918–21*
Anselmi, Guido	Languages	1917–21
Banzecar, Mlle. Gilberte	Languages	1919–20
Barbieri, Eduardo	Violin	1913–14
Belov, Samuel	*Viola*	*1920–21*
Benson, Frederick Richards	*Voice*	*1916–17, 1918–21*
Brownell, Mildred	*Piano*	*1917–21*

Call, Lucy Lee	*Voice*	*1919–21*
Castellanos, Margarita	Languages	1913–16, 1919–20
Clemens, Edna Gray	Voice	1916–17
Cooper, Mabel	*Piano*	*1913–21*
Dean, Marie	Piano	1916–17
Dossenbach, Hazel	*Violin*	*1920–21*
Dossenbach, Hermann	Violin	1913–14, 1915–17
Dossenbach, Theodore	Double Bass	1913–17
Foley, Anne	Violin	1913–14
Fuller, Jeannette	Piano, Dunning System	1913–21
Gareissen, Oscar	*Voice*	*1914–17*
Gillette, Dorothy	*Piano*	*1920–21*
Ginsberg, Bessie	Piano	1916–17
Gleason, Harold	*Organ*	*1919–21*
Griffith, Rose Cummins	*Dunning System*	*1916–17, 1918–21*
Guerne, A.	Piano	1918–19
Handry, Hermann	Wind Instruments	1916–17
Hartmann, Arthur	*Violin*	*1919–21*
Henricus, George	Viola	1913–14
Hochstein, David	Violin	1915–16
Howland, Mrs. C. A.	Voice	1915–19
Jack, Emma	Opera	1916–17
Johnson, Lucile	*Harp*	*1920–21*
Karl, Tom	Voice	1913–15
Klingenberg, Alf	*Piano*	*1913–21*
Klinzing, Ernestine	*Piano*	*1914–21*
Knauss, Effie	*Violin*	*1913–21*
Knoepke, Emil	Cello	1913–15
Kunz, Gerald	*Violin*	*1920–21*
Maas, Gerald	*Cello*	*1920–21*
McKelvie, Norma	Dunning System	1916–21
McMath, Elsie	Piano	1913–15
Morse, Leila Livingston	Voice	1914–19
Mumford, Jeanne	*Piano*	*1914–21*
O'Ryan, Anne Wynne	Drama, Elocution	1917–18
Paddon, James	Violin	1913–14
Penny, George Barlow	*Organ, History, Harmony*	*1913–21*
Pfaff, J.	Clarinet	1913–14
Polah, Andre	Violin	1919–20
Renard, Rosita	Piano	1916

Rummel, William	Violin	1916–18
Rummel, Mrs. William	Voice	1916–17
Schenck, Ludwig	*Violin, Viola*	*1913–21*
Schrader, Frank	Flute	1913–14
See, Arthur	*Piano*	*1914–21*
See, Genevieve	Languages	1920–21
Smith, Virginia	Dancing	1915–16, 1917–21
Stoll, Flora	Languages	1913–14
Suarez, Miguel	Languages	1915–16
Torrens, L.A.	Voice	1917–18
Van Halen, Mme. Tircher	Languages	1917–19
Varillat, Henri	Voice, Opera	1913–15
Vaska, Bedrich	Cello	1915–20
Warner, John Adams	Piano	1913–18
Weeks, Florence	Opera, Drama Elocution	1916–18
Werner, Clara Louise	Languages, Dunning System	1914–18
Wilbur, Laura	Voice	1915–17

Members of the Eastman School of Music Faculty, 1921–1932

The following is a listing of individuals who taught at the Eastman School of Music during the period from September 1921 through June 1932. The dates of their faculty service are indicated. Especially during the school's earliest years, this information is difficult to ascertain with absolute certainty. Various individuals may have started teaching at the school prior to being listed in any of the school's publications. Conversely, some individuals may have been listed without actually having any students whom they might be teaching. Further confusion may arise from the fact that, at this point in its history (and for many years afterward), the Eastman School of Music did not confer any academic rank nor did it clearly indicate a distinction between collegiate-level teaching and instruction offered through its Preparatory Department.

Abele, Catherine Eaton	Public School Music	1924–28
Agnisy, Karl	Double Bass	1921–22
Alexander, Arthur	Voice	1921–22
Alexander, Florence (*see* Schoenegge, Florence Alexander)		
Ames, William Thayer	Composition and Theory	1928–38
Arey, Rufus	Clarinet	1927–54
Augieras, Pierre	Piano	1921–25
Austin-Ball, Thomas	Voice	1922–43
Bacon, Ernst	Opera Department	1925–28
Balaban, Emanuel	Opera Department	1925–44
Barnett, Marjorie	Physical Education	1927–29
Barr, Grace	Public School Music, Appreciation	Summer 1925
Beckwith, Helen Hatch	Public School Music	1931–61

Belov, Samuel	Violin and Viola	1921–49
Benson, Frederick	Voice	1921–30
Berentsen, Robert	Motion Picture Organ	1923–30
Bigelow, Lucile Johnson (*see* Johnson, Lucile Bigelow)		
Biracree, Thelma	Dance	1925–26
Bishop, Eugene	Trumpet	1926–29
Bloch, Ernest	Composition	1924–25
Bonnet, Joseph	Organ	1921–23
Botsford, Enid Knapp	Ballet (Opera Department)	1924–25
Bowen, George Oscar	Public School Music	Summer 1931
Brownell, Mildred (*see* Mehlenbacher, Mildred Brownell)		
Call, Lucy Lee	Voice	1921–55
Carter, Russell	Public School Music	Summers 1930, 1931
Castellanos, Margarita	Languages	1922–23
Catalano, Lewis	Oboe	1924–25
Chamberlin, Rachel	Piano	1927–29
Clute, Sherman	Public School Music	1924–49
Coates, Albert	Opera Department, Conducting	1924–25
Colgan, Marion	Public School Music	Summer 1931
Conrad, Otto	Clarinet	1924–27
Cooper, Mabel	Piano	1921–41
Croxford, Lyndon F.	Piano	1924–47
Cummins, Anne Theodora	French	1924–66
D'Angelis, Frederick	Oboe	1925–26
D'Antalffy, Deszo	Motion Picture Organ	1922–23
Davis, Ralph	Physical Education	1931–58
Decaux, Abel	Organ	1923–37
DeLorenzo, Leonardo	Flute	1924–35
Diamond, Jerome	Piano	1926–66
Dossenbach, Hazel (*see* Smith, Hazel Dossenbach)		
Duncan, Barbara	Librarian	1922–47
Duncan, Hazel Sampson	Piano	1929–41
Dykema, Peter W.	Public School Music	Summer 1930

Eaton, Catherine	Public School Music	1924–28
Eaton, Rachel Winger	Piano	1929–32
Eccleston, Marion (*see* Sauer, Marion Eccleston)		
Edwards, Norman	Opera Department	1924–25
Erhart, Marie	Piano	1923–71
Fauver, Edwin	Physical Education	1929–39
Fay, Jay W.	Public School Music	1921–??
Fermin, Adelin	Voice	1921–35
Finckel, George	Cello	1928–37
Fitch, Theodore	Theory and Composition	1928–32
Foreman, Arthur	Oboe	1926–36
Freeman, Henry (Harry)	Trumpet	1924–27
Fryberger, Agnes	Public School Music, Appreciation	Summers 1926–30
Fuller, Jeannette	Piano	1921–29
Gareissen, Oscar	Voice	1921–24
Gartlan, George	Public School Music	Summer 1930
Gehrken, Warren	Organ	1924–31
Gehrkens, Karl	Public School Music	Summer 1931
Genhart, Cecile Staub	Piano	1926–82
Genhart, Herman	Opera Department, Chorus	1925–64
Gillette, Dorothy (*see* Scott, Dorothy Gillette)		
Gleason, Harold	Organ	1921–55
Goossens, Eugene	Conductor, Opera	1924–31
Graham, Martha	Dance	1925–26
Greene, Carlotta	Public School Music	1930–45
Griffith, Rose	Piano	1921–26
Gustafson, Ester	Dance	1925–26
Hall, Clarence	Opera Department	1929–58
Halliley, Richard	Voice	1924–35
Hammond, John	Motion Picture Organ	Summer 1924
Hanson, Howard	Director, Theory and Composition	1924–64
Harrison, Guy Fraser	Organ, Conducting	1922–25
Harrison, Lucile Bigelow (*see* Johnson, Lucile Bigelow)		
Hartmann, Arthur	Violin	1921–22
Haywood, Frederick	Voice	1924–54

Hoskam, Jessie (*see* Kneisel, Jessie Hoskam)		
Hoss, Wendell	French Horn	1924–26, 1928–30
Houston, George	Voice	1924–27
Inch, Herbert	Composition	1925–28, 1930–31
Jamieson, Margaret	Piano	1924–26
Johnson, Lucile Bigelow	Harp	1921–38
Johnson, Mark	Opera	1927–29
Kammerer, Hope	Piano Normal Course	Summers 1930–32
Kaun, Bernard	Theory	1926–28
Keenan, Gertrude	Piano and Theory	1927–36
Kefer, Paul	Cello	1924–41
Kelley, Dorothy	Public School Music	1928–30
Kimball, Marian Cramton	Physical Education	1929–36
Kinscella, Hazel	Public School Music	Summers 1925–28
Klingenberg, Alf	Director, Piano	1921–23
Klinzing, Ernestine	Piano	1921–57
Knauss, Effie	Violin	1921–54
Kneisel, Jessie Hoskam	German, Dean of Women	1931–76
Konraty, Nicholas	Voice and Opera	1929–57
Kramer, Clair	Physical Education	1929–31
Kunz, Gerald	Violin	1921–32
Lamond, Frederic	Piano	1923–25
Landow, Max	Piano	1922–45
Larson, Arthur	Secretary, Registrar	1930–61
Larson, William	Public School Music/ Psychology	1929–54
Leventon, Gladys Metcalf	Piano	1928–74
Liddell, Donald	Piano	1923–56
Loeffler, Kathryn Makin	Piano	1927–29
Loysen, Hilda Carlson	Physical Education	1929–32
Luening, Otto	Opera	1926–28
Maas, Gerald	Cello	1921–22
MacKown, Marjorie Truelove	Piano and Theory	1921–57
MacNabb, George	Piano	1922–60
Malone, Eileen	Harp	1931–89

Mamoulian, Rouben	Opera	1923–26
Maslinkowsky (Masling), Samuel	Cello	1924–26
Mattern, David	Public School Music	1924–27
May, Hilda	Physical Education and Dance	1926–28
McCleery, Kathleen	Piano	1924–27
McHose, Allen Irvine	Theory	1929–67
Mehlenbacher, Mildred Brownell	Piano	1921–26
Mellon, Edward	Trumpet	1929–41
Metcalf, Gladys (*see* Leventon, Gladys Metcalf)		
Miller, Charles	Public School Music	1924–38
Miller, Dorothy Hawkins	Public School Music	1927–28
Mohler, Louis	Public School Music/ Appreciation	Summer 1925
Montjoy, Harry	English	1925–26
Moore, Fannie Helner	Piano	1923–29, 1930–32
Morlock, Leroy	Voice	1929–67
Mumford, Jane	Piano	1921–32
Nabokin, Jacob	Bassoon	1926–32
Northrup, Ruth (*see* Tibbs, Ruth Northrup)		
Olson, Clair Colby	English	1926–32
Palmgren, Selim	Theory and Composition	1922–27
Penny, George Barlow	Theory and History	1921–34
Pettis, Ashley	Piano	1925–32
Press, Joseph	Cello	1922–24
Puttick, Olive	Piano	1922–24
Quillen, James	Opera Department	1928–29
Rader, Catherine Bodler	Opera	1929–31
Remington, Emory	Trombone	1922–71
Remington, Frederick	Trumpet	1930–35
Resnikoff, Vladimir	Violin	1923–25
Rich, Mabel	Public School Music	Summer 1926
Riker, Charles	Humanities	1930–68
Rogers, Bernard	Composition	1929–67

Rose, Edgar	Piano	1921–31
Rosing, Vladimir	Opera	1923–28
Royce, Edward	Theory	1923–47
Sauer, Marion Eccleston	Violin	1926–36
Schenck, Ludwig	Violin	1921–29
Schmidt, Paul	Tuba	1925–42
Schonegge, Florence Alexander	Piano	1924–38
Scholl, Evelyn	English	1926–30
Scott, Dorothy Gillette	Piano	1921–35
See, Arthur	Piano and Administration	1920–53
Sinding, Christian	Theory and Composition	1921–22
Sisson, Margaret	Opera Department	1928–30
Skinner, Laila	Piano	1924–29
Slonimsky, Nicolas	Opera Department	1923–25
Smith, Hazel Dossenbach	Violin	1921–26
Smith, Harold Osborn	Organ and Opera	1924–54
Smith, Melville	Theory	1925–32
Soderlund, Gustave	Theory	1928–52
Spurrier, Merle	Physical Education	1922–37
Stanton, Hazel	Psychology	1921–32
Stevens, Marian	Physical Education	1929–36
Street, William	Percussion	1927–67
Thorpe, Christina	Public School Music	1931–37
Tibbs, Ruth Northrup	Theory	1924–52
Tinlot, Gustave	Violin	1925–42
Trotter, Thomas Henry Yorke	Theory	1921–23
Tweedy, Donald	Theory	1923–29
Van Hoesen, Karl D.	Violin and Public School Music	1926–66
Vas, Sandor	Piano	1923–54
Waite, Ellen	Piano and Organ	1929–32
Waller, Frank	Conductor	1924–25
Waterhouse, George	Percussion	1924–29
Watson, Nelson	Double Bass	1924–45
Watts, Harry	Piano	1921–24, 1926–61
Weed, Marian	Voice, Dean of Women	1921–38

Weiss, Adolph	Bassoon	1924–25
White, Paul	Violin, Conducting	1928–65
Wilbraham, Hazel	Physical Education	1931–36
Wilson, Raymond	Piano	1921–53
Wonderlich, Elvira	Piano, Theory	1925–66
Woodcock, Edith	Piano	1923–27
Woolford, Jeanne	Voice	1922–48
Wylie, Norma MacKelvie	Piano, Dunning System	1921–24
Yegudkin, Arkaty	French Horn	1926–53

Artists Who Performed in Eastman Theatre Concerts, 1922–1932

Bauer, Harold (pianist): 6 February 1924
Bonnet, Joseph (organist): 24 January 1923
Boston Symphony Orchestra: 8 November 1922, 4 November 1927, 29 October 1928
Calvé, Emma (soprano): 21 March 1923
Casals, Pablo (cellist): 6 February 1924
Chaliapin, Feodor (bass): 7 March 1923
Chamlee, Mario (tenor): 23 October 1924
Civetti, Lydia (soprano): 25 October 1922
Cortot, Alfred (pianist): 5 February 1925, 6 January 1927, 29 November 1929
Crooks, Richard (tenor): 15 January 1925
D'Alvarez, Marguerite (contralto): 20 November 1924
Damrosch, Walter (conductor): 29 November 1922, 28 November 1923
Detroit Symphony Orchestra: 13 February 1924, 6 December 1929
Diaz, Rafaelo (tenor): 5 March 1925
Don Cossack Russian Male Choir: 30 October 1931
Dux, Claire (soprano): 12 March 1925
Easton, Florence (soprano): 2 February 1928
Elman, Mischa (violinist): 6 December 1922, 26 February 1925, 14 January 1926, 16 November 1928, 15 January 1932
English Singers: 8 December 1927, 7 December 1928
Farrar, Gerladine (soprano): 9 November 1928
Festival Chorus of Rochester: 4 April 1923
Friedman, Ignaz (pianist): 10 January 1923
Gabrilowitsch, Ossip (pianist): 12 November 1925
Gabrilowitsch, Ossip (conductor): 13 February 1924, 6 December 1929
Galli-Curci, Amelita (soprano): 10 December 1925, 1 December 1927
Garden, Mary (soprano): 6 November 1924, 28 October 1926

Georgi, Yvonne (dancer): 31 October 1930
Giannini, Dusolina (soprano): 29 January 1925, 5 January 1928, 14 February 1930
Gigli, Beniamino (tenor): 21 October 1926, 17 January 1930
Gogorza, Emilio de (baritone): 20 November 1924, 10 February 1927, 9 February 1928
Goldsand, Robert (pianist): 20 November 1931
Graveure, Louis (tenor): 18 January 1929
Hayes, Roland (tenor): 21 January 1926, 20 January 1927, 11 January 1929, 10 January 1930, 8 January 1932
Heifetz, Jascha (violinist): 26 March 1924, 13 November 1924, 12 January 1928, 21 February 1930
Hempel, Frieda (soprano): 12 February 1925
Hess, Myra (pianist): 8 February 1929
Hofmann, Josef (pianist): 7 November 1923, 19 November 1925, 11 November 1926, 17 November 1927, 7 November 1930
Homer, Louise (contralto): 7 Feburary 1923, 6 January 1927
Horowitz, Vladimir (pianist): 8 November 1929
Iturbi, José (pianist): 30 January 1931, 4 December 1932
Jeritza, Maria (soprano): 22 October 1925
Keener, Suzanne (coloratora soprano): 20 February 1924
Kochanski, Paul (violinist): 30 January 1924, 23 October 1924, 5 November 1925, 21 October 1926, 20 November 1931
Koussevitzky, Serge (conductor): 4 November 1927, 29 October 1928
Kreisler, Fritz (violinist): 14 December 1928, 5 December 1930
Kruetzberg, Harald (dancer): 31 October 1930
L'Argentina (dancer): 18 October 1929
Laubenthal, Rudolf (tenor): 5 January 1928
Lazzari, Carolina (contralto): 22 November 1922
MacBeth, Florence (soprano): 31 January 1923, 5 March 1924, 15 January 1925, 3 February 1927
Martinelli, Giovanni (tenor): 25 October 1922, 29 January 1925, 3 March 1927, 19 February 1932
Matzenauer, Margaret (contralto): 5 March 1925
McCormack, John (tenor): 24 October 1923, 7 January 1926, 27 October 1927
Meisle, Kathryn (contralto): 3 November 1927
Menuhin, Yehudi (violinist): 16 January 1931
Metropolitan Opera Company (New York City): 5 May 1924, 6 May 1924, 6 May 1925, 7 May 1925, 6 May 1926, 7 May 1926, 9 May 1927, 10 May 1927, 7 May 1928, 8 May 1928, 6 May 1929, 7 May 1929, 12 May 1930, 13 May 1930, 4 May 1931, 25 April 1932
Milkail Mordkin Ballet & Orchestra: 18 November 1926

New York Philharmonic: 7 March 1929
New York Symphony: 29 November 1922, 14 March 1923, 28 November 1923
Onegin, Sigrid (contralto): 19 March 1924, 25 February 1926, 10 February 1927, 24 January 1930
Paderewski, Ignace (pianist): 15 November 1922, 5 February 1932
Pavley-Oukrainsky Ballet: 7 December 1923, 30 October 1924
Pavlova, Anna (ballerina): 14 October 1923, 14 November 1923
Pons, Lily (coloratura soprano): 13 November 1931
Ponselle, Rosa (soprano): 19 October 1928, 7 March 1930, 26 February 1932
Quaint, Robert (tenor): 19 March 1924
Rachmaninoff, Sergei (pianist): 25 January 1929, 6 February 1931
Rethberg, Elisabeth (soprano): 9 January 1931
Ricci, Ruggiero (violinist): 13 February 1931
Robeson, Paul (baritone): 23 January 1931
Rosenthal, Moritz (pianist): 2 February 1928
Russian Symphonic Choir: 4 February 1926, 25 October 1929
Salvi, Alberto (harpist): 22 November 1922
San Carlo Opera Company: 16 October 1922, 17 October 1922, 18 October 1922, 19 October 1922, 20 October 1922, 21 October 1922, 5 December 1923, 6 December 1923, 7 December 1923, 8 December 1923
Schipa, Tito (tenor): 20 February 1924, 12 November 1925, 2 December 1926, 7 February 1930
Schumann-Heink, Ernestine (contralto): 3 January 1923, 31 October 1923, 11 Feburary 1926, 10 November 1927
Seidel, Toscha (violinist): 2 December 1926
Shawn, Ted (dancer): 1 November 1922, 21 November 1923, 13 January 1927
St. Denis, Ruth (dancer): 1 November 1922, 21 November 1923, 13 January 1927
Szigeti, Joseph (violinist): 9 February 1928
Thibaud, Jacques (violinist): 10 January 1923
Thomas, John Charles (baritone): 31 January 1923, 5 February 1925, 3 February 1927, 1 February 1929, 29 January 1932
Tibbett, Lawrence (baritone): 21 November 1930
Toscanini, Arturo (conductor): 7 March 1929
Ukrainian National Chorus: 21 February 1923
Werrenrath, Reinald (baritone): 30 January 1924, 5 November 1925, 3 November 1927
Whiteman, Paul (and his orchestra): 3 December 1925
Zimbalist, Efrem (violinist): 1 November 1929

Conductors of Rochester Philharmonic Orchestra Concerts, 1923–1932

Alexander, Arthur
  1923: 28 March
Coates, Albert
  1924: 16 January, 23 January, 30 January, 6 February, 20 February, 27 February, 5 March, 19 March, 26 March, 7 April (Carnegie Hall),
  1925: 9 April, 22 January, 29 January, 5 February, 12 February, 19 February, 26 February, 5 March, 12 March, 19 March
Dobrowen, Issay
  1932: 8 January
Golschmann, Vladimir
  1932: 15 January
Goossens, Eugene
  1923: 17 October, 24 October, 31 October, 7 November
  1924: 16 October, 23 October, 6 November, 13 November
  1925: 29 October, 5 November, 12 November, 19 November, 10 December
  1926: 28 January, 11 February, 11 March, 28 October, 11 November, 2 December
  1927: 6 January, 20 January, 27 January, 10 February, 3 March, 10 March, 10 November, 17 November, 1 December, 8 December
  1928: 5 January, 12 January, 2 February, 9 February, 16 February, 1 March, 9 November, 16 November, 23 November, 7 December, 14 December
  1929: 11 January, 18 January, 1 February, 8 February, 15 February, 1 November, 8 November, 15 November, 29 November, 6 December

1930: 10 January, 17 January, 31 January, 7 February, 14 February, 7 November, 14 November, 21 November, 5 December
1931: 9 January, 15 January, 23 January, 30 January, 6 February, 13 February, 27 February
Hanson, Howard
  1925: 12 March
  1926: 25 February
  1927: 3 February
  1932: 19 February
Harrison, Guy Fraser
  1930: 24 January
  1931: 20 November
  1932: 15 January
Mengelberg, Willem
  1926: 14 January
Molinari, Bernardino
  1932: 22 January, 29 January, 5 February
Reiner, Fritz
  1931: 6 November, 4 December
  1932: 19 February, 26 February
Rodzinski, Artur
  1929: 25 January
Shavitch, Vladimir
  1923: 12 December
  1924: 9 January

Appendix 5

Soloists with the Rochester Philharmonic Orchestra, 1922–1932

Balaban, Emanuel (pianist): 6 February 1931
Bigelow, Lucille Johnson (harpist): 7 December 1928
Daniels, Mark (baritone): 27 January 1927
De Sylva, Richard (violinist): 10 February 1927
Genhart, Cecile (pianist): 10 March 1927, 5 January 1928, 23 November 1928, 5 December 1930
Gleason, Harold (organist): 6 January 1927, 10 January 1930, 19 February 1932
Halliley, Richard (baritone): 6 November 1924, 11 November 1926, 29 November 1929
Hedley, Charles (tenor): 24 October 1923
Hoss, Wendell (French hornist): 26 February 1925
Houston, George Fleming (baritone): 31 October 1923, 11 February 1926
Kefer, Paul (cellist): 5 February 1925, 17 November 1927, 6 December 1929
Klingenberg, Alf (pianist): 28 March 1923
Kochanski, Paul (violinist): 31 January 1930
Konraty, Nicholas (baritone): 7 February 1930, 23 January 1931
Lamond, Frederic (pianist): 16 January 1924, 22 January 1925
Landow, Max (pianist): 28 January 1926, 9 February 1928, 1 February 1929, 13 February 1931
Lerner, Tina (pianist): 12 December 1923
Leventon, Alexander (violinist): 21 November 1930
Luening, Ethel Codd (soprano): 10 November 1927
MacNabb, George (pianist): 3 March 1927, 14 December 1928, 4 December 1931
Maier, Guy (pianist): 7 April 1924 (Carnegie Hall)
Martin, Olivia (soprano): 7 November 1923

Miller, Clyde (baritone): 7 November 1923
Naegele, Charles (pianist): 14 November 1930, 20 November 1931
Palmgren, Selim (pianist): 20 February 1924, 12 November 1925
Pattison, Lee (pianist): 7 April 1924 (Carnegie Hall)
Peebles, Brownie (soprano): 6 January 1927
Press, Joseph (cellist): 17 October 1923, 9 April 1924
Resnikoff, Vladimir (violinist): 27 February 1924, 19 March 1925
Rosing, Vladimir (tenor): 6 February 1924, 19 February 1925, 5 November 1925, 1 December 1927
Ruggles, Archie (tenor): 23 October 1924
Salmond, Felix (cellist): 15 November 1929
Schumann, Henrietta (pianist): 16 February 1928, 25 January 1929
Silveira, Mary (coloratura soprano): 20 January 1927
Tinlot, Gustave (violinist): 29 October 1925, 28 October 1926, 8 December 1927, 16 November 1928, 14 February 1930, 30 January 1931
Travis, Katheryne (soprano): 19 November 1925
Vas, Sandor (pianist): 9 January 1924, 12 February 1925, 11 March 1926, 2 December 1926, 2 February 1928, 18 January 1929, 16 January 1931
Weisberg, Roslyn (pianist): 10 December 1925
Wilson, Raymond (pianist): 16 October 1924, 3 February 1927, 24 January 1930, 22 January 1932

Appendix 6

Eastman Faculty and Guest Artists in Kilbourn Hall Recitals, 1922–1932

This compilation does not include individuals who were soloists with the Rochester Little Symphony, nor does it include performers appearing under auspices other than the Eastman School of Music. Eastman faculty members are shown in italics. The term "faculty" has been broadly interpreted to include people associated with the opera department and with the Eastman School of Dance and Dramatic Action.

Alexander, Arthur (tenor): 19 May 1922
Alexander, Caroline Hudson (soprano): 24 March 1927
Allen, Warren (organist): 26 May 1926
Augieras, Pierre (pianist): 24 March 1922, 15 January 1923, 17 November 1924
Auguilar Lute Quartet: 12 November 1929
Bacon, Ernst (pianist): 20 May 1927
Bailey, Parker (pianist): 24 March 1927
Balaban, Emanuel (pianist): 13 June 1929
Bartlett, Ethel (pianist): 2 February 1932
Bauer, Harold (pianist): 22 November 1926, 20 November 1928, 24 November 1931
Belov, Samuel (violist): 12 May 1922, 27 January 1928, 9 July 1930, 9 July 1931
Bonnet, Joseph (organist): 26 February 1923
Brahms Quartette: 6 February 1928
Burt, Allan (baritone): 20 May 1927
Call, Lucy Lee (soprano): 23 February 1928
Cecelians (vocal ensemble): 9 May 1932
Chamber Music Art Society of New York: 23 March 1923, 24 March 1923, 4 April 1924, 5 April 1924

Chamber Music Society of San Francisco: 30 November 1925
Coates, Albert (conductor): 9 February 1925
Connell, John (organist): 23 November 1931
Conrad, Otto (clarinettist): 17 December 1923
Cortot, Alfred (pianist): 7 November 1922
Croxford, Lyndon (pianist): 9 December 1929
Decaux, Abel (organist): 21 February 1924
DeLorenzo, Leonardo (flutist): 9 November 1923, 17 December 1923, 15 March 1932, 21 July 1932
Draper, Paul (vocalist): 12 March 1923
Dupré, Marcel (organist): 14 January 1924, 5 December 1924
Elshuco Trio: 20 April 1922, 7 November 1924, 19 February 1929
Finckel, George (cellist): 9 July 1925, 13 June 1929, 9 July 1929, 12 June 1930, 9 July 1930, 31 March 1931, 2 July 1931, 21 July 1932
Flonzaley Quartet: 11 January 1924, 12 January 1925, 16 November 1925, 14 November 1927, 1 November 1928
Ganz, Rudolph (pianist): 25 October 1927
Garden, Mary (soprano): 7 February 1927
Gehrken, Warren (organist): 14 January 1925
Genhart, Cecile (pianist): 6 February 1928, 24 July 1930, 9 July 1931
Gieseking, Walter (pianist): 18 January 1927, 27 February 1928
Gleason, Harold (organist): 26 September 1922, 1 February 1924, 8 May 1924, 22 July 1924, 20 January 1925, 21 July 1925, 13 July 1926, 28 June 1927, 6 July 1928, 13 June 1929, 26 June 1930, 9 July 1931, 23 March 1932, 7 July 1932
Gondre, Mona (soprano): 24 February 1923
Goossens, Eugene (conductor): 15 December 1925, 15 March 1926, 13 December 1926, 14 December 1926, 14 March 1927, 12 December 1927, 10 December 1929, 2 December 1930
Goossens, Eugene (pianist): 27 January 1928, 8 March 1928, 16 January 1929, 31 March 1931
Goossens, Leon (oboist): 27 January 1927, 16 January 1929
Gordon String Quartet: 10 October 1927, 10 October 1929, 24 November 1930
Graham, Martha (dancer): 27 March 1926
Hailliley, Richard (baritone): 12 June 1930
Harrison, Guy Fraser (pianist): 19 February 1923
Harrison, Lucile Johnson (see Bigelow, Lucile Johnson)
Hartman, Florence (soprano): 4 March 1927
Hartmann, Arthur (violinist): 24 March 1922
Hart House String Quartet: 25 October 1926, 16 December 1926
Henri Casadesus' Old Instrument Society: 14 January 1930

Hess, Myra (pianist): 9 February 1923, 6 November 1923, 16 February 1928, 10 November 1930

Hewitt, Helen (organist): ?? July 1925

Hochstein String Quartet: 17 July 1929, 11 December 1929, 21 July 1930, 30 June 1931, 14 December 1931

Hoss, Wendell (French hornist): 29 November 1927

Houston, George Fleming (bass): 9 November 1923

Humphrey, Doris (pianist): 2 November 1931

Inch, Herbert (pianist): 24 March 1927

Järnefelt-Palmgren, Maikki (soprano): 12 December 1922

Johnson, Lucile Bigelow (harpist): 12 May 1922, 15 January 1923, 17 December 1923, 20 January 1925, 16 November 1926, 17 November 1926, 15 March 1932

Kedroff Quartet (vocal): 26 January 1932

Kefer, Paul (cellist): 10 November 1925, 6 July 1927, 27 January 1928, 17 July 1928, 15 March 1932

Kilbourn Quartet: 4 March, 1922, 10 March 1922, 31 March 1922, 28 November 1922, 9 April 1923, 29 October 1923, 9 November 1923, 17 December 1923, 19 February 1924, 21 March 1924, 30 January 1925, 21 January 1926, 18 February 1926, 30 June 1926, 26 July 1926, 21 October 1926, 29 November 1926, 29 December 1926, 2 February 1927, 24 March 1927, 28 April 1927, 12 July 1927, 23 February 1928, 5 April 1928, 10 July 1928, 16 January 1929, 26 April 1929, 13 January 1931, 31 March 1931, 18 November 1931, 23 March 1932

Klingenberg, Alf (pianist): 4 March 1922

Klingzing, Ernestine (pianist): 5 November 1923, 1 March 1928, 23 July 1931

Konraty, Nicholas (bass): 25 October 1929, 16 February 1931, 30 June 1932

Kunz, Gerald (violinist): 12 May 1922, 19 February 1923, 25 November 1924, ?? July 1925, 9 July 1925, 6 July 1927, 29 November 1927, 17 July 1928, 25 February 1930, 7 December 1931

Lamond, Frederic (pianist): 22 October 1923, 10 October 1924

Landow, Max (pianist): 12 April 1922, 18 December 1922, 29 January 1923, 19 February 1923, 30 January 1925, ?? July 1925, 9 July 1925, 26 July 1926, 6 July 1927, 17 July 1928, 14 November 1928, 28 June 1929, 23 July 1929, 25 February 1930, 2 July 1930, 13 January 1931, 7 December 1931, 14 July 1932

Landowska, Wanda (pianist/harpsichordist): 9 March 1926, 21 February 1927

Leone, Santina (soprano): 12 June 1930

Lerner, Tina (pianist): 29 February 1924
Letz Quartette: 15 March 1922, 17 November 1922, 17 January 1928
Leventon, Gladys Metcalf (pianist): 12 March 1930
London Singers: 3 March 1931, 29 February 1932
London String Quartet: 27 November 1923, 17 February 1925, 12 January 1926, 8 February 1927, 28 January 1930, 11 January 1932
Maas, Gerald (cellist): 28 April 1922
MacKown, Allison (cellist): 21 January 1931, 17 December 1931
MacKown, Marjorie T. (pianist): 10 January 1927, 24 March 1927, 19 March 1928, 12 June 1930, 21 January 1931, 17 December 1931
MacNabb, George (pianist): 26 March 1923, 11 March 1926, 4 March 1927, 9 July 1929, 9 July 1930, 2 July 1931
Maier, Guy (pianist): 27 January 1923: 22 October 1928, 28 October 1930
Makin, Kathryn (pianist): 28 May 1928
Malone, Eileen (harpist): 21 July 1932
Marmeins (dancers): 2 February 1931
McGill, Donald (baritone): 24 October 1924, 28 April 1930
Metcalf, Gladys (see *Leventon, Gladys Metcalf*)
Morlock, Leroy (baritone): 2 July 1931
Morse, Charles H. (organist): 6 February 1924
Murphy, Lambert (tenor): 27 February 1925
Musical Art Quartet: 4 December 1928
New York Trio: 10 October 1922
Palmgren, Selim (pianist): 12 December 1922
Pattison, Lee (pianist): 22 October 1928, 28 October 1930
Peterson, Norman (organist): 12 June 1930
Poister, Arthur (organist): 19 January 1931
Press, Joseph (cellist): 1 February 1924
Pro Art Quartet: 12 March 1929
Resnikoff, Vladimir (violinist): 19 February 1923, 22 January 1924, 15 July 1924
Robinson, Rae (pianist): 2 February 1932
Rochester American Opera Company: 14 October 1925, 15 October 1925, 16 October 1925, 5 April 1926, 6 April 1926, 7 April 1926, 8 April 1926, 9 April 1926, 10 April 1926, 1 November 1926, 2 November 1926, 3 November 1926, 4 November 1926, 5 November 1926, 6 December 1926, 7 December 1926, 8 December 1926, 9 December 1926, 10 December 1926, 11 December 1926, 7 February 1927
Rochester Little Symphony: 9 February 1925, 17 March 1925, 27 March 1925, 15 December 1925, 15 March 1926, 13 December 1926, 14

December 1926, 14 March 1927, 12 December 1927, 8 March 1928, 10 December 1929, 2 December 1930

Rochester Woodwind Quintet: 10 April 1929, 10 March 1930

Rosing, Vladimir (tenor): 19 November 1923, 28 October 1924, 16 November 1926, 17 November 1926

Roth String Quartet: 28 October 1929

Royce, Edward (pianist): 14 March 1924

Samuel, Harold (pianist): 4 March 1926

Schmitz, E. Robert (pianist): 7 January 1926, 7 January 1929

Schumann, Henrietta (pianist): 28 April 1930

Scott, Dorothy Gillette (pianist): 5 November 1923, 23 July 1931

Segovia, Andres (guitarist): 10 February 1930

Silveira, Mary (soprano): 9 November 1923

Slonimsky, Nicholas (pianist): 10 May 1924, 24 October 1924

Sorelle, Elise (harpist): 24 February 1923

Tinlot, Gustave (violinist): 10 November 1925, 27 January 1928, 9 July 1929, 23 July 1929

Torpadie, Greta (soprano): 29 February 1924

Trio de Lutece: 29 January 1929

Vas, Sandor (pianist): 10 March 1923, 22 January 1924, 15 July 1924, 25 January 1926, 29 November 1927, 23 February 1928, 22 March 1929, 16 February 1931, 18 February 1932

Verbruggen Quartet: 9 October 1923

Vierne, Louis (organist): 21 March 1927, 7 April 1927

Warner, John Adams (pianist): 12 March 1923

Watts, Harry (piano): 25 March 1929, 13 June 1929

Wendling Quartet: 24 October 1922

White, Paul (violinist): 13 June 1929, 31 October 1929, 12 June 1930, 9 July 1930

Wilson, Raymond (pianist): 28 April 1922, 11 July 1922, 1 December 1922, 24 July 1924, 25 November 1924, 25 January 1926, 28 July 1927, 18 July 1930

Woodside, James (baritone): 10 May 1924

Woolfold, Jeanne (mezzo-contralto): 12 April 1922, 1 December 1922, 17 November 1924, 9 July 1925, 24 March 1927, 26 April 1929, 13 June 1929

Appendix 7

List of Compositions Played in the American Composers' Concerts and Festivals of American Music, 1925–1932

Ernst Bacon	Prelude and Fugue
	Two Songs with Orchestra
John Beach	Ballet, *The Phantom Satyr*
Evelyn Berkman	Symphonic Poem, *The Return of Song*
Ernest Bloch	Concerto Grosso
	Four Episodes for Chamber Orchestra
Jeanne Boyd	*Andante Lamentabile*
Radie Britain	*Heroic Poem*
Gertrude M. Brown	*Prelude and Allegro*
Charles Wakefield Cadman	Cantata-Opera, *The Sunset Trail*
John Alden Carpenter	*Adventures in a Preambulator*
	Skyscrapers for Ballet, Chorus, and Orchestra
George W. Chadwick	*Symphonic Sketches*: Suite for Orchestra
	"Tantum Quando" from *Noel*
	Mary's Lullaby
	Silently Swaying
	Symphonic Poem, *The Angel of Death*
	Symphonic Poem, *Tam O'Shanter*
	Overture, *Rip Van Winkle*
Joseph Clokey	*When the Child Christ Came*
Aaron Copland	"Cortège Macabre" from *Grohg*
	Prelude from *Music for the Theatre*
Henry Cowell	*Symphonietta*, Second Movement
	Concerto for Piano and Orchestra (First Movement)
Mabel Wheeler Daniels	*Exultate Deo*

Eric DeLamarter	Suite from *The Betrothal*
	The One Hundred and Forty-Fourth Psalm
Edward Delaney	Suite, *The Constant Couple*
Anthony Donato	*Three Intimations* for String Quartet
Martha Alter Douglas	Orchestral Introduction and Song, "Bill George"
Herbert Elwell	Ballet, *The Happy Hypocrite*
George Foote	*Variations on a Pious Theme*
Henry F. Gilbert	Chamber Music Suite (Two Movements)
Henrietta Glick	Symphonic Suite, *Paris, 1927*
Charles Griffes	*The Pleasure Dome of Kubla Khan*
C. Hugo Grimm	*Abraham Lincoln—A Character Portrait*
Rev. Ignatius Groll	Symphonic Poem, *Memengwa*
Henry Hadley	Overture, *In Bohemia*
Howard Hanson	Prelude and Ballet from *The California Forest Play*
	The Lament for Beowulf, for Chorus and Orchestra
	Pan and the Priest
	Symphony No. 2, "Romantic"
	String Quartet in One Movement
Roy Harris	Andante from An Unfinished Symphony
Walter Edward Howe	Symphonic Poem, *Outside the Tent*
Herbert Inch	*Variations on a Modal Theme*
	Barcarolle
	Suite for Small Orchestra
	Symphony No. 1
Frederick Jacobi	Nocturne from Symphony No. 1
Dorothy James	*Paolo and Francesca*
	Three Fragments for Orchestra
Werner Janssen	Symphonic Poem, *New Year's Eve in New York*
Werner Josten	Concerto "Sacro" (for strings and piano)
	Suite, *Frolics*
	Symphony in E-Flat Major
Bernard Kaun	Suite of Sketches for Orchestra
Edward Kurtz	Scherzo from First Symphony
A.C. Kroeger	Symphonic Poem, *S. P. D. S.*
Wesley LaViolette	*In Memoriam—Armistice Day 1919*

Charles Martin Loeffler   *Hymn of St. Francis*
Otto Luening   *Serenade*
Leopold Mannes   Suite for Orchestra
Daniel Gregory Mason   Festival Overture, *Chanticleer Cathedral Prelude*, for Organ and Orchestra
        Prelude and Fugue for Piano and Orchestra
Allen Irvine McHose   Concerto for Oboe and Orchestra
George F. McKay   Symphony "From the Black Hills," First Movement
Colin McPhee   Concerto for Piano and Seven Wind Instruments
Douglas Moore   *The Pageant of P. T. Barnum*
        Symphonic Poem, *Moby Dick*
        A Symphony of Autumn
Harold Morris   *Tone Poem*
Robert Nelson   Prelude and Orientale from *Ballet Suite*
Frank Patterson   Overture to the Opera *Mountain Blood*
Quincy Porter   *Ukrainian Suite* for Strings Suite in G Minor
John Powell   *Natchez on the Hill*
Wallingford Riegger   *Caprice* for Ten Violins
Bernard Rogers   *Soliloquy* for Flute and Strings
        Symphony "Adonais" *Pastorale*
        Prelude to *Hamlet*
        Symphony in A-Flat Major (in One Movement)
        The Marriage of Aude, A Lyric Drama in Three Scenes
        Cantata, *The Raising of Lazarus*
Edward Royce   Tone Poem, *The Fire-Bringers*
        Tone Poem, *Far Ocean*
Beryl Rubinstein   Scherzo for Orchestra
Robert Sanders   Suite
Mark Silver   Symphonic Poem, *Peace and War*
David Stanley Smith   *The Fallen Star* for Chorus and Orchestra
Melville Smith   *The Weeping Earth* for Orchestra, Organ, Chorus, and Tenor
Leo Sowerby   *Medieval Poem* for Organ and Orchestra
        A Set of Four Ironics
        Symphonic Poem, *Prairie*
        "Northland" Suite

	Overture, *Comes Autumn Time*
	Serenade for String Quartet
Alexander Lang Steinert	Tone Poem, *Southern Night*
William Grant Still	*Darker America*
	Suite, *From the Journal of a Wanderer*
	Suite, *Africa*
	Afro-American Symphony
	Sahdji for Ballet and Chorus
Albert Stoessel	*Suite Antique*
Edwin Stringham	*Three Pastels*
Deems Taylor	*Through the Looking Glass*
Randall Thompson	*Pierrot and Cothernus,* Prelude to a Play Edna Vincent Millay
	Symphonic Poem, *The Piper at the Gates of Dawn*
	Concerto for Piano and Orchestra
	Symphony No. 1
	Symphony No. 2
Donald Tweedy	Symphonic Study, *L'Allegro*
David Van Vactor	*Chaconne* for Strings
Bernard Wagenaar	*Divertimento*
	Symphony No. 1
	Symphony No. 2
	Sinfonietta
F.M. Warnke	Suite, *Impressions of a Mountain*
Adolph Weiss	Tone Poem, *I Segreti*
	Chamber Symphony (Second Movement)
Mark Wessel	*Burlesque* for Piano and Orchestra
	Concertino for Flute and Orchestra
	Symphony-Concertante for Horn, Piano, and Orchestra
	Sextet for Woodwinds and Piano
Paul White	String Quartet
Emerson Whithorne	*Saturday's Child*

Bibliography

Primary Sources

A. Sibley Music Library

Ruth T. Watanabe Special Collections and Eastman School of Music Archives

Individual Collections

Harry Freeman Papers. Freeman was the first trumpet teacher at the Eastman School of Music and the grandfather of Robert Freeman, fourth director of the school. The collection contains diaries, personal correspondence, and a biographical sketch by his son Henry Freeman.

Howard Hanson Papers. Howard Hanson served as director of the Eastman School of Music from 1924 to 1964. The collection contains various papers including drafts of speeches and reports.

Paul Horgan Collection. Horgan was associated with the Rochester American Opera Company and was the author of the prize-winning novel *The Fault of Angels*, which was based on his experiences in Rochester. The collection mainly contains manuscript drafts of his novel.

Jean Ingelow Papers. Jean Ingelow was a graduate of the D.K.G. Institute of Musical Art and later studied organ at the Eastman School of Music. The collection contains her theory workbooks from the Institute of Musical Art, some of her compositions, her personal notes on the Institute of Musical Art, and a 1975 article from *Theatre Organ* on her life.

Official Publications and Collections

Eastman School of Music Programs. A collection of programs of major recitals and concerts sponsored by the Eastman School (1922–).

Eastman School of Music Board of Managers. Minutes and other documents (1919–85).

Eastman School of Music Magazines. Includes *The Note Book* (1921–25), a publication by and for students during the school's first four years, and the Alumni Bulletin (1929–32).

Eastman School of Music/University of Rochester Publications. Includes Eastman School of Music annual catalogues (1921–) and Reports of the President and Treasurer (1915–26, 1926–31).

Eastman School Yearbooks. A complete collection of student yearbooks (1925–).

Eastman Theatre Contracts. Contracts (1919–21) overseen by George Eastman during the construction of the school and theater.

Eastman Theatre/School Correspondence. Correspondence relating to the theater and school from its earliest years (1919–30).

Eastman Theatre Scrapbooks. Scrapbooks filled with press clippings and programs of motion picture screenings and live performances at the Eastman Theatre (1922–28). Specific scrapbooks contain clippings on the building of the Eastman School and Eastman Theatre, on George Eastman as patron, and on the first performances in the theater. Two additional scrapbooks contain clippings on film screenings at two other Rochester theaters, the Piccadilly and the Regent.

Faculty File. Sundry documents on almost all individuals who have held teaching positions at the Eastman School of Music.

Festivals of American Music. Bulletins and programs of the American Composers' Concerts and the Festivals of American Music (1925–71).

Institute of Musical Art. A scrapbook on the Institute of Musical Art, containing newspaper clippings, concert announcements, articles on music, and programs (1919–21). Yearbook of the Dossenbach-Klingenberg School of Music (1913–14). Yearbooks of the D.K.G. Institute of Musical Art (1914–18). Yearbook of the Institute of Musical Art (1918–19). Yearbooks of the University of Rochester Institute of Musical Art (1919–21).

Rochester Scrapbooks. Approximately 200 scrapbooks compiled by the Sibley Music Library containing newspaper clippings (1921–79) on musical life in Rochester and musical events relating to the Eastman School of Music.

B. Rush Rhees Library

Department of Rare Books, Special Collections, and Preservation

Corner Club, Rochester. Information about the Corner Club, its organization, membership, and activities.

Eastman-Butterfield Collection. Nine notebooks, four boxes, and one package containing notes for an unpublished biography of George Eastman, including interviews, clippings, and printed material.

Rush Rhees Papers. Correspondence of Rush Rhees during his tenure as President of the University of Rochester.

Helen Rochester Rogers Papers. Letters, photographs, sketches, and memorabilia of Helen Rochester Rogers, the great-granddaughter of Colonel Nathaniel Rochester, one of the founders of the city of Rochester.

C. George Eastman House

George Eastman Archive and Study Center

George Eastman Correspondence. Letters by George Eastman (1879–1932) and incoming correspondence to George Eastman (1890–1932).

Secondary Sources

Ackerman, Carl W. *George Eastman.* Boston and New York: Houghton Mifflin Company, 1930.

Brayer, Elizabeth. *George Eastman: A Biography.* Baltimore and London: Johns Hopkins University Press, 1996.

Cahn, William L. *Rochester's Orchestra: A History of The Rochester Philharmonic Orchestra and Its Education Programming, 1922 to 1989.* Rochester: Citizens for a Quality Philharmonic, 1989.

Duncan, Barbara. "The Sibley Music Library." *University of Rochester Library Bulletin* 1, no. 1 (1945).

Foreman, Edward R. "An Appreciation of David Hochstein." In *Centennial History of Rochester, New York*, edited by Edward R. Foreman, vol. 2. Rochester: Rochester Historical Society, 1932.

Gleason, Harold. "Please Play My Funeral March." *University of Rochester Library Bulletin* 26, no. 3 (1971).

Goldberg, Louise, and Charles Lindahl. "Gathering the Sources: A Case History." In *Modern Music Librarianship: Essays in Honor of Ruth Watanabe*, edited by Alfred Mann, 3–26. Stuyvesant, N.Y.: Pendragon Press, 1989.

Graham, Martha. *Blood Memory / Martha Graham.* New York: Doubleday, 1991.

Hanson, Howard. "Music Was a Spiritual Necessity." *University of Rochester Library Bulletin* 26, no. 3 (1971).

Kalyn, Andrea. "Constructing a Nation's Music: Howard Hanson's American Composers' Concerts and Festivals of American Music, 1925–71." Ph.D. diss., University of Rochester (Eastman School of Music), 2001.

Klinzing, Ernestine N. "Music in Rochester: A Century of Musical Progress." *Rochester History* 29, no. 1. Edited by Blake McKelvey. Rochester: Rochester Public Library, 1967.

Kraut, Grace N. *An Unfinished Symphony: The Story of David Hochstein.* Rochester: Author, 1980.

Lansing, Richard H. "Music in Rochester from 1817 to 1909." In *The Rochester Historical Society Publication Fund Series*, vol. 2, edited by Edward R. Foreman. Rochester: Rochester Historical Society, 1923.

Lenti, Vincent A. "David Hochstein: Rochester's Promising Violinist." *Rochester History* 56, no. 3 (1994).

——. "The Eastman School of Music" *Rochester History* 58, no. 4 (1996).

——. "Hermann Dossenbach and the Rochester Orchestra." *Rochester History* 42, no. 3 (1980).

——. "A History of the Eastman Theatre." *Rochester History* 49, no. 1 (1987).

May, Arthur J. *A History of the University of Rochester, 1850–1962.* Rochester: University of Rochester, 1977.

McKelvey, Blake. *Rochester: The Quest for Quality, 1890–1925.* Cambridge, Mass.: Harvard University Press, 1956.

Rhees, Mrs. Rush [Harriet Seyle]. "Rochester at the Turn of the Century." In *The Rochester Historical Society Publication Fund Series*, vol. 20, compiled by Dexter Perkins. Rochester: Rochester Historical Society, 1942.

Riker, Charles. *The Eastman School of Music: Its First Quarter Century, 1921–1946.* Rochester: University of Rochester, 1948.

Rosenberger, Jesse Leonard. *Rochester: The Making of a University.* Chicago: University of Chicago Press, 1927.

Rosing, Ruth Glean. *Val Rosing: Musical Genius, an Intimate Biography.* Manhattan, Ks.: Sunflower University Press, 1993.

Sabin, Steward B. "Music in Rochester from 1909 to 1924." In *The Rochester Historical Society Publication Fund Series*, vol. 3, edited by Edward R. Foreman. Rochester: Rochester Historical Society, 1924.

——. "A Retrospect of Music in Rochester." In *Centennial History of Rochester, New York*, edited by Edward R. Foreman, vol. 2. Rochester: Rochester Historical Society, 1932.

Shilling, Donovan A. *Rochester Labor and Leisure.* Images of America. Charleston, S.C.: Arcadia Publishing, 2002.

Sibley, Hiram W. "Memories of Hiram Sibley." In *The Rochester Historical Society Publication Fund Series*, vol. 2, edited by Edward R. Foreman. Rochester: Rochester Historical Society, 1923.

Slater, John Rothwell. *Rhees of Rochester.* New York and London: Harper & Brothers Publishers, 1946.

——. "Rochester Forty Years Ago." In *The Rochester Historical Society Publications*, vol. 20, compiled by Dexter Perkins. Rochester: Rochester Historical Society, 1942.

Slonimsky, Nicholas. *Perfect Pitch: A Life Story.* New York: Oxford University Press, 1988.

Stanton, Hazel M. *Prognosis of Musical Achievement: A Study of the Predictive Value of Tests in the Selection of Degree and Certificate Students for the Eastman School of Music.* Rochester, 1929.

Watanabe, Ruth. "The Sibley Music Library of the Eastman School of Music, University of Rochester." *Notes* 33, no. 4 (1977): 28–29.

Index

This index refers only to the main text of the book and consists (for the most part) only of personal names and titles of Rochester and Eastman School institutions and performing groups.

For a complete name search (and for American compositions), the reader will want to consult Appendices 1–7 as well (pp. 244–69).

Page numbers in italics refer to illustrations.

For the Enrichment of Community Life is the first part of the history of the Eastman School of Music, beginning with the events that led to the establishment of the school in 1921 and ending in 1932 with the death of the school's benefactor, George Eastman. It was Eastman, the founder of Eastman Kodak, and Rush Rhees, the remarkable president of the University of Rochester, who really made it all possible.

Though the Eastman School of Music is not the oldest music school in the United States or the largest, it has had an enormous influence on music education in the United States. Creating a professional music school within the context of a university was a bold experiment at the time. American music education had traditionally followed the European model of training performers in conservatories and creating musical scholars in universities. The Eastman School would be a home to both performer and scholar, as well as to both composer and educator. It would be a professional music school, but one committed to a broadly based education leading not to a professional diploma but to a baccalaureate degree. The Eastman School would be in the forefront of national efforts to establish and regulate the curriculum for the bachelor of music degree. It would be a leader in the training of musicians at the graduate level through the awarding of the master of music degree and through the creation of a new professional doctorate in music, the doctor of musical arts.

Even more important was the effort to establish the Eastman School as a truly American institution, dedicated to American ideals and to the encouragement and support of American music. Howard Hanson, chosen as the school's second director in 1924, led the school for the next forty years. Under his leadership the Eastman School of Music became known throughout the world for its advocacy and support of American music.

The story related here is not simply that of a music school. It also involves a symphony orchestra, an American opera company, a ballet company, a school of dance and drama, a music library, and a commercial radio station dedicated to broadcasting live classical music. It includes efforts to support the musical education of Rochester's elementary and secondary school children and the involvement of the symphony orchestra in their musical education. It is the story of the school's Eastman Theatre, which became the location of concerts and recitals by the world greatest musicians.

Upon the facade of the Eastman Theatre is the inscription "For the Enrichment of Community Life," words selected by Rush Rhees to dedicate the theater to that purpose. In a broader sense also, these words embody the mission of the Eastman School of Music.